Library of
Davidson College

Michael Wolffsohn

German-Saudi Arabian Arms Deals 1936-1939 and 1981-1985

With an Essay on West Germany's Jews

PETER LANG

German–Saudi Arabian Arms Deals
1936–1939
and
1981–1985

Michael Wolffsohn

German-Saudi Arabian Arms Deals 1936-1939 and 1981-1985

With an Essay on West Germany's Jews

Verlag Peter Lang
Frankfurt am Main · Bern · New York

CIP-Kurztitelaufnahme der Deutschen Bibliothek

Wolffsohn, Michael:

German-Saudi Arabian arms deals 1936 – 1939 and 1981 – 1985 : with an essay on West Germany's jews / Michael Wolffsohn. – Frankfurt am Main ; Bern ; New York : Lang, 1985.
   ISBN 3-8204-7490-0

Library of Congress Cataloging-in-Publication Data

Wolffsohn, Michael.
  German-Saudi Arabian arms deals 1936–1939 and 1981–1985.

      Bibliography: p.
      1. Munitions—Germany—History—20th century.
  2.   Munitions—Germany (West)—History—20th century.
  3.   Germany-Military relations—Saudi Arabia.
  4.   Saudi Arabia—Military relations-Germany.
  5.   Germany (West)—Military relations—Saudi Arabia.
  6.   Saudi Arabia—Military relations—Germany (West)
  7.   Jews—Germany (West)—History—20th century. I. Title.
UF535.G3W65   1985   355'.032'538   85–14061
ISBN 3-8204-7490-0

ISBN 3-8204-7490-0

© Verlag Peter Lang GmbH, Frankfurt am Main 1985
Alle Rechte vorbehalten.
Nachdruck oder Vervielfältigung, auch auszugsweise, in allen Formen wie Mikrofilm, Xerographie, Mikrofiche, Mikrocard, Offset verboten.

Druck und Bindung: Weihert-Druck GmbH, Darmstadt

TABLE OF CONTENTS

page

INTRODUCTION 5

ABBREVIATIONS 7

PART I: THE PAST: 1936 TO 1939

I. Methodological Approach 11
II. Dominant Macro- and Micro-Environmental Factors 12
III. German-Saudi Relations: The Decision Flow on the Bilateral Level (A Chronological-Analytical Account) 15
IV. German Actors: Their Images, Arguments, Preferences, Actions and Importance (A Systematical Account Instead of a Conclusion) 34

    Adolf Hitler 34
    The Economy 34
    The Ministry of Foreign Affairs 36
    The Aussenpolitisches Amt of the NSDAP (APA) 38
    The Military 39
    Conclusions 39
    Annex: The Decision-Making Process: A Quantitative and Qualitative Survey 41
    Legend to the Annex 45

PART II: THE PRESENT: 1981 TO 1985

I. Economic Structures and Cycles 51
II. Political Structures and Cycles
    1. The Polls 52
    2. West Germany as an Off-Middle East Theater of War 52
    3. Bilateral Relations with Middle Eastern States and Actors 55
        a. Iraq 55
        b. Relations with the PLO 55
        c. Relations with Israel 58
        d. Bonn's Iranian Connection 64

	page
4. Germans to the Gulf?	66
III. The Arms Deal with Saudi Arabia	69
A. The SPD-FDP Coalition 1981/82	69
1. The Disclosure	69
2. The Decision Process	70
a. The Governmental Level	70
b. The Social Democratic Party	76
c. The Free Democratic Party	78
d. The Christian Democrats (CDU/CSU)	79
e. Industry	81
f. Trade Unions	83
g. Jewish Influence	84
3. Less Visible Actions	84
B. Epilogue: The CDU/CSU-FDP Coalition, 1982-1985	91
1. Flow of Events	91
a. Compensation for Israel?	94
b. The Snowball Effect: German Weapons to other Arab States	95
c. A Pre-Emptive Israeli Strike against Saudi 'Leopards'?	95
d. 'Tornado' Planes for Saudi Arabia?	95
2. Economic Aspects	96
a. The Macro-Economic Level	96
b. The Micro-Economic Level	96
3. Bureaucratic Politics	97
a. The Rise and Fall of Jürgen Möllemann	98
4. The Political Parties	99
a. The CDU/CSU	99
b. The Free Democratic Party	100
c. The Social Democrats	100
d. The Greens	100
5. Interest Groups	101
a. Trade Unions	101
b. The Protestant Church	101
c. German Jews	101
6. The American Connection	102

	page
C. The Past as Present: The Shadows of the Holocaust	104

APPENDIX: WITHOUT IDENTITY AND FUTURE? GERMAN JEWS
    BETWEEN DIASPORA AND ISRAEL   107

I.   The demographic situation   108

II.   Self-image and behavior   110

III.   The Diaspora and Israel. Or: The Double Dilemma of the German Jews   113

IV.   Perspectives   119

NOTES

    Part I   121
    Part II   136
    Appendix   161

SELECTED BIBLIOGRAPHY   169

INTRODUCTION

On 27 April 1981, at the state dinner in honor of the West German delegation led by Chancellor Helmut Schmidt, the late King Khalid of Saudi Arabia reminded his guest of tradition. "In the 1930s", the monarch explained, Germany had been the first foreign supplier of arms to his country.(1)

The hint was unequivocal. As in the 1930s, Germany this time the Federal Republic of Germany should again send weapons to the desert kingdom. Above all the Saudis were now interested in buying the Leopard 2 tank, supposedly the most sophisticated weapon of its kind. (2)

Chancellor Schmidt was either too polite or simply uninformed about the German-Saudi Arabian arms deal of the 1930s, for otherwise he would have contradicted the very substance of King Khalid's short historical lecture. After all, historians seemed to agree that the Third Reich had not exported arms to Saudi Arabia in the 1930s, despite repeated requests put forward since 1937.(3) Or did the Chancellor know more than the historians dreamed of in their historiography? Moreover: It was somebody in Saudi Arabia, the King himself, and not anybody who contended that Germany did, in fact, deliver weapons asked for by his late father Ibn Saud. Implicitly casting doubts on historiography, the King referred to history. Maybe the King had access to sources and information hitherto unknown. In short, King Khalid's remarks may justify a fresh look at the German-Saudi Arabian arms deal of 1936 (not 1937, as will be shown) to 1939. A reconsideration may be overdue; a reconsideration based mainly on German archival material - to begin with.

At the same time such a reconsideration may also shed more light on the foreign policy decision-making process of the Third Reich prior to World War II.

ABBREVIATIONS

AA	Auswärtiges Amt; Foreign Office
APA	(Foreign Policy Office of the NSDAP)
BAK	Bundesarchiv Koblenz (Archives of the Federal Republic of Germany), Koblenz
BAM	Bundesarchiv/Militärarchiv (Military Archives of the Federal Republic of Germany), Freiburg/Brsg.
EC	European Community
FM	Foreign Minister
IfZ	Institut für Zeitgeschichte (Institute for Contemporary History), Munich
ME	Middle East/Middle Eastern
MECS	Middle East Contemporary Survey
NA	National Archives, Washington, D. C.
NSDAP	National-Socialist German Workers' Party
PA	Politisches Archiv des AA (Archives of the Foreign Office at the Federal Republic of Germany), Bonn
PIW	Petroleum Intelligence Weekly
PM	Prime Minister
PRO	Public Record Office, London
WG	West Germany/West German

PART I:
THE PAST: 1936 TO 1939

I. METHODOLOGICAL APPROACH

This essay tries to identify the most important political actors in Germany's external as well as internal environment, as far as the arms deal with Saudi Arabia is concerned. All these political actors are considered to be input-factors relevant to the decision which, in the end, has to be taken by the government. The government, in turn, is not perceived as a monolithic actor but rather a heterogeneous one with its subsystems (the government itself being a subsystem of the overall supra-system of the German state) at times competing with one another, at times cooperating with one another. "Bureaucratic politics" is the key term. I distinguish between the **micro** (= individual) and **macro** (= extraindividual) environment of the decision-makers.(4) Both are surrounded by internal and external factors or environments. The micro environment consists of private and non-private interpersonal relationships of the individual political actor or actors. The external factors of the macro environment are the global system, regional subsystems, dominant bilateral relations, other bilateral relations.

The internal factors of the macro-environment are the economy, military, society, political structure (government, parliament, judiciary - if they are, in fact, operating) competing elites (even within an omnipotent party or state executive), the cultural system.

Individuals have images not only of themselves and their micro-environment but also of others and their macro-environment. We shall, therefore, take images into consideration. They, in turn, are reflections of and on reality rather than reality itself. But people act according to their images of reality rather than according to reality itself.(5)

Clearly, the importance and intensity of all these input-factors varies from country to country and from issue to issue. I shall therefore only refer to those relevant for our issue. Finally, I shall try to weigh actions and the importance of the actors quantitatively.

II. DOMINANT MACRO- AND MICRO-ENVIRONMENTAL FACTORS

It is doubtless safe to state that German-Saudi Arabian relations were a direct result of **German-British relations**. To put it more correctly: They could be derived from what Germany's key foreign policy decision-makers, primarily Adolf Hitler, wanted German-British relations to be. Moreover, German-British relations depended (from Hitler's perspective) on the **global role of the Third Reich**.

"Hitler's aims were of world-wide scope," Andreas Hillgruber has contended and succinctly documented.(6) Automatically, this had to lead to an all-out confrontation with England. This strategy, however, consisted of several stages three of which are relevant to the German-Saudi Arabian arms deal of 1936 to 1939.(7) From 1933 to 1935, during the first stage, the "Führer" aimed at "reaching on alliance with England at the expense of his colonial and maritime ambitions."(7)

During stage two, from March 1935 to autumn 1938, "Hitler had increasing doubts as to whether England could in fact be either wooed into an alliance or forced into one by the application of pressure", for instance by repeatedly insisting on the "return of the farmer German colonies."(8)

The third stage, lasting from autumn 1938 to September 1939, was "marked by Hitler's decision to persevere in his continental expansion, even if this meant war with England."(9)

Stage three should be subdivided into the periods preceding and following the invasion of the rest of Czechoslovakia (March 1939). Only then did it become crystal clear that the German "Führer" was deliberately running the risk of a military confrontation with the Western powers. (10) Any factor and actor disturbing British policies was welcome during stage three. It goes without saying that the Middle East, a traditional English domain, could well support this aim: the periphery as a destabilizer of the center. And the more troublesome the peripheries, the weaker the center. Clearly, Saudi Arabia was designed to be such a peripheral troubleshooter or, at least a prospective "hinterland" for Germans in the Middle East.

The target was Britain, the British Empire, which represented an obstacle to the would-be German **Weltherrschaft**. The target was not Saudi Arabia. This country was a means to an end. This strategy, however, misperceived Saudi Arabia's limited manoevreability vis-à-vis Great Britain. "British domination of the Red Sea and the Persian Gulf was decisive; it meant control of Saudi Arabia's food supply, the dependence of Ibn Saud on British financial support and British preponderance in the neighbouring Arab lands."(11)

Due to tactical considerations between 1933 and 1939, Germany failed to develop a coherent political concept to realize the original strategy.(12) The reasons for this failure are beyond the scope of this article. Suffice it to state that until September 1938/March 1939, the latest, the Third Reich was guided by tactical considerations towards Britain in the Middle East. Strategic encroachments into her domain were not tolerated by Germany's key decision-makers until then. And the prospective arms deal would have clearly represented an encroachment endangering friendly relations with Britain which the Reich wanted to maintain.(13) Nicosia claimes that even after 1938/39 Hitler aimed at maintaining good relations with Britain to secure an Anglo-German racial alliance.(14)

Whatever Hitler's genuine strategy vis-à-vis Great Britain may have been, relations with Saudi Arabia resulted from German-British relations on the tactical as well as strategic level.

The incoherence of Germany's Middle East policy was partly dictated by her alliance ("axis") with **Italy** which, contrary to Germany, did have direct "ambitions" in the Middle East, particularly in Palestine and Yemen. These, however, could not have been realized without British and French resistance.(15)

On October 24, 1936, the day preceding the conclusion of the axis, the "spheres of interest" of Germany and Italy were defined by Hitler and the Italian foreign minister Count Ciano, Mussolini's son-in-law. "La Méditerranée est une mer italienne. Toute modification future de l'équilibre méditerranéen doit se faire en faveur de l'Italie."(16) ("The Mediterranean is an Italian sea. Any future modification of the balance in the Mediterranean must be in Italy's favor"). In return, Germany got a free hand in Eastern Europe.

German priorities vis-à-vis Britain and Italy did not match. Besides, Italy met with much skepticism in the Arab world.(17) Undoubtedly, the axis partner was a burden for Germany in the Middle East. Italy, in turn, frowned upon German activities in that region, her sphere of influence.(18)

Even if Hitler really was "pushed" only reluctantly(19) into the closer relationship with Italy and if he did make "it clear that he would not support Italian ambitions in the Mediterranean and Africa if they were in conflict with the interests of the British Empire,"(20) German priorities remained on a collision course.

Micro-environmental factors: The Ideology of the "Master Race"

Rather than facilitate Germany's Middle East policy **the Jewish factor** complicated things further. "The supposed bond of Germans and Arabs in their common enmity to the Jews ... was on closer inspection a delusion."(21) Anti-Semitism became an integral part of Germany's **foreign** policy only as late as 1938(22) and even then the "Endlösung" (the "Final Solution", the physical liquidation) had not yet been decided upon. This happened in January 1942. Prior to this, Nazi Germany wanted to get rid of her Jews, but not necessarily kill them.(23)

Germany had therefore agreed to the "Haavara" (transfer) arrangements allowing Jews to leave Germany without taking foreign exchange with them and providing for the promotion of German exports to Palestine. (24) Jewish emigration from Germany and immigration into Palestine did, of course, arouse the opposition of Arab nationalists(25) who, in turn looked for cooperation with Nazi Germany – against England and the Jews. But this ran directly counter to Germany's British as well as economic priorities, for the Third Reich was short of foreign exchange.

Furthermore, the Jewish factor complicated German-British relations. After Austria's **Anschluß** Hitler felt free to let his anti-Semitic ideology become part of his foreign policy. He was most upset about British reactions to the Crystal Night (9 November 1938): "What's the use of Chamberlain's willingness to accomodation if he is unable to quiet down the press and opposition," the "**Führer**" reasoned.(26)

Hitler's prejudiced personality, his "image" of racial hierarchy which clearly affected his more ideologically oriented entourage did not only concern Jews but Arabs as well. For the super-ideologues like Alfred Rosenberg this caused quite a dilemma, as will be demonstrated. In 1939 (!) Hitler expressed his feelings about the Arabs whom he called "lacquered half-apes who want to feel the whip."(27) Two years later, for pragmatic reasons, he discovered the Aryan physiognomy, the blond hair and the blue eyes of Haj Amin el-Husseini thus whitewashing Arabs racially.(28) Moreover, people like Grobba, Germany's envoy to Baghdad and, from January 1939 also to Jidda, were impressed with the national awakening of the Arabs, their belief in authoritarianism and force as well as their abhorence of individualism.(29) The German Model was attractive there.

At best, the attitude of Hitler and German foreign policy makers toward the Arabs was ambivalent. Again, no coherent policy was followed. Friends and foes alike had to be confused. Were the Arabs mongrels or worthy allies of the master race?

To sum up: Macro- as well as micro-environmental factors prevented Germany to pursue a clear and unequivocal course in the Middle East.

The dominant actors and factors were Great Britain, Italy and National Soialist racism. Ever and again principles were diluted by pragmatic considerations which were, in part, contradictory.

III. GERMAN-SAUDI RELATIONS: THE DECISION FLOW ON THE BILATERAL LEVEL (A CHRONOLOGICAL-ANALYTICAL ACCOUNT)

No, contrary to common accounts and assumptions the history of the German-Saudi Arabian arms deal did not begin in late 1937 but rather in late 1936 or in February 1937. True, some sources – first hand information as well as most authors – refer to the "fall of 1937", whereas Nicosia speaks of February 1937.(30) The latter is right as to the timing but wrong as to the substance, because he confuses German arms for Polestinians ordered by and delivered via Saudi Arabia with weapons the Saudis themselves wanted to buy.(31) These two packages have to be distinguished as clearly as possible.

On 15 June 1937 the United States' Military Attaché in Berlin, Major Truman Smith, reported that according to "one of the most prominent figures in the foreign business field of the **German armament industry**" the Saudis were interested in German weapons.(32) His unnamed "prominent figure" explained: "... In recent months every European arms concern has noticed a sudden and quite remarkable interest in armaments throughout the Near East countries. Turkey, for several years has been a steady arms customer of Germany ... **Since February** (my italics, M.W.), however, Afghanistan, Persia, Iraq and the Hedjaz (Ibn Saud) have all decided simultaneously on a modernization of armaments on a scale which is quite surprising. Hardly a fortnight goes by without a new commission from one of these lands appearing in Berlin. All wish only the newest and most modern weapons. Each commission stands ready to pay cash for what they want but all equally demand prompt delivery.

The reason given by these Near Eastern nations (my italics, M.W.) for their armaments orders is their desire to escape the fate of Abysinnia. There are, possibly other, as yet unrevealed, reasons in the background."(33)

Again, Germany's ally Italy was feared by the Middle Eastern decision-makers, and this could hardly make life easier for the Third Reich. On the one hand, Germany would offend Italy and Britain, on the other hand having to reject the Arabs. In 1937, however, there were no motivations for Germany's key decision-makers to either offend the British or the Italians, and they did not care too much about the Arabs. We shall realize later that the Foreign Ministry reluctantly registered the Saudi overtures. Saudi timing in 1937 was poor and manifested a dismal misperception of the basic orientation of Nazi Germany's foreign policy.

But this failure can be explained easily. The Saudis had the wrong contacts, and were therefore misled. Fritz Grobba, the German envoy to Baghdad was too pro-Arab compared with other key officials of the Auswärtiges Amt, and the super-ideologues of the NSDAP's Außenpolitisches Amt (APA) were unrepresentative of Germany's foreign policy line. Necessarily, their image of German foreign policy did not correspond to reality.

There is, however, one indication that the German-Saudi Arabian arms deal did, in fact, begin in 1936, at least on a sub-governmental or semi-governmental level.

In July 1939, "Berlin" (who? which office?) "denied the fact" that "three years ago" **Khalid (al-Hud al Qargani)**, adviser to King Ibn Saud and his envoy to contact German firms and the APA in 1938, "had signed several **contracts with German firms** providing for the delivery of weapons, ammunition and several aeroplanes until November 1938." (34)

If the denied "fact" was more than an allegation then the the semi-governmental deal had started in 1936, "three years ago." (Semi-governmental because a governmental adviser of one country had acted here, whereas the other government had not played any role.)

It cannot be ruled out that this had, indeed, happened because the Saudis were interested in German weapons and Khalid al-Hud did undoubtedly contact German officials and firms to obtain the desired goods.

In any case, these contracts could not be carried out by the unnamed German firms because the government of the Reich had not granted the necessary permission.(35)

Whatever had or had not happened in 1936, from February 1937 things moved forward.

Again, months before most later historians and contemporaries had realized the intensification of the German-Saudi relations on the transnational, i.e. sub-governmental level, the **U.S. Military Attaché** in Berlin filed to Washington that "on a recent visit of an American ordinance officer to a **Rheinmetall** demonstration at the Unterlüss proving grounds a number of delegations were present from foreign countries which were obviously involved in the process of negotiating for the purchase of armaments. In addition to the American representative, groups of officers and engineers from Austria, Greece, Ethiopia and the Hedjas were present ... the representative of the Hedjas seemed to be solely interested in the Rheinmetall 20mm anti-aircraft and anti-tank machine guns."(36)

Until November 1937 neither international (governmental level) nor transnational bilateral steps could be retraced. Then, in Baghdad, in November 1937, **representative of the Otto Wolff enterprise** were asked by Sheikh **Yusuf Yasin**, the King's private secretary, "and other confidential agents" if they would supply the Kingdom with 15,000 rifles "on credit or for cash."(37) It could not be ascertained how this firm reacted and what political initiatives they undertook to secure the export permission. Maybe Otto Wolff did not react at all. The question remains open.

In the same month, on 5 November 1937, **Fritz Grobba** had a **meeting with** - yes, **Yusuf Yasin**. But in his talk Yusuf Yasin did not mention military aspects, i.e. arms requests, at all. They discussed the Palestinian problem and its implication for Arab-British relations in general and Saudi-British relations in particular. Ibn Saud's secretary and Grobba emphasized their generally intact connection with England and the German diplomat unequivocally instructed his interlocutor that his country would not jeopardize its "friendly relations" with England. Asked what kind of support Germany could muster for the Palestinian Arabs Yasin contented himself with "diplomatic means" which "for the time being" might be enough.(38)

This, however, was a misleading piece of information because at about the same time Palestinians did try to buy German arms which they hoped to smuggle into the British Mandate via Saudi Arabia.(39)

Yusuf Yasin did make a suggestion, though: King Ibn Saud would welcome the idea of Germany sending a diplomatic envoy to Jidda. The case of Palestine (where Grobba thought that the Saudis as well as other Arabs were not unanimous in their rejection of the establishment of a Jewish state) proved, said Yasin, "that it might be helpful to both governments if they had the opportunity to exchange views on questions of mutual interest."(40)

Grobba, too, welcomed this proposal but added that his country, for economic reasons might be unable to send a permanent **representative to Jidda**. The Reich would have to ask her envoy in a neighbouring country to be in charge of Saudi Arabia as well. The King's secretary accepted this modus unhesitantly.(41)

It might be worth recollecting that the very same Yusuf Yasin had asked representatives of the Otto Wolff firm about possible arms purchases. Why did he hide this intention from the German diplomat? After all, Grobba was favorably inclined towards the Arabs. Did he prefer to give the APA connection a first try?(42)

There may be two other plausible explanations, neither of which can be proved but only guessed at. During their 5 November 1937 talk, Grobba had reminded Yasin that his government owed the former German Honorary Consul to Jidda, Mr. Heinrich de Haas, a **debt of £ 2,000 in gold**. A repayment might ease the way to diplomatic relations which King Ibn Saud desired, added the German diplomat.(43)

Yasin might have thought that this reminder destroyed the psychological environment for far-reaching requests such as arms purchase.

The second explanation is less psychological but rather political. **Grobba maintained contacts to exiled Hashemites** opposed to King Ibn Saud.(44)

"Introduced by a merchant living in Berlin and close to the Außenpolitisches Amt (of the NSDAP, M.W.) the young Sherif Seif Ibn Basir turned up" at Grobba's "in late November" 1937.(45) The young prince was the son of the commander of former Hejaz King Ali's troops defending Jidda against Ibn Saud.(46) Seif ibn Nasir was sent by Prince Abdul Ilah, a powerful man at the Iraqi Hashemite royal court.

And this was the latter's message: Six years ago, the members of the exiled Hashemite family had secretly founded the "Association of the Sherifs" to topple the regime of Ibn Saud. They referred to the latter as the "leader of a gang of robbers," "usurper" and "missionary of teachings alien to Islam (Wahabism)." Emir Abdul Ilah was to replace Ibn Saud as the "legitimate successor to the crown, "The only members of the Hashemite family who had not joined the Association were King Ghazi of Iraq ("for political reasons") who "did not build up obstacles, however," Emir Abdullah of Jordan and his son Tallal who claimed the Hejaz for themselves. The Association's operational center was located in Baghdad but they had agents in "all Arab countries." Abdul Ilah was the President.

Seif ibn nasir continued with a vivid and colorful description of the

17

alleged dissatisfaction of the Hejaz population with Ibn Saud. People there were "starving" and the King developed the Nejd at the expense of the Hejaz. There, the situation was "desperate".(47)

Moreover, Ibn Saud followed the British line "completely" and acted as a "policeman for the English in the Arab world."(48) At the request of the English he had even menaced other Arab states militarily - "when King Faisal had had differences of opinion with the English". When the Imam of Yemen has cooperated too closely with the Italians he acted similarly, and "recently" he amassed troops at the southern border of Transjordan to prevent Emir Abdullah from joining forces with the Palestinian Arabs.(49)

The Association hoped to reconquer the Hejaz and later the Nejd by mustering the support of tribes loyal to the Hashemites. The best time to carry out the strike would be in about seven to eight months (= June/July 1938) when Ibn Saud would have spent all the money he had got from the pilgrims.(50

Finally, Seif ibn Nasir disclosed the purpose of his visit: "The Sherifs would sacrifice their lives and fortune but they needed outside support," namely "weapons and money."(51) A thousand rifles would do, he added.(52) The Association had also asked for Italian support "during the Abyssinian War") but Italy insisted on Jidda as a war port, Unfudha (Asir) as a war and commercial port as well as on a "military base" in Hail and the economic concessions granted to Great Britain (the right to search for and exploit minerals in the Western part of the Arabian peninsula, except for an area of 30 km. around Mecca and Medina; oil concessions in el-Hasa for 99 years; exploitation of gold in the Medina area by the English Rothschild Bank; oil concessions in the Aquaba area.)(53)

The Hashemites agreed only to the latter demand. Now they offered the economic opportunities as well as "friendly propaganda in the Islamic World" to the Germans.(54)

On 22 December 1937, Grobba met with Abdul Ilah himself.(55) Grobba told him outrightly that, in his view, the Association underestimated Ibn Sauds position in the Hejaz and Nejd. The King was supported by peasants to whom he had given weapons, water and money. Besides, he had succeeded in playing off the different tribes against each other. Finally, the English would back him. Any attempt to overthrow Ibn Saud was premature. Nevertheless, the long-term prospects seemed to be more promising for the Hashemites. The sons of Ibn Saud were "weak personalities" and "in disagreement with one another". The King himself was aged and of "frail health". After his death Abdul Ilah's prospects would be more favorable.(56)

Surprisingly, Abdul Ilah agreed with Grobba and confined to him that he shared his doubts and implied that Sherif Seif had pushed him. Grobba should once again talk to Seif, lest he thought that Abdul Ilah wre "irresolute".

Together with Sherifs Shahin and Nami, both from Medina, Seif met with Grobba in Baghdad on 27 December 1937.(57) The two Medinians were, indeed, not convinced by Abdul Ilah's behavior. They had the impression that he did not believe in the success of their attempt. Moreover, he was not the right **"Führernatur"** (person to lead). Since he was the legitimate successor to the throne of the Hejaz, his rights were undisputable. After all, they wanted their undertaking to succeed.

Sherif Shahin tried vehemently to correct Grobba's image of the domestic situation in Saudi Arabia. Yes, the King had settled the Bedouins - only to lead them into "misery." The tribes in the Nejd, too, were dissatisfied with him because he had killed their leaders or sent them into exile. The Shaqra, Muteir, Adjman and Shammar tribes were all opposed to him and the traditional "enmity" between the House of Saud and the House of Rashid of Hail was far from over. Some tribal leaders in the Hejaz like the Sheikh of Teima had not even surrendered to Ibn Saud.

Then Seis informed Grobba about the details of the prospective revolt. He did not expect the British to support Ibn Saud save financially. They would not interfer militarily for fear of an Italian intervention. The revolt would remain an inner-Arab affair.

Again the three Sherifs asked for German weapons and promised later cooperation with Germany. By implication, they hoped for the yet non-existent British-German antagonism.

Grobba immediately indicated that the German government would probably not interfer with these inner-Arab affairs and would, therefore, not send the requested weapons. The Sherifs should feel free, however, to **buy arms in Germany via "trustworthy firms"** familiar to them.

This reaction fell just short of an outright rejection because Grobba must have known that German arms exports were subject to strict governmental scrutiny.(58) Without official authorization it was almost impossible for the firms to send weapons abroad. "Some time ago" the Italian once again tried to win the Association over for cooperation but Abdul Ilah reportedly refused "to be bluffed by the Italians", Grobba added to his file.(59)

When Yusuf Yasin met with Grabba on 5 November 1937 he might have been informed about the latter's Hashemite connection without being able to evaluate it correctly. True, Yasin talked to the German diplomat in early November and the delegates of the Association in late November and December 1937, but there must have been earlier efforts to communicate with the Saudi opposition. Otherwise Seif and his collaborators would not have confined to Grobba as much as they had.

In late December 1937 Grobba had practically refused to recommend German arms exports to the insurgents. On 1 January 1938, Yasin informed (he did not ask!) the envoy that Khalid(al-Hud) al-Qarqani had been commissioned by the Saudi Arabian government to go to Germany and buy weapons. The only request put forward by Yasin: the diplomat should ask his government to support this mission so as to enable the delegate to buy the weapons "at moderate prices" and "by installments."(60)

Moreover, despite the important matters Yasin had to discuss with Grobba, he "was very busy and in a hurry" before leaving Baghdad and regretted not to have found time for a second meeting with the German envoy.(60)

One way or other, Yasin seems to have mistrusted Grobba. The reason remains open to more or less informed speculation, although other than these alternative explanations are hard to find.

Grobba's reaction to Yasin's request: He gave no recommendation whatsoever and submitted it to the judgement of his superiors ("weitere Veranlassung in dieser Angelegenheit gemäss dortigem (= in Germany, the officials al-Qarqani would meet) Ermessen ergebenst anheimstellen.)(62)

Two more documents, one of which has not yet been referred to by historians(63), seem to prove, once more, that Yasin was not willing to inform Grobba completely. Either that, or he himself was not completely informed about the Saudi Arabian foreign policy decision process with Germany.(64)

In the **"fall of 1937"** King Ibn Saud's personal physician Midhat Shaikh al-Ard turned up at the APA. His King feared that the **anti-Semitic campaign** of the German Reich would not only be directed against the Jews, but also against the Arabs as Semites.(65) The reaction of the APA (headed by the super-ideologue Alfred Rosenberg!) seemed to be soothing because another Arab serving as a "private courier" transmitted the gratitude of the King and his foreign minister to the office.(66) This "private courier" was the very same Khalid al-Hud al-Qarqani.(67)

But anti-Semitism seems not to have been the only topic discussed between the physician and the APA officials in the fall of 1937. Von Hentig, in charge of the Oriental Department at the Auswärtiges Amt, noted in February 1939 that "already then", i.e. fall 1937, the APA had informed the Foreign Office about **arms deliveries asked for** by the personal physician of the King.(68)

Yasin's letter to Grobba was dated 1 January 1938. In other words, the Saudis had put forward their requests for arms earlier and via different channels.

Since it was Yusuf Yasin who in November 1937 had spoken to representatives of the Otto Wolff firm about "15,000 rifles on credit or for cash" and since, at about the same time, Madhat al-Ard made a similar request at the APA in Berlin we may conclude that Yusuf Yasin was, in fact, informed about the Saudi Arabian foreign policy decision process with Germany, but he wanted to conceal something from Grobba.

In the **spring of 1938 Khalid al-Hud arrived in Berlin**.(69) The "Saudi minister of commerce and intimate of the King"(70) had already had previous commercial contacts with Germans. He had once been the partner of the former German honorary consul de Haas(71) to whom the Saudi Arabian goverment was indebted (see Yasin-Grobba meeting, 5 November 1937).

Al-Hud submitted two requests: 1) He wanted an intensification of German-Afghanian trade. Rifles and a cartridge factory should be financed by a German credit of "about" a million Reichsmark. Germany should offer her cooperation for the exploitation of Saudi resources, such as "wool, furs, skins, etc." 2) The opening of diplomatic relations; "At this occasion al-Hud explained that after earlier unsuccessful contacts with German circles Saudi Arabia had trust only in the Party."(72)

No wonder: because von Hentig of the AA was reluctant to respond positively to the demand of "15-20,000 modern rifles." Germany needed most modern weapons for her own rearmament and had refused similar demands put forward by Saudi Arabia's neighbour countries.(73)

Al-Hud talked business with the **business community**. The **APA** acted as a go-between. These "basic talks" dealt with the intensification of commercial exchange. "Promises were made to begin with the delivery of war material (rifles, construction of a cartridge factory) and cars to pursue the motorization of the country."(74) This promise was more than surprising: after all, arms exports had to be agreed to by the government. The APA had undoubtedly overestimated its influence and was most upset when the permission had not arrived by late July 1938 because in the meantime al-Hud had submitted an ultimatum. If he did not have a final decision by 1 August 1938, he informed the APA, he would have to consider his mission a failure.(75)

Ibn Saud was outraged, too. He would not let the Crown Prince go to Germany and would not allow him to represent the kingdom at the NSDAP Reichsparteitag in Nürnberg (Party Rally) unless the invitation were put forward by a German representative in his country.(76)

Von Harder contended that **von Hentig**, of the Oriental desk of the AA, the **foreign minister, Ribbentrop**, as well as **Canaris** (Military Intelligence) had favored the establishment of diplomatic relations in the spring of 1938.(77)

Between "spring" and July 1938 the key decision-maker in the AA (**von Hentig** who chanelled the communication as the man in charge of the responsible desk?) had obviously changed his mind, for neither the permission nor the establishment of diplomatic relations followed - much to the dismay of the APA.

The Ministry of the Economy, however, did cooperate and approved of the credits for the sales.(78)

Meanwhile the **Ferrostall** enterprise (based in Essen, in the Ruhr area had submitted its offer in Juni 1938.(79) After having "consented to undertake economic pioneering for Germany in Saudi Arabia,"(80) the firm reacted quickly. The Ferrostaal connection had been initiated by the APA.

On 5 July 1938, Grobba recommended to Foreign Minister Ribbentrop that Germany - take advantage of Britain's confusion about the Palestinian problem and cooperate with Ibn Saud against the partition plan. The envoy felt encouraged to express this suggestion because the Iraqi foreign minister, Tawfik as-Suwaidi, had told them about Ibn Saud's outspoken opposition to the partition plan. This rejection had been admittedly underestimated by Grobba.(81)

On 28 July 1938, the APA expected Ibn Saud's personal physician to turn up once more. Since no decision had been made on the opening of diplomatic relations von Harder feared that the King might interpret this as "an expression of a negative political attitude toward his country."(82)

But the next visitor was the Saudi deputy foreign minister. **Fuadbey Hamza** who stayed in **Berlin** from **23 to 27 Aug. 1938**.(83) He explained the basic constraints of Saudi foreign policy to von Hentig stressing the economic as well as political conditions which "did not allow the King to act according to his own preferences."(84) Ibn Saud, whom he described as an "ever watchful" man, would therefore not act against but only with **England**.

As to **Italy**, relations had improved, he continued, and indicated that the King had refused to accept Italian arms, lest he lose his freedom to act the way he wanted. **Germany** was of "long-term" interest to the Saudis, despite a desire to keep the friendship with his country low-keyed. He did not refer to "details such as the secondary question of diplomatic representation" and emphasized that he did not wish immediate help, if this would represent a burden to Germany". The Reich was trusted because it would not have "interests in power politics in the Arab region."(85)

Clearly, this document suggested that Fuad Hamza or Saudi Arabia in general was representing two different positions. Either this, or that the different German actors, AA and APA, perceived Saudi policies differently. Only a few weeks before, the APA feared for the worst when Ibn Saud threatened to boycott Germany because no diplomatic relations had been established. Fuad Hamza now called this a problem of "secondary" importance.

Since 1936 the Saudis had repeatedly asked for weapons. Here, the deputy foreign minister came and understood the "burden" which immediate help, in other words, weapons, could become for the Reich.

A few weeks before, Ibn Saud would not let his foreign minister, Prince Feisal, go to the Party rally at Nürnberg, and now Fuad Hamza expressed his "appreciation" at the invitation, indicating that he might be present.(86) In fact, he did turn up.(87) It could well be that the Saudis had perceived (correctly) that the AA had to be treated less harshly, with more diplomacy and sophistication than the APA.

In any case, Fuad Hamza did succeed in making this impression, for von Hentig noted that "of all the Arabs who had negotiated with us Fuad Hamza was the most reasonable ("nüchtern"); the one who was least guided by momentary aspects."

This remark, in turn, suggests that von Hentig had met with other representatives from Saudi Arabia before, maybe al-Hud, because the Desert Kingdom was referred to by the AA simply as "Arabien." In other words, von Hentig had been directly involved in the negotiating process, face-to-face with the Saudis, earlier than generally realized.

Whereas von Hentig stated in his 27 August 1938 note that Fuad Hamza had not asked for immediate help," i.e. weapons (for no other plausible explanation of this help can be found), he wrote in his note of 28 February 1939 that Fuad Hamza did, in fact, "again raise the question of the arms delivery."(89)

Whatever the substance of the August 1938 talk, after having consulted with Ministerialrat Prüfer of the AA(90) von Hentig introduced Fuad Hamza to Viceadmiral Canaris of military intelligence.(91)

But von Hentig's cooperativeness did not have so much to do with the good impression Fuad Hamza had made. In order to build up pressure on England and France with respect to the **Czechoslovakian issue**, Hitler had decided to cause the British trouble in the periphery. **Palestine** seemed like a good spot to start and it was up to the "Abwehr" led by Canaris to smuggle weapons into the Mandate.(92) The Saudis were more than willing to take part in this transaction. In his negotiations with the Oberkommando der Wehrmacht (OKW, the chiefs of staff), Fuad

Hamza "insisted not only on deliveries for his King but also for Palestine and explained that the route via Saudi Arabia was safe."(93)

Between Hamza's visit and the **Munich conference** everything seemed to gear up for the delivery. The **Abwehr** had organized the transport, the "steamer was ready for sailing when there arrived definite information claiming that Fuad Hamza had been bought over by the English."(94) The delivery was suspended instantly. OKW and AA then agreed that politically as well as economically the arms transfer would be unacceptable. The weapons could ultimately be used against Germany. But these prepared-for-but-undelivered weapons were not identical to those negotiated with **Ferrostaal** (which had **submitted a detailed offer to al-Hud's firm on 9 August 1938**)(95) because on **1 September 1938 von Harder** of the APA asked Woermann and the AA to agree to the "delivery of rifles and the construction of a cartridge factory in Saudi Arabia."(96) Von Harder added that the **Ministry of the Economy** (Ministerialrat Schottky) was "very interested" in the transaction - "if the Auswärtiges Amt would agree to it for political reasons". **Canaris**, too, had "shown most urgent interest."(97)

After this meeting Woermann asked von Hentig to instruct the APA on the "actions already initiated" ("das Veranlaßte"). In other words, the above-mentioned transport prepared ("actions"!) by the Abwehr was enough, for the time being, and that was it.

During the same meeting Woermann did, however, promise to investigate the possibility of accrediting the German envoy to Baghdad to Jidda as well. This reportedly satisfied von Harder.

And, indeed, on **29 September 1938** Woermann informed Malletke (APA, Department of foreign trade)(98) whom he had met on 25 September(99) that "we have decided **to establish official relations** with Saudi **Arabia very soon**". Germany's envoy to Baghdad should simultaneously be accredited at Jidda.(100) Unofficially, Woermann had obviously spoken about this decision before, as he emphasized the fact that Malettke did, in fact, know of it.(101)

As to the arms deal, the position of the AA had remained unchanged, despite renewed efforts by the APA. Malettke had, of course, pressed for it again when he met with Woermann.(102) **Von Harder** did the same during his own discussion with Woermann.(103)

Woermann had been prepared for this unequivocal reply by **von Hentig** on 6 September. The head of the Oriental desk at the AA denied the contention of the APA which quoted officials of the **Ministry of the Economy** who supposedly supported the arms deal. On the contrary, wrote von Hentig, they were opposed to it because it would not supply Germany with foreign exchange in cash. Moreover, the economic as well as the Oriental department of the **AA rejected** it on economic and political grounds.(104)

And these were the reasons given by Woermann who had signed the letter formulated by von Hentig:(105) According to the "best source one could think of", the Foreign Minister of Saudi Arabia (did he mean the Deputy Foreign Minister Fuad Hamza who had recently visited Berlin?). Even if he could, Ibn Saud would not act against England. Von Hentig/Woermann realized the basically pro-German attitudes of the King but took his Realpolitik necessities into consideration.(106)

The letter was dated 29 September 1938, the day of the Munich Conference, which seemed to "normalize" relations with Britain once again. Von Hentig/Woermann seemed to be pleased by this turn of events: "Fortunately", he concluded the letter, "things have changed since yesterday" (the day the Conference was agreed upon).(107) In other words, arms to the Saudis would have been a means to an end, to cause trouble to England, and not an end in itself. Business could now go on as usual for the AA. This meant no arms to the Saudis, but diplomatic relations in order not to offend the King. Moreover, the risk was very limited. After the Munich Conference, this was even less risky, for English good will could be taken for granted – for the time being.

But the **APA** was neither satisfied nor prepared to give up, and **von Hentig** felt compelled to react once more. Meanwhile, "German **military officials**" seemed to have contacted the Saudi foreign minister (where? when? did von Hentig actually refer to Hamza?) and were told, once more, that Ibn Saud could not possibly provoke Britain. "Our help could never reach the level of English aid. Besides, the Arab coastline is heavily guarded. In sum, these circumstances prove that the deal is politically unfeasible for the time being."(108)

By now, **Ferrostall** had made an official offer(109) to which the Saudi Minister of Finance referred in a letter to al-Hud on 20 December 1938. He agreed in principle and asked the merchant/economic adviser to the King to pursue contacts with the firm. There is a revealing detail in this letter, though. The cartridge factory should be able to produce cartridges for the "German rifle Mauser" – and "for English rifles".(110) Despite the blocking by the AA the enterprise had not lost hope. But risk guaranties asked for by the firm because of Saudi insistence on installment payment were unobtainable.(111)

Giving in to renewed(?) demands by the **APA** and the **Ministry of the Economy** on the question of trade relations ("establish and enlarge them"), the **AA** continued to reject the arms deal – also for economic reasons. The sale of arms would not provide Germany with foreign exchange in cash (the Saudis wanted a barter agreement) and "considering past experiences" with that country (since 1932, Saudi treasury bonds had not been respected it was not "undelicate". To bolster its position the AA had consulted the **OKW** (Oberkommando der Wehrmacht) which reemphasized the "political unreliability" of Ibn Saud and instructed the foreign office that "legally, no weapons had been delivered to Saudi Arabia"; illegally, there had been "some unimportant models".(112)

On 21 January 1939 **Grobba** flew to Jidda to formally open the German mission there.(113) The arms deal was high on his priority list, for he wrote to **Ferrostall** as soon as 26 January 1939. This must have been one of his first actions in Jidda and he behaved like a real intermediary between al-Hud and Ferrostall. The Saudis wanted 5,000 "Mauser" rifles (not 8,000 ? M.W.) with 1,000 cartridges per rifle for £ 11 cif Jidda and a cartridge factory capable of producing of 20-30,000 cartridges per working day (not only 20,000, M.W.). **The Italians** were actively competing with the Germans and had allegedly offered 5,000 Belgian "Mauser" rifles with 1,700 old cif Jidda for only £ 11 per rifle. But al-Hud agreed to wait for Ferrostall's reaction. He was also interested in "old Austrian army rifles" and suggested that the two companies cooperate on Saudi exports to Germany (dates, furs, wool). A collaboration in Egypt would also be feasible.(114)

Between 12 and 18 February 1939 Grobba was received by the King and Yusuf Yasin, an old acquaintance. His report to the AA was dated 18 February 1939.(115) He stressed the "openness" and mutual "confidence" of the interlocutors, explained Ibn Saud's basically anti-British position and his merely tactical considerations vis-à-vis this power. "At the very beginning" of the talk (13 February) the monarch identified **the common "Todfeind" ("deadly enemy")**, "namely the Jews" (did Ibn Saud really not distinguish between Jews and Zionists?). The "Jewish question" was a "matter of existence" to both. People who had visited Berlin continually told him of the "practices" ("Treiben") of the Jews in Germany. "Grobba quoted the King as saying that it was a shame that the children of that country had to lead a miserable life, whereas the Jews and their families turned up ostentatiously ("großprotzerisch") at the big hotels of Unter den Linden" (then Berlin's most attractive street). No, the monarch did not make any distinction between Jews and Zionists. On the contrary, he tried to win over his German counterpart by out anti-Semitizing (anti-Judaizing) the Nazis.

To preserve his independence, the King asked for moral as well as material support, first and foremost in the form weapons "at low prices and favorable conditions." He, in return, offered his "sincere friendship", "at least friendly neutrality, if not even more in case of actual fact."

But the King was very cautious and demanded "discretion", lest "other countries" undertake counter.

The King also mistrusted **Italy** which had concluded an agreement with Britain (16 April 1938) on the spheres of interest in the Mediterranean and Red Sea areas. During the Ethiopian War Ibn Saud had not applied sanctions against Italy and even sold her food, sheep and camels. He was among the first to recognize Italy's annexation of Ethiopia - all this much to the dismay of the English.(116) An Italian envoy arrived in Jidda in the spring of 1937 and was received by Ibn Saud in March. The Italians promptly expressed their gratitude by selling arms on favorable terms, made him a present of several planes, trained Saudi pilots at their own expense and sent flight instructors to the Desert Kingdom. The April 1938 agreement, however, alarmed the monarch, and in February 1939 he insisted that the mission of flight instructors be withdrawn.(117)

Clearly, Ibn Saud tried to counterbalance British influence by establishing diplomatic relations with Germany (and the United States of America)(118) But at least as important as that; he aimed at taming the Italians by explicitly wooing their most powerful ally. For Germany, of course, this was a dilemma.

Finally, Ibn Saud suggested that Germany and his country conclude a) a treaty of friendship, b) a treaty on commerce, and c) an agreement on the exchange of goods.(119)

Knowing, by now, Grobba's position fairly well (hopefully), the reader will not be surprised to hear the envoy's recommendation. Yes, definitely, Germany should fulfill Ibn Saud's expectations and requests. His was a strategically located country and Ibn Saud's "importance" was beyond doubt. If turned down, he may turn his back on Germany "for good". Therefore, he asked for an immediate answer by cable but was also willing to come to Berlin to explain everything personally.

But the AA was in no hurry. Unexpectedly, on **24 February 1939**, Herr **Joachim Rohde of Ferrostaal** arrived **at the Foreign Office**. Contrary to what one might think, Mr. Rohde, "a representative of the firm" (his position was not mentioned), did not press for the realization of the arms deal for which his enterprise had worked so hard. The enterprise had taken up the deal very hesitantly because the economic, as well as the political prospects seemed unpromising. Herr (in fact, Freiherr, M.W.) von Harder had pressed for it ever and again but his explanations had always seemed "fantastic". Rohde himself had been reminded of "a Karl May story."

When the official revealed the AA's ??? Rohde reportedly felt relieved.(116)

Hardly a month later, the **office checking installations for the production of war material** (V.A.K. = "Vorprüfstelle Anlagen zur Herstellung von Kriegsmaterial und Wehrmachts-Ausrüstungen") **forbade Ferrostaal to pursue the deal with the Saudis**.(121)

Far away from Berlin, in Saudi Arabia, King **Ibn Saud** could not know this. Four days later, **on 27 March 1939**, he tried to reach a breakthrough by **writing a personal letter to** "Seine Exzellenz den Kanzler des Deutschen Reiches Herrn **Adolf Hitler**."(122)

The King expressed his gratitude for sending Dr. Grobba to his country "to strengthen the friendly ties between our Kingdom and the German Reich." This letter, to be delivered by (yes) Khalid al-Hud, "may be one of the strong factors contributing to the furthering of good understanding that we aim at with Your Excellency and the great German Reich." He asked Hitler to support al-Hud's mission which he did not specify except for a remark on "economic matters" and referred to the contacts his government had had with Grobba.(123)

On 17 June 1939, at last, al-Hud was received by the Führer. But before things went less than smoothly; despite the fact that on **15 March 1939 the "rest" of Czechoslovakia had been "liquidated"**, as Hitler put it.

Did Ibn Saud speculate on that? In other words: Did he realize that Hitler would then again be willing (as he was in 1938 - before the Munich Conference) to cause harm to Britain on the periphery? If he did, the speculation of the King was intelligent and to the point. For the time being, however, the AA kept blocking. Significantly, the V.A.K. had sent its order after, and not before, the invasion of Czechoslowakia.

Because of (and not despite) the "events in Europe which absorb us completely",(124) "we do not plead for a basic revision of our traditional policy on the Arabian Peninsula." In his letter to Grobba, Woermann unequivocally rejected the proposed treaty of friendship with and the delivery of weapons to the Kingdom. His only compromise: Grobba should inform the Saudi government with "all due caution."(125)

The AA remained convinced that Saudi Arabia would be lost, in case of war - lost to Britain.

At about the same time, sometime **in April, von Hentig met with Grobba in Baghdad.** Hirszowicz(126) contends that the diplomat's trip to the Near East (in February)(127) "effected, to a certain extent, a change in the German Government's view on strengthening relations with Saudi Arabia." To some extent yes, but more tactically than strategically, as we shall see. The AA, primarily von Hentig, basically stuck to traditional views.

Still in April, during von Hentig's trip, his assistant Schlobies remarked that his superior did not share Grobba's "optimism" as far as German opportunities to increase influence in "this region" (= Near East) were concerned.(128) Grobba claimed, however, that von Hentig had changed his mind, explaining to the envoy that his earlier attitude had been based "on incorrect premises." Now the AA official would be willing to "work for the acceptance of Ibn Saud's suggestions and for cooperation with him."(129)

This perception - rather than fact (as we shall see) - encouraged **Grobba (2 May 1939)** to ask the AA (Woermann as the key person) to change its, i.e. his mind.(130) Moreover, he was told by Yusuf Yasin that Fuad Hamza had been neutralized in the Saudi decision-making process. Yasin and al-Hud were the only real people to negotiate with. Finally, events in Europe (Czechoslovakia) made the outbreak of a war ever more likely, in which case Saudi Arabia, having promised "friendly neutrality," would provide facilities for an evasion ("Ausweichstellung"), both "politically and militarily." After having met with the King three times Grobba had "no doubt whatsoever" that Ibn Saud would not keep his promise.

Again, he described what he saw as the merely tactical gestures of the King towards the English whom he allegedly "hated". This was why he granted oil concessions in al-Hasa and at the border with Kuwait to the Americans and not to the International Petroleum Company run by England.

The **Italian envoy, Sillitti**, had also recognized the mistrust of Saudi Arabia towards his country and was willing to pay the price of German-Saudi cooperation lest, in case of war, the axis be placed at a disadvantage.

This letter seems to be Grobba's first success ever, in this decision-making process, for Woermann remarked, on 5 May 1939, that he "had been convinced by this letter".(131)

Hirszowicz contends that the **Anglo-Turkish declaration of 12 May 1939** and the ensuing Franco-Turkish declaration issued six weeks later (23 June) appear" in the notes of Auswärtiges Amt" as "a prime reason for the change of the policy toward Saudi Arabia."(132) But whereas Woermann had been convinced by 5 May 1939, the Anglo-Turkish Agreement followed on 12 May, a week later. It wasn't until 9 June 1939, that the Foreign Office registered the British-Turkish step.(133)

It goes without saying that the "Führer" was less than happy about Turkey's decision to back the Western powers. He tried to comfort himself as well as the chiefs of staff by declaring, on 22 August 1939, that "since Kemal's death Turkey has been governed by cretins and half-idiots".(134) At the same time, he did not flatter the Arabs, to say the least. In the very same speech he had called them "at best lacquered half-apes who want to feel the whip".(135)

No, strategically, his micro-environment had not undergone significant changes and since ideology played such a decisive role in his policy making we may pretty well assume that the basic input-data, as far as Saudi Arabia was concerned, had not changed either.

The AA obviously had **second thoughts on Italy's willingness to cooperate**, despite Sillitti's reaffirming remarks to Grobba. On the occasion of the signing of the Steel Pact, during Foreign Minister Ciano's visit to Berlin, Woermann conferred with Ambassador Buti who seemed less than enthusiastic. The foreign minister himself would have to decide and, besides, Italian rather than German firms should be granted the weapons deal. On the other hand, he conceded that German-Italian competition for the Saudis was undesirable. Woermann promised to seek further clarifications from the Italian decision-makers.(136)

On 25 May, Woermann asked his staff at the AA to consult the Italian government before proceding with the Saudi deal(137). On 10 June he sent a cable to the German embassy in Rome instructing it to inform the Italian government of Germany's intentions and to report back regarding the Italian reaction.(138)

The southern axis partner took its time, though. First of all Italy had to lose something (it had to practically acknowledge the failure of her Saudi Arabian policy and had to renounce on an economically not too unattractive deal). Moreover, the Saudi representative negotiating with Germany was less than well liked by the Italians. Al-Hud was a Tripolitanian who had fought them "and did not conceal his hostility toward Italy during his talks with the Germans."(139) But this was not a unique onto characteristic al-Hud. His King and Yusuf Yasin, just to name two decision-makers, were not enthusiastic about Italy either.

The Italians probably made a final attempt not to lose the Saudi connection by trying to win time. Finally, on 14 1939, Count Magistrati informed Woermann that his government would not object to Germany's steps in Saudi Arabia but reminded him of the Jidda based Italian firm "Sana" which could also serve the Germans in dealing with Arab countries on the Red Sea.(140)

According to Grobba's prediction, **von Hentig** really did recommend a new Saudi Arabian policy – on **22 May 1939**. "The past months have proven", he wrote, that 1) Egypt has completely turned to England (has "thrown herself into England's arms"); 2) resistance in Palestine has evidently died out; 3) Syria is unable to conduct an independent policy, Iraq has openly sided with England; 4) Turkey does not endanger England's flank; 5) oil has enabled Ibn Saud to get regular revenues 6) the "growing mistrust" Italy has met in the Arab world has led her, according to envoy Sillitti whom von Hentig quoted (he did not refer to other Italian reactions) to "welcome" German cooperation.(141)

"In accordance with the **Minister of War**" von Hentig suggested that (142) 1) the foreign minister receive Khalid al-Hud (who had arrived in Germany in "early May")(143) 2) the latter be authorized to hand over the letter of Ibn Saud to the "Führer" 3) Ibn Saud's desire for "economic cooperation" be met.

True, von Hentig seemed to have revised his earlier position. True, those people who had to deal with al-Hud in the deal knew what it was about, namely weapons (first and foremost). But why, then, did von Hentig not recommend, clearly, unequivocally and openly to send weapons? Instead, he only spoke of "economic cooperation". We may well assume that von Hentig was not innocent and naive enough not to know about al-Hud's mission, but the problem remains: Why did he not recommend to deliver arms? After all, this note was an internal paper written for his superiors. He was the man who was supposed to inform them, he was supposed to know more than they did so as to enable them to make the decisions for which he, the AA professional, made the preparations, i.e. had to gather information and make evaluations. **No, this note is far from being a verification of von Hentig's new Saudi Arabian policy.** There are also other proofs of this contention to which I shall return.

Finally, weeks after his arrival in Berlin, **al-Hud was received on 8 June 1939 by Foreign Minister Ribbentrop.** The very fact that despite von Hentig's and the AA's supposedly new policy the Saudi negotiator had to wait approximately four weeks is also indicative of the not too new line.

After the routine exchange of niceties al-Hud proved that he had learned the German vocabulary quite well. Saudi Arabia and Germany had "the same aims and a common adversary [note: He did not speak of the "enemy", M.W.], Judaism," (Note: Like his King, he did not refer to Zionism but Judaism and Jews respectively.) England, which for tactical reasons had to be treated "carefully" by the Saudis and which was a "natural adversary," limited Arab "Lebensraum" (living space, one of the National Socialist key-words).

Saudi Arabia wanted to build up her armed forces independently of England. The case of Palestine had demonstrated that an independent supply of ammunition was also necessary.

Therefore, he was "especially interested" in rifles and "a small ammunition factory". The following wishes would be armoured cars and light anti-aircraft guns.(144)

Ribbentrop agreed to al-Hud's proposals "in principle" and referred him to von Hentig with whom he should negotiate the details. The Saudi delegate seemed to be "very satisfied".(145)

Officially, this was the first time the Saudis had put forward their request for anti-aircraft guns and armoured cars. Or at least it seems to have been the first official request. The military attaché of the United States had been informed of anti-aircraft and anti-tank gun interests of the "Hedjas" long ago, in May 1937 the latest.(146) We may assume that "Rheinstahl", which produced the desired and already inspected guns, knew about these desires too.

Also on **8 Juni 1939**, Herr Willy **Jäger**, of the board of Ferrostaal, turned up **at von Hentig's** office. Contrary to Herr Rohde, he reaffirmed his firm's interests in the Saudi deal. He went so far as to deny that his representative (he meant Rohde) had signaled a lack of willingness to pursue it. Jäger had evidently sent this information by letter to Grobba combining these instructions with attacks on both von Hentig and Rohde.(147) In his talk with von Hentig Jäger tried to play this down, wanting to conceal the fact that the APA had initiated the Saudi deal. The Ministry of the Economy had referred it to Ferrostaal, he claimed, but von Hentig dismissed this interpretation categorically. Ferrostaal could, of course, have as many business contacts as he wished, but political deals would be decided upon by the Auswärtiges Amt exclusively, von Hentig stated. Moreover, the AA "would not tolerate the interference and pushes of any other institution" without prior information from the Foreign Office. The upcoming negotiations would procede after a "reception (of al-Hud, M.W.) by the Führer" under "different circumstances" and were conducted by the foreign minister and his representatives. "Herr Jäger understood and said good-bye.(148) The following day von Hentig suggested that Hitler receive al-Hud. Now he openly wrote about the arms deal and supported it.(149) Now, that Ribbentrop had met with the Saudi delegate, now that "resistance" would not have made sense. To repeat: On 22 May, he had not yet given up.

On **17 June 1939, the "Führer" and al-Hud came together** at the Obersalzberg and Hitler finally received Ibn Saud's letter. He explained that Germany had no territorial ambitions in Arabia, that both countries fought the same "enemies" and together "fight the Jews." He would not rest until the "last Jew had left Germany." Al-Hud seemed to like this idea and mentioned analogous approaches in the past. Prophet Mohammad had acted similarly, he elaborated, by "expelling all the Jews from Arabia." Yes, indeed, the Prophet had not only been a "religious leader", but also a "great statesman", al-Hud philosophied.

Other philosophical topics of their talk dealt with the burning question of what would have happened if Karl Martell had not defeated the Saracenes but had, instead, infused "Germanic spirit" into them, modifying Islam with "Germanic dynamism". "Very remarkable" was the impression al-Hud had won from the "Führer". More important, Hitler had obviously promised a credit of one and a half million Reichsmark for the "immediate" purchase of 8,000 rifles including 8 million cartridges, a "small ammunition factory, light anti-aircraft guns and armoured cars."(150) He did, however, seem to have insisted on prior Italian approval.(151)

Two days later, on 19 June 1939, Willy Jäger submitted a detailed summary of the actual developments and the substance of the negotiations with the Saudis.(152) Ferrostaal, seemed to win the day, at last.

The German-Saudi Arabian honeymoon was not to last for long because press reports about the al-Hud/Hitler meeting had alarmed Ibn Saud. (153) Here, already, Germany could see that the King was unable to initiate any basic foreign policy change at the expense of **Britain**, least of all in times of crisis with Germany and Britain at the brink of war. After all, the visit of Ibn Saud's emissary to Herr Hitler was "said to have caused consternation in London."(154)

The King seemed so incensed by the German and Italian press coverage that he thought of cancelling the deal altogether should another report be published.(155) Clearly, the publicity of the German-Saudi connection turned out to be an embarrassment to the King. The dominant bilateral relations with England were in jeopardy and that would have proved more disadvantageous to the Desert Kingdom than the deal with Hitler could prove advantageous. On 5 July, an excited al-Hud came to von Hentig telling him that the King had instructed him to leave Germany. Yes, the German radio station broadcasting in Arabic had, once again, given the details published earlier by the Italian press.(156)

In the end, he did stay in Berlin and got the written German promise to deliver the desired arms.

But before, **the negotiations proved to be more difficult** than might be believed by those who considered Hitler's word omnipotent. the AA, first and foremost von Hentig, had some additional techniques in store.

Encouraged by the political-philosophical dialogue with Hitler al-Hud did, in fact, ask for a credit of six, instead of one and a half million Reichsmark conceded by the Chancellor.(157) Von Hentig was in no hurry to come to terms with al-Hud. Detailed negotiations could follow later and al-Hud could well carry out other orders and then return to Berlin.(158) Undoubtedly, von **Hentig wanted to win time** to get rid of the affair.

Meanwhile, "**military and economic**" officials (they remained unnamed) had pointed out "difficulties". Von Hentig was not at all unhappy about them. "If military officials are not interested in the strengthening of our position in Saudi Arabia, and I had to learn this from the recent report, we could easily lead Khalid al-Hud and his high commissioner to renounce upon further negotiations."(159)

Could **von Hentig** really have been of Grobba's line? More and more, we realize that the AA official had not changed his mind. Whenever and whereever he could, he **tried to torpedo** the deal.

But he was overoptimistic - from his point of view. Or else he had overstated his case. Whatever the case, on 4 July, at 11:20 a.m., the phone rang in his office - and Canaris was on the line. No, the Oberkommando der Wehrmacht had no objections to the obligations to which it felt committed, even if the Saudis could not pay. Von Hentig was on the defensive. On 12:15 p.m. Canaris once again phoned von Hentig and informed him that "the delivery would be made" and had, in fact, been packed.(160)

All this had been a misunderstanding, though. Canaris had spoken of **weapons destined for Palestine** to which von Hentig had no objection either.(161)

The **Abwehr**, headed by Canaris, had promised **4,000 rifles as a present** to the King,(162) but this step was not well liked by von Hentig. First of all, he was told by Major Stolze of the Canaris staff, that only 1,000 rifles could be organized, possibly another 200 pistols. Second, and more important, compared with the support the "Führer" had promised this was a very poor result.(163) They had also asked Captain Koch of the "Wehrwirtschaftsabteilung" only to find out that 4,000 rifles were unavailable.(164)

But on **12 July 1939 Canaris and Keitel** were able to mobilize them, or at least they **decided upon the delivery**.(165) Von Hentig had lost.

Woermann and two representatives of the OKW divided the costs between the two institutions on 13 July. The Army would pay for the rifles, the AA for the packing.(166) The OKW/Abwehr behavior was all the more surprising considering **Hitler's previous decision not to export arms to states whose position in a future war between Germany and the West was in doubt.** The only "safe" areas for German arms exports were South America, the Baltic states, Norway and Bulgaria.(167) Maybe von Hentig knew about Hitler's vacillations? Why, then, did Keitel and Canaris proceed at all? Whatever the explanation, on **18 July 1939, the letter carrying the detailed list of Germany's promises was handed over to al-Hud.**(168) Fearing that on al-Hud's trip to Paris (why did he go there instead of returning to Saudi Arabia immediately?) the letter "might be read by unauthorized persons," the formal information was written on neutral paper (carrying no sign of the AA or any other official German institution) and it did not contain the passage on the **present of 4,000 rifles.**(169)

Yes, the Saudis were promised a **credit of six! million Reichsmark** to purchase German arms. They could buy an unspecified number of **"Mauser" rifles** for £ 11 including **1,000 cartridges; machine-guns** (Rheinstahl-Borsig enterprise); **ammunition and the ammunition factory** often referred to (Ferrostaal firm). An **interest rate of six per cent annually** had been fixed. Moreover, another offer concerning **light machine guns** coming from Brünn (formerly, Czechoslovakia!) and **light armoured cars with machine guns** was to be submitted later, "as soon as it would be here."(170) In September 1939, shortly after the outbreak of the War, al-Hud left Berlin for Saudi Arabia.(171)

Were these weapons ever delivered? Hirszowicz writes that the "deal may not have been realised, for the war broke out about six weeks later and the transport of arms to the Red Sea ports became extremely difficult not to mention the other changes in this respect brought about by the war."(172)

Nicosia states that the "package, which included 4,000 rifles, anti-aircraft guns and the munitions factory, was never delivered."(173)

Alfred Rosenberg noted in his diary, in 1941, that the outbreak of the war prevented the weapons from being delivered.(174)

Most of the weapons referred to in the letter handed over to al-Hud on 18 July 1939 should have been delivered within 14 to 18 months. (175) The only delivery which had, in fact, been packed contained 4,000 rifles organized by Canaris and Keitel in July 1939. Indeed, these weapons could pose serious problems as to whether or not they had arrived in Saudi Arabia.

As to the other weapons, the answer is beyond any doubt: No, impossible. There may be some doubts about the ammunition factory, for there were no delivery dates mentioned in the letter. But even this part of the package could not have been constructed until German-Saudi relations took a turn to the worse.

Whereas Schröder contends that Saudi Arabia broke off diplomatic relations with Germany on 11 September 1939 (the British had allegedly pressed for this step)(176), Hirszowicz claims that Saudi Arabia "did not break off diplomatic relations but did not permit the presence of a German envoy at Jidda"(177). Grobba denies this. Saudi Arabia did, in fact, break off diplomatic relations with the Reich - on 28 February 1945, a few weeks before the end of the war. Grobba reproaches the AA with having missed an opportunity to gather information on Arab countries during the war in an Arab country. The AA had told him to return to Berlin instead of following up on an invitation by the Saudi King. But Grobba, too, concedes that "later on" during the war the King might have been "pressed" by the British to insist on his departure from Saudi Arabia.(178) In other words, Saudi Arabia could neither politically nor militarily live up to the expectations of the APA and Grobba. Saudi Arabia was unable to do so, even if it had wished to act differently. Structurally, this was impossible. Von Hentig and Woermann had been right, from the very beginning. From the German point of view Saudi "neutrality" was unfriendly. Formally, Saudi Arabia remained "neutral". As a matter of fact, she was pro-British and her oil was used against the Reich.(179)

IV. GERMAN ACTORS: THEIR IMAGES, ARGUMENTS, PREFERENCES, ACTIONS AND IMPORTANCE (A SYSTEMATICAL ACCOUNT INSTEAD OF A CONCLUSION)

Images, arguments, preferences and actions of the political actors in Germany have already been dealt with in the chronological section. Here, some sketchy remarks rounding the general picture may suffice. The importance or weight of the actors has been reached via the table, "The Decision-Making Process" (see annex). True, such a quantitative evaluation carries the risk of being subjectively biased as far as the respective historian is concerned. On the other hand, the data can easily be checked by others as well. The method of measuring resembles the principle of "attitude scales" often used in the social sciences.(180)

There is one obvious shortcoming to this method, though. Hierarchy is considered less than function and may thus lead to distorting results. Thus, Ministerialrat Prüfer and the minister of war obtain better results than Hitler. A single successful action may distort the whole picture. These shortcomings can, however, be easily recognized and the overall impression remains instructive. As an additional, not an exclusive instrument, this scale may be rather helpful in attempting to weigh the importance of decision-makers when using historical material, i.e. sources of and in diplomatic history. A chronological and systematic survey of the actors and actions is provided for.

ADOLF HITLER

Although being highly motivated by ideology, he was more pragmatic than those who were most often referred to Nazi ideology, i.e., the APA people. Hitler's anti-Semitism did not consist only of anti-Judaism but of anti-Arabism as well. This made the deal with the Saudis even more difficult.

He hardly interfered in this decision-making process in particular but rather set the parameters according to which the lower echelons could act with one another as well as against one another.

There remains an enigma, though: Why did Keitel and Canaris finalize the deal after Hitler's evaluation of "safe" and "unsafe" areas for German arms exports? Had he been overruled? What had happened? This question remains unanswered by the sources. Or perhaps Hitler and the OKW considered the volume of this deal to be of such limited scope as not to take it too seriously, and they went ahead.

THE ECONOMY

On the **macro economic level**, Saudi Arabia's attractiveness to Hitler's Germany was more than limited.

In the "spring of 1933" Germany was offered oil concessions in the al-Hasa province but refused to accept.(181) Hitler argued that they could not be defended in times of war. Besides, Germany had not enough foreign exchange to buy these concessions. Instead, Germany hoped to sell drilling equipment to British and U.S. firms.(182) English goodwill was not to be jeopardized. As far as raw materials in general and oil in particular were concerned, Germany wanted to be as independent as possible. The fields supplying her with oil should in any case be "adjacent to the Reich, not overseas".(183) Rumania was therefore more interesting, and the production of synthetic oil was economically as well as strategically important.(184)

On the **micro economic level** one should not overstate the interest on the part of German firms to enter the Saudi arms market.(185)

The **Otto Wolff** enterprise was not heard of any more after November 1937. In June 1939 the enterprise had a surprising but late comeback. Herr de Haas, the former German honorary consul and associate of al-Hud, introduced himself to the latter as the future representative of Otto Wolff and the NSDAP to Saudi Arabia(186) a disadvantageous choice. Saudi contracts and joined forces with Grobba and the APA - the two weakest allies in the decision-making process. The "average weight per actor" of this most active micro economic actor was the lowest of all (2.1; see annex). The impact of economic influence was minimal to non-existent.(187)

Al-Hud's own Jidda-based firm "Khalid Qarqani" had imported 40 **Büssing** motor trucks, and he wanted to import another 300 trucks as well as 60 buses produced by that manufacturer.(188) He had subsequently suggested that Büssing open a repair workshop in Saudi Arabia but the Hannover enterprise refused.(189) **Auto-Union, Siemens and Bosch**, too, had not shown much enthusiasm.(190) The Saudis were an unattractive business partner wooing the German addresses rather than being wooed. Besides, they had obviously chosen the wrong go-between to win the support of German enterprises. But the choice of Ferrostaal's Herr Jäger had been made by the APA.(191)

Rheinmetall Borsig, which was to produce the anti-aircraft weapons, if acting politically, acted silently. Nothing could be observed as to actions by **Mauser**, the producer of the desired rifles.(192) Other firms mentioned in files of the AA(193) in connection with weapons to Saudi Arabia clearly belong to the other category of arms referred to repeatedly. This material was destined for Palestinian insurgents and sent via the Desert Kingdom. (The files do not make the distinction.)

We have also realized that "**bureaucratic politics**" were not limited to the governmental bureaucracy. For how are we to offer to the behavior of two top managers of Ferrostaal, Rohde on the one hand and Jäger on the other one?

Infighting seems to have been going on within the **Ministry of Economic Affairs** as well. Some (APA) claimed support for the arms exports by this office, others (the Oriental desk of the AA) contended that this ministry was opposed to the deal. Misperceptions can hardly explain the divergent impressions. The "average weight" of this inhomogenous ministry was low (2.7).

This in turn, may well be due to the lack of a consistent line within the ministry; and this, again, may well be the result of bureaucratic politics.

In general, the Ministry of Economic Affairs acted rather timidly. Even von Harder had to admit that the Ministry of Economic Affairs would only agree to the export of German arms to the Saudis if the AA supported it for political reasons.(194) Economically, the deal was uninteresting because it would not improve Germany's foreign exchange situation, the argument ran in the Ministry of Economic Affairs.(195) Here this office agreed with the AA.(196)

THE MINISTRY OF FOREIGN AFFAIRS (AA)

This office held the key to any decision on the issue. **Woermann** may have been the more influential person (as to hierarchy and function) compared with **von Hentig**. But the latter was clearly the more active man, and his influence (weight) fell just short of the importance of his superior. At the beginning of his tenure, in the spring of 1938, **Ribbentrop** seemed to have been in favor of sending the arms to the Saudis, but then von Hentig and Woermann took over. Here, we are confronted with a discrepancy between function and hierarchy. By September 1938, the foreign minister was uninterested in the affair, despite the pressure of the APA. At the Party rally in Nurnberg he refused to meet with and talk to its chief, Alfred Rosenberg.(197)

Even in September 1938 and March 1939, when the Czechoslovakian crisis and its repercussions for German-British relations encouraged the supporters of the deal, the AA (Woermann and von Hentig) were successful in trying to block it. Their only concession: the establishment of diplomatic relations which was decided upon in September 1938. Had Ribbentrop not sided with them by now, he would undoubtedly have gone farther.

Political as much as economic reasons were given by the AA. **Politically**, Ibn Saud was considered unreliable, from the German point of view. In case of a German-British war he would side with the English, it was predicted correctly.(198) A possible worsening of German-Italian relations was also taken into consideration by von Hentig and Woermann who cooperated very closely with the former. Hentig, not a member of the NSDAP, formulated the letters Woermann (belonging to the SS) signed; a functional coalition.

Economically, foreign exchange aspects were not the only argument. Until 1939, Saudi Arabia had not repaid her treasury bonds issued in 1932.(199) The Kingdom's reputation as a creditor-nation was bad. Later references to the prospective oil wealth partly neutralize this argument. But why did von Hentig mention this fact in May 1939 and not in January of that year? He must have known about oil earlier. There remains only one explanation: He had remained opposed to the deal.

Nevertheless, a certain **lack of knowledge about Saudi Arabia** cannot be denied. Neither von Hentig nor Woermann knew much about their partners and their intentions.

Whereas the U.S. military attaché in Berlin was informed about what he called "Hejazi" interest in anti-aircraft guns as early as February 1937, the AA was confronted with this fact in June 1939, during the al-Hud/Ribbentrop meeting.

Fuad Hamza was repeatedly referred to by von Hentig as the Saudi foreign minister.(200) He was, however, deputy foreign minister. Al-Hud was called the Saudi minister of commerce but he was only an economic adviser to the King.(201)

Whereas Woermann knew about al-Hud's status,(202) he also spoke of Deputy FM Fuad Hamza.(203)

Yes, von Hentig did not support the export of German arms to Saudi Arabia Contrary to Hirszowicz' remarks(204) "the Germans", especially von Hentig, did not show a "willingness to please Ibn Saud".

But despite his counter-efforts in the 1930s, al-Hud and the ruling Saud family would not bear a grudge against him. After the Second World War, Ibn Saud's son and successor was looking for a political adviser. Khalid Abul Walid, prior to the war named al-Hud, recommended von Hentig and the latter got the post.(205)

Fritz Grobba was neither a genuine diplomat nor a member of the NSDAP. After the First World War he somehow slid into the diplomatic service to which he had belonged as an interpreter before. Among all the "Vons", the aristocrats who had traditionally dominated the German diplomatic service, he was looked upon as a "homo novus."(206) Being a member of the "Free Masons,"(207) he had, of course, difficulties with the Party. It was, therefore, more than natural (from the perspective of careerism) that he tried to prove his ideological as much as his diplomatic efficiency by joining forces with the super-ideologues of the APA. Unfortunately, the APA was active in the Saudi affair, but also unsuccessful. So was Grobba, and his average weight per actor is even lower than that of the APA. No wonder, he was the client of an already weak patron. His 2 May 1939 letter was not pivotal in favor of the arms export, despite Woermann's handwritten marginal note. Rather, the political parameters had been changed.

His anti-Judaism was vehement, at least in his official dispatches (the Jews as "deadly enemy")(208). Considering his Free Masonism it may well have been a tactical manoeuvre rather than a reflection of his own political/racial conviction.

His image of Arabs was not too flattering either. Telling lies was "typical of Saudi Arabian mentality."(209)

Similar to numerous politicians of the late 1970s and early 1980s, Grobba had **misperceived** Saudi power and prestige, with a striking difference, though. Thus, he contended that an improvement of German-Saudi relations would enhance his country's position in the Islamic World in general because of the Kingdom's influence there. He indicated that Ibn Saud's position in time of war would be "decisive" for "Palestine (not an independent state! M.W.), Transjordan (the archrival of the Saudis! M.W.), Iraq (also Hashemite! M.W.) and Syria."(210) Grobba had either forgotten his own talks with Iraqi Hashemites trying to overthrow Ibn Saud or believed in the ignorance of his superiors who he wanted to win over for the deal.

37

Another pattern of the 1930s and the 1980s: By morally supporting the Palestinian course Germany would buy itself into Arab hearts and markets.(211)

Strategically and politically Grobba misperceived two additional points. He believed in the possibility of exploiting Saudi oil in times of a German-British war and had "no doubts" that Ibn Saud would reject "even the most tempting English offers" if "cooperation with us had been realized" before.(212) The aimed at cooperation had been realized but Ibn Saud acted differently.

THE AUSSENPOLITISCHES AMT OF THE NSDAP (APA)

The APA was another loser, an active one though (15 actions per actor). Its activities were more noticeable when others hardly acted at all, namely in 1936/37. Contrary to the pragmatic "Realpolitik" approach of the AA, the APA tried to use the Czechoslovakian crisis as a catalyst.

Even von Hentig had to admit that the "Oriental experts" of the APA had been active in the "Near and Middle East" prior to the Foreign Office.(213)

It was the APA which had made the contacts with the Saudis. It was the APA which had made the contacts with the Iraq-based Hashemite opposition to Ibn Saud(214) and it was the APA which had made contacts with Egyptians as early as 1933/34 to undermine the British position in the Middle East.(215)

These activities met with opposition from the NSDAP establishment(216) which had opted for the traditional bureaucracy and fought the "Old Fighters" who wanted to revolutionize the whole political system (see the liquidation of the SA, 30 June 1934). It goes without saying that the traditional AA bureaucracy itself tried to sabotage the APA efforts. Von Hentig, the man in charge of the Oriental desk of the Foreign Office, naturally became the main target of the APA activists. Rosenberg and von Harder made bitter complaints about him.(217) Malettke was only the APA man in charge of the "Oriental desk" (from Asia Minor, Egypt to India).(218) "Coalition" partners of the APA were, apart from Grobba, some industrial enterprises, first and foremost Ferrostaal, another loser. Or at least, the powerless winner of the contract that never materialized.

The APA, too, misperceived Saudi Arabian power and prestige, claiming that Ibn Saud's kingdom had become a "spiritual power center of the orthodox-Muslim and national-Arabic currents". Its "völkisch" (ethnic) unification movement had allegedly reached Iraq, Syria, Palestine, Transjordan (and) the Yemen."(219) The same argument put forward by Grobba. Like him, the APA had overlooked (or wanted to overlook) the rivalries between Ibn Saud and the Hashemites.

As to the role of the APA in the decision-making process of the Third Reich, we have to modify Jacobsen's conclusion that until 1938 it had not been possible to realize any active participation of this office in diplomatic decisions.(220) The establishment of formal relations with

Saudi Arabia and later the decision to export arms were cases of APA participation, though not power.

With its very limited staff (80 in 1938),(221) the APA was at least a serious challenger of traditional foreign policy actors.

Rosenberg, the head of the APA, and his staff were obviously so obsessed with their anti-Judaism as to overlook (willingly?) the fact that the Arabs were Semites as well. The Saudis were aware of this contradiction and this is why they asked about the consequences of NSDAP anti-Semitism. As mentioned, they got a satisfactory answer; satisfactory from their point of view.(222)

THE MILITARY

The **Minister of War** participated rarely but successfully in this decision-making process but it seems that foreign policy rather than security considerations were preponderant.

Canaris actively supported an involvement in the Saudi-Palestine-Germany triangle until September 1938 and then changed his mind after the Fuad Hamza affair, like the **OKW**; both influential decision-makers. Afterwards, they considered Ibn Saud to be unreliable. Contrary to Hirszowicz' contention,(223) they did not intend to use Saudi Arabia as a potential military equivalent to Turkey which was "lost" to Germany after the Turco-British Declaration of April 1939. One enigma has been mentioned already: the Canaris-Keitel agreement to go ahead with the delivery despite Hitler's arms exports list to "safe" areas not including Saudi Arabia. In this latest phase of the decision-making process the Canaris-Keitel (military) axis clearly dominated the Foreign Office staff.

CONCLUSIONS

Among the great powers on the sidelines, Hitler's Germany was a nation reluctant to get involved in Saudi Arabia, in the Middle East in general. Germany was wooed by the Arabs rather than the Arabs by the Germans. Neither was any German threat possible, intended or necessary.

As in many other foreign and general policy decision-making processes of the Third Reich, we have been able to observe the struggle of Nazi internal politics. As Browning put it, "the chieftains of the Third Reich were in perpetual competition to out-perform each other. Like a feudal monarch, Hitler stood as arbiter over his squabbling vassals." (224) Surprisingly, however, some of his vassals, at least in the Foreign Office, even tried to out-perform the feudal monarch. The negotiations with al-Hud after 17 June 1939 are a point in case. The same seems to be true as to the Canaris-Keitel agreement, although there remain certain doubts here. The "pluralism" immanent in the foreign policy decision-making system of the Third Reich (Michalka) (225) has, again, been verified. "Bureaucratic politics" might be the better term, for "pluralism" would wrongly imply democracy.

We have been confronted with Saudi anti-Judaism (and not only a predictable, from the Arab point of view, anti-Zionism) which hardly fell short of National Socialist ideology as far as Jews were concerned.

Historians may rest assured. They are still better historians than kings and politicians. No, either the late King Khalid nor German Chancellor Schmidt knew more than the historians dreamed of in their historiography. Fortunately, the Chancellor did not refer to the traditional German-Saudi friendship. After all, he would have identified himself with the super-ideologues and racists of the APA, at least in the context of arms relations between the two countries. And King Khalid? Had he known that Hitler, after having met with his envoy al-Hud, called Arabs "at best lacquered half-apes who want to feel the whip," he would have preferred not to lecture on tradition.

The tradition of the mutual friendship and the friends of Saudi Arabia in Germany is not too flattering - for either side.

ANNEX

THE DECISION-MAKING PROCESS: EVENTS, ACTIONS, ACTORS. A QUANTITATIVE AND QUALITATIVE SURVEY
(Only domestic actors)

Actors / Events/Actions	A.H.	Economy Firms	For.Office Gr. v.H.	FM Pr.	W.	APA	EcM.	Mil. C.	OKW	M/War Notes
1936? contract al-Hud with unnamed German firms	(2) (3)									
May? 1937 Rheinmetall		2								
Nov. 1937 Otto Wolff		1								
Nov. 1937 Gr.-Yasin			2	5						
22 Dec. 1937 Gr. turns Abdul Ilah to German firms		1	2							
Fall 1937 M. al-Ard			5			5/5/1				rally+ anti-Sem.5 weapons 1
Spring 1938 al-Hud, APA, AA			5/5			2/2				
June 1938 Ferrostaal offer		2								
July 1938: Dipl.rel.+arms exp.			5	2		2	2	2		
July 1938,Gr.: Use S.A. against Great Britain			2	5		2	5	5		
Aug.1938 v.H.-Fuad Hamza	(5)		5		5	2		2		
Aug.1938 Ferrostaal offer										
1 Sept. 1938 v. Harder-W.		2								
CZECHOSLOVAKIAN ISSUE										
Sept.? 1938 Fuad Hamza bought over, no arms exported			(5) (5)							
6 Sept. 1938 v.H. opposed					5	3				
Mid Sept. v. Harder-W.					5	3				
25 Sept. 1938 W.-Malettke						4			5	4 dipl.rel. 3 weapons
26 Sept. 1938 letter Malettke-W.						3 4				

Events/Actions	A.H.	Economy Firms	For. Office Gr. v.H. FM Pr. W.	APA	EcM	Mil. C. OKW	M/War	Notes
27 Sept. 1938 v.H.: Arms to S.A.=to GB								
28 Sept. 1938 W.: "Friendly reply to APA"			5					
29/30 Sept. MUNICH CONFERENCE (v.H.)/W.								
letter to APA			4	5				
22 Oct. 1938 V.H.–Malettke			5	3				
Dec.? 1938 Ferrostaal offer Dec.1938/Jan. 1939 pressure by APA+EcM		2		4/3	4	5		
26 Jan. 1939 letter Gr. to Ferrostaal		2						
18 Feb.1939 letter Gr. to AA (13 Feb. received by Ibn Saud)		2				4		
24 Feb.1939 J. Rohde (Ferrostaal) at v.Hentig's		4						Not line of firm (=Jäger)
15 March CZECHOSLOVAKIA "LIQUIDATED"								
23 March 1939 V.A.K. stop to Ferrostaal							5	Supervised by this office
27 March letter King to A.H. (handed over 17 June 1939)								
18 Apr. W.to Gr.:No arms ? Apr. v.Hentig meets Gr. in Baghdad			5					

Events/Actions	A.H.	Economy Firms Gr.	For. Office v.H.	For. Office FM	For. Office Pr.	For. Office W.	APA	EcM	Mil. C.	Mil. OKW	M/War Notes
2 May letter Gr. to W.		5				5				5	
12 May ANGLO-TURKISH DECL.											
22 May note v. Hentig			4	4	4						4
25 May W.:Consult Italy					5						
?May? letter Jäger to Gr.		2									
8 June Jäger (Ferrostaal) at v.Hentig's		1	5								
9 June v.Hentig: A.H. should receive al-Hud			4								
17 June al-Hud at Hitler's	5										
19 June letter Jäger to v.H.		4									
Late June/early July: Press reports endangering the deal (GB!)											
22 June 1939 negotiations v.H. with al-Hud			4								
23 June FRANCO-TURKISH DECL.											
? June "difficulties" reported by military + ec. officials			3					3	3?		
4 July Canaris: Deliver!			5							5	? Because of Canaris 4 July v.H. Palestine yes
? July Abwehr: Present of 4,000 rifles			3							5	

Actors Events/Actions	A.H.	Economy Firms	Gr.	v.H.	For. Office FM	Pr.	W.	APA	EcM. C.	Mil. OKW	M/War	Notes
6 July al-Hud asked to leave Germany												
Early July A.H.: No arms to "unsafe" areas	3											
12 July Canaris-Keitel agreement (payment regulations on 13 July)				3								
18 July letter with list weapons handed over to al-Hud									5	5		
7 Sept. 1939 al-Hud returns via Berlin				2								
Total Actions per actor	3	12	6	20	3	1	9	15	4	5	10	2
Total points per actor	13	26	15	87	11	5	44	46	11	22	41	9
Average weight per actor in the German-Saudi Arabian arms deal decision-making process (Points/actions)	4.3	2.1	2.5	4.3	3.6	5	4.7	3.0	2.7	4.4	4.1	4.1

LEGEND

Quantification

5 – Decision; successful influence
4 – advice followed (as decision input)
3 – unsuccessful attempt at influencing decision-maker(s)
2 – advice given, but not decision-input; action undertaken but no political results
1 – passive; having to accept a decision without being able to do anything
( ) uncertain (re)action (to request); derived from other decisions

Actors

A.H.	Adolf Hitler
Gr.	Fritz Grobba (not a member of the NSDAP)
v.H.	von Hentig (not a member of the NSDAP)
FM	Foreign Minister
Pr.	Ministerialrat Prüfer (manpower department of the AA)
W.	Woermann (then, member of the SS)
APA	Außenpolitisches Amt der NSDAP
EcM	Ministry of Economic Affairs
Mil.	Military
C.	Canaris (Abwehr)
OKW	Oberkommando der Wehrmacht
M/War	Ministry of War

PART II:

THE PRESENT: 1981 TO 1985

1980/81 was the decisive year of the contemporary German-Saudi Arabian arms deal. To achieve an in-depth understanding of West Germany's policy toward Saudi Arabia in this "crucial" year it may be helpful to look at the wider perspective of its general political and economic priorities and its policy toward other Middle Eastern states in these two years.

I. ECONOMIC STRUCTURES AND CYCLES

Sluggish economic growth, conservation and improved energy efficiency caused an impressive fall of West German oil demand of roughly 13 %.(1) The attempt to decrease vulnerability vis-à-vis Middle Eastern developments was partly achieved by diversifying oil-supply sources. British and Norwegian oil became more important.(2)

Turning from the level of **macro-economic** import to the macro-economic export it can be seen that Saudi Arabia and Iraq, as well as Algeria and Libya have played increasingly larger roles.(3)

This becomes even more evident when analyzing the **micro-economic** level. Branches afflicted by the recession found support in contracts from these countries - such as the building industry. The yearly reports of practically all larger construction firms stressed the importance of ME activities without which profits would have been far lower. These activities compensated for domestic setbacks.(4) The sluggish steel industry also profited from ME contracts.(5)

To be in more immediate proximity to the ME market, Audi/Volkswagen and Daimler-Benz decided to open assembly plants in Egypt.(6) Characteristically, ME countries have bought shares in structurally weakened or crisis-ridden branches of German industries: Iran possesses 25.01 % of Fried. Krupp Ltd. Essen(7) (steel), Kuwait controls 6 % of Volkswagen, 10 % of Volkswagen do Brasil, 20 % of Metallgesellschaft, 14 % of Daimler-Benz (an exceptional enterprise), 25 % of Korf (steel).(8)

For the second year in a row, the Saudis, in November 1980, pledged to purchase $ 2.75 billion worth of notes from the West German treasury. The Germans borrowed a total of 9 billion Deutschmark (DM) or $ 3.96 billion) from the Saudi government and Saudi businessmen in 1980.(9)

By mid-1981, West Germany was indebted to the Desert Kingdom by 13.6 billion DM or $ 6 billion. It had become West Germany's biggest creditor-nation.(10) West Germany was the recipient of twice the total amount of Saudi credit in 1981 than in 1980.(11) This, of course, resulted in a structural, i.e. longer-term, dependence and the Saudis let their presence be felt. Reluctantly, the West German government had to postpone the arms deal with the ME nation because of tough opposition from parliamentary coalition fractions. In June 1981, there were repeated rumours about a possible Saudi credit freeze which WG treasury correctly denied.(12) But the conditions were somehow worse with a yearly interest rate of 10.3 %. Considering the market, this was not too bad.(13)

II. POLITICAL STRUCTURES AND CYCLES

1) THE POLLS

1980/81 marked a clear setback for Israel. It was, of course, partly self-inflicted (Begin's attacks on Chancellor Schmidt and the "whole German People"). Based on comparison with previous opinion polls, this trend may well indicate new (long-term) structures rather than (short-term) cycles.(14) In May **1981** (after Begin's 3 May attacks on 8 and 9 May 1981), 21 % of the West German public "sided more with Israel", 24 % "more with the Arabs", 43 % "with neither one", 12 % had "no opinion". In May **1970**, however, 45 % sided more with Israel, 7 % with the Arabs, 33 % with neither one. In May **1978**, Begin having been in office for a year, the structures remained stable: 44 % felt closer to Israel, 7 % to the Arabs, 33 % to neither one.(15) The poll may possibly have been influenced by the fact that it was conducted only a few days after Begin's speech. But parallel West European reactions as well as the drastic cracks in Israel's image (less than half the sympathy of 1978) may well suggest that structural rather than cyclical forces were at work.(16)

2) WEST GERMANY AS AN OFF-MIDDLE EAST THEATER OF WAR

Contrary to the beginning of 1980 when a **Libyan** opposition politician was murdered in Bonn(17), the period surveyed was calm as far as Libyan infighting in the Federal Republic of Germany was concerned. The Bonn incident had no far reaching repercussions for German-Libyan relations and after the meeting between Major Jallud, the Libyan number two man, and Foreign Minister Genscher, it was made publicly known that Qadhafi was interested in an official visit to the Federal Republic.(18)

According to the Bavarian Minister of the Interior, Gerold Tandler, Libya continued not only arms deliveries to extreme leftist terrorists but more recently, also to extreme rightist ones.(19) This did not prevent official relations between the federal government and Libya from continuing intact. At the climax of the U.S.-Libyan dispute, in early December 1981, FM Genscher offered the U.S. Bonn's "good contacts" with Libya in the case of mediation.(20)

After all, Qadhafi had recently kept the extreme left terrorist group "Red Army Fraction" at arm's length(21).

With all due reservation it may be safe to state that Libya attempted to pursue normal foreign policy relations with Germany on the governmental level while pursuing more unconventional approaches on the subgovernmental level. There were many indications that neither line was followed exclusively.

Syria's Muslim Brothers, (first and foremost 'Isam al- 'Attar) who found refuge in W-Germany continued oppositional activities.

In May 1979(22), for instance, they held secret conventions in Germany in 1980.(23) Two other members of the Muslim Brothers granted an interview to the daily newspaper "Die Welt".(24) On 20 March 1981, Isam al- 'Attar's wife was slain by two Syrians in her Aachen appartment. The two Syrians who killed her were apparently looking for her husband.(25) In 1980, according to the German Ministry of the Interior, Syria also used "her" Palestinian group, "Saiqa", in "activities against members of the fundamentalist Muslim Brotherhood in Germany".(26)

About 1,000 **Iranian** students staged a protest rally against the Khomeiny regime in Bonn (28 June 1981) and 30-50 persians occupied their country's consulate in Hamburg on 23 June.(27) This was clearly part of the Iranian power struggle between Bani Sadr and Khomeiny. The Iranian government reacted by confiscating passports of opposition countrymen in Germany but reportedly also warned them of pending executions.(28)

German authorities were most concerned with a phenomenon which the weekly "Der Spiegel" called "The **War of the Turks** in Germany".(29) The Bavarian and Lower Saxonian institutions charged with the observation of extremist groups in Germany ("Verfassungsschutz"; this exists on a state=Land as well as national=federal level) spoke of a increasing "polarization" (Bavaria) and "hardening" (Lower Saxony) between Turks of the extreme left and right in their host country.(30) In Lower Saxony alone there were an estimated 2,900 Turkish **Gastarbeiter** (foreign workers) who supposedly belonged to organizations of the extreme left and 2,000 to the extreme right.(31)

According to the federal "Verfassungsschutz" there were 18,850 "orthodox communists" from Turkey living in Germany in 1980 (21,250 in 1979), and an additional 7,810 were categorized as "new left" (7,750 in 1979). (32) The Grey Wolves were actively proselytizing among the 1.2 million Turks in West Germany, and this was far from being non-violent.(33) Moreover, protests against the military government in Turkey were coordinated by Turks and Germans of the extreme left, both fighting "West German imperialism" and international "fascism".(34)

Leftist Turks of Kurdish origin(35) stormed the Turkish consulate in West Berlin in October 1980.

More peaceful means (hungerstrike(36) and nonviolent demonstrations) were practiced as well.(33) Members of the German parliament (Bundestag), belonging mainly to the social-democratic left (Coppik, Heidemarie Wieczorek-Zeil), as well as the youth organizations of the two coalition parties ("Young Socialists" and "Young Democrats" = FDP, the liberal junior partner) participated and held speeches expressing their solidarity with these contesting military rule in Turkey.(37) Thus, Turkish and German politics became interwoven.

The absolute climax of extremist activity was reached when connections were ascertained linking the assassin of Pope John Paul II with the Grey Wolves in Germany.(38)

It is no wonder that even less prejudiced Germans and their liberal/ "progressive" publicized opinion ("Die Zeit" or "Der Spiegel") complained of foreign infighting in Germany.

This must be viewed against the background of a certain distance to and sometimes dislike of foreigners in West Germany, especially with respect to foreign workers.(39) More and more the issue of **"Ausländerstopp"** (halt to the influx of foreigners) became a focal point of German politics, not just limited to the extreme right.

Problems of integration, of a society within a society, - and, above all, growing unemployment have led to an increasingly restrictive immigration policy on the part of Land (= state) and federal authorities.(40)

An opinion poll conducted by the Allensbach Institute in August 1981 showed that 80 % of the West Germans supported restrictions of that kind. 79 % claimed that there were too many foreigners living in W-Germany. In West Berlin where there are 1.75 million Germans and 238,000 foreigners, among them 116,000 Turks, 89 % complained of what they considered an exaggerated number of non-Germans.(41) It goes without saying that even a minimal transformation of West Germany into an off-ME theater of war is far from helpful to a rational approach to the approximately 4.5 million foreigners in that country, a third of them being Turks. Among foreigners younger than 18 about half are Turks.(42)

On 5 September 1980 two German terrorists, Christof Wackernagel und Gert Schneider, were convicted of attempted murder and sentenced to fifteen years imprisonment. Both belonged to the "Red Army Faction". Their trial brought to light connections linking them to **Iraq** where several other members of that group had found refuge.(43)

On 1 August 1980, two staff members of the Iraqi embassy in East Berlin (German Democratic Republic) the first secretary and a technician, were arrested in West Berlin. They were charged with having planned to plant explosives at a congress of Kurdish students in West Berlin. According to police experts, a "catastrophy" would have ensued, had the plot not been detected in time.(44) Iraq and the East German news agency ADN spoke of a "campaign against Iraq" and accused the West Berlin authorities of having violated" diplomatic conventions".(45) The affair led to a dispute between the West German government and the executive body ("Senat") of West Berlin. The former wanted to extradite the two diplomats because of "foreign policy considerations" whereas the latter insisted on bringing them to trial.(46) According to the Frankfurter Allgemeine Zeitung,(47) FM Genscher, his party (Free Democrats) colleague Baum, Minister of the Interior, and the chief of the Chancellery, Schlüter (SPD who was in charge of security matters), pressed hardest for extradition. Genscher did not want to torpedo Iraq's recent advances toward the West and Baum (probably Schlüter too) hoped to continue collaboration with Iraqi authorities in fighting German terrorists.(48) At first the Berlin Senat refused to act accordingly, then demanded "assurances" from Iraq; among them the promise to "put an end to all terrorist activities" (in West Berlin? West Germany?) and "concrete help in terrorist problems".(49) On 17 September 1980 the two Iraqi diplomats were sent back but it was not made known whether or not the conditions of the Senate had been met. The only Iraqi "assurance" which was publicly announced stated that these men would not reenter German "legal territory".(50)

Why did Germany act like this?

3) BILATERAL RELATIONS WITH MIDDLE EASTERN STATES AND ACTORS

a) Iraq

The federal government was guided by what it perceived to be questions of national interest; obviously, these were mainly economic.

Despite the August/September 1980 affair and the Iraq-Iran war, West German companies were regaining their momentum in Iraq. In January 1981, credit guarantees ("Hermes") for Iraq were eased after an initial restriction following the outbreak of the war in October 1980(51) in early February 1981, a German-Italian consortium led by Hochtief AG was awarded a $ 1.5 billion contract to dam the Tigris River near Mosul by 1986 and another West German building contractor (recession-ridden branch!) won approval for its $ 270 million bid to construct sixteen agricultural colleges in Iraq.(52) On 25 May 1981, Iraq's Deputy PM arrived for a three day official visit and on 26 May an agreement on economic, technical and scientific cooperation was signed.(53) This trip undoubtedly "crowned the economic relations between Iraq and the Federal Republic of Germany."(54) (In 1983, however, Iraq's debts which had, in fact, been foreseeable, became a liability to West German companies.)(55)

b) Relations with the PLO

This relationship, too, had two dimensions; the first being the bilateral, the second internal. The latter entailed neo-Nazi as well as leftist terrorist activities and all their accompanying transnational connections. As to the cooperation between **neo-Nazi terrorists and the PLO**, the German Ministry of the Interior stated in its "Verfassungsschutzbericht 1980" that former members of the illegal (since 30 January 1980, confirmed by the German Supreme Court, "Bundesverfassungsgericht", on 2 December 1980) **Wehrsportgruppe Hoffmann** as well as its leader, Hoffmann himself, underwent military training in PLO camps in Lebanon. The report named four people,(56) who returned voluntarily to Germany and were sentenced to terms ranging from sixteen months imprisonment to seven months probation.(57)

Abu Ijad, himself, Fatah's number two man, admitted in an interview with "Der Spiegel" that twelve Hoffmann members had, in fact, stayed at Lebanese Fatah camps.(58) He denied, however, that they had been trained militarily.(59) This version was only partly confirmed by the West German Minister of the Interior, Gerhard Baum, who based his statement in the Bundestag (= parliament) on the accounts of the ex-Hoffmann men said he had no reason to doubt these reports as there was no evidence contradicting their contention that they had, indeed, actively participated in "paramilitary exercises"(60). The PLO connection with German neo-Nazis had been observed since spring 1980.(61)

On 19 December 1980, the Jewish editor Shlom, Levin an ex-Israeli, and his life companion Frida Poeschke were murdered at their Erlangen home. First reports had it that this was "probably unpolitical".(62) But on 19 August 1981, Karl-Heinz Hoffmann and his friend Franziska

Birkmann were arrested as suspects of this murder.(63) The main suspect, Uwe Berendt, also a member of the Wehrsportgruppe, presumably went underground – in the ME with the PLO.(64) In a way the PLO-connection also involved Germany as an off-ME theater of war.

This proposition is not far-fetched. In late August 1981, unnamed Arab diplomats made it known that not only the "Steadfastness Front" but also el-Fatah with Arafat presiding decided on 14 August 1981 "to carry the struggle of the Palestinian People into Europe".(65) The main targets were to be Jewish institutions. This new Fatah line was decided upon because Israel's actions in Lebanon had increased "the psychological willingness in Europe to tolerate measures against Israel and European Jews supporting her".(66) The PLO's Abu Jihad was charged with contacting illegal groups in the Federal Republic of Germany, Spain, Italy and Turkey in order to carry out this plan.(67)

In late October 1981, Belgian police arrested four West German extreme rightists who were allegedly connected with the 20 October bomb explosion at a synagogue in Antwerp killing three and injuring about a hundred people. Results of the investigators also indicated a possible connection between the rue Copernic (Paris) explosion of October 1980 and extreme rightists from France and the Netherlands.(68)

The attack on a Viennese synagogue probably carried out by Abu Nidal men (breakaway faction of Fatah; opposed to political approaches or solutions) also occured in the fall of 1981.

The West German government was clearly worried about PLO-neo-Nazi collaboration well before Fatah's decision to step up its campaign in Europe. In June/July 1981 the "Haaretz" correspondent for Western Europe in Bonn repeatedly reported on federal as well as state (Bavarian) contacts with the Palestinian organization in order to prevent future PLO-neo-Nazi undertakings. The PLO seemed willing to cooperate but demanded, in return, official recognition by Bonn. The German government would not accept this.(69) As a result, West German police feared increased striking capabilities of the extreme right, the journalist claimed. Quoting unnamed "social-democratic sources" he added that Willy Brandt was most disappointed because after his 1980 talk with Arafat in Vienna he had hoped that PLO activities in Western Europe would come to an end.(70)

The Minister of the Interior's "Verfassungsschutzbericht 1980" referred to the PLO connection to Germany's **extreme leftist terrorism** as follows: "As before, the RAF (= Red Army Faction) maintained close relations with a radical splinter group, the 'Peoples' Front for the Liberation of Palestine' (PFLP)".(71)

German authorities are also aware of the immanent "security risks" and extremist intentions" of certain Palestinians. Again, they realize that Germany, too, has remained an off-ME theater of war.

Whereas there were 76 active Arab "branch-groups" in 1978 and 110 in 1979, the number reached 166 in 1980. This "considerable increase" was explained by the "intention of several Palestinian associations to step up their efforts to organize a Palestinian state."(72) The number of mother-organizations was 20 in 1980 compared with 18 in the previous year and 21 in 1978.(73)

Membership in Arab "extremist group" climbed from 2,540 in 1979 to 2,800 in 1980.(74) Most of them evidently belonged to Palestinian organizations whose 1980 membership reportedly reached 2,670. Fatah members in Germany numbered "approximately 400 to 500".(75) Violent internal strife among PLO members practically paralyzed their activities in Germany but "at year's end the relatively moderate Fatah forces seemed to have gained the upper hand."(76) The PFLP, on the other hand, continued to be viewed as a "high security risk still planning commando actions in Germany or against German institutions abroad."(77)

Whether or not Thomas Reuter and Brigitte Schulz, detained by Kenyan authorities on 27 January 1976 in connection with an intended attack on an El Al plane at Nairobi airport and later extradicted to Israel where they were sentenced to ten years prison did, indeed, belong to the PFLP (W. Hadad faction) remained unclear. Both denied it categorically, Israel insisted. But since the affair contributed to the already aggravated German-Israeli relations, the Israeli government released them on Christmas Eve 1980. After their return, the two Germans accused Israeli authorities of having tortured them. This, in turn, was categorically denied by Israel.(78)

Shortly after their return to Germany, on 2 January 1981, an explosion at the Nairobi Norfolk Hotel (owned by a Jew, Jack Block) killed fifteen people and injured another eighty-five.(79) According to Kenyan police, the main suspect, Qaddura Mohammad Abd el-Hamid, belonged to the PFLP. The latter categorically rejected the accusation.(80) The British "Guardian", the French "Le Monde" and the West German "Frankfurter Allgemeine Zeitung" speculated that the explosion might represent an act of revenge for Reuter's and Schulz's treatment in Kenya and Israel now that they were out of danger.(81)

In sum, West Germany could not escape being drawn into ME issues on an international as well as transnational level.

On the bilateral inter"national" level there are **two essentials** which guide West Germany's policy vis-à-vis the PLO. Both have much to do with Germany's contemporary history. The first essential refers to the **right of any people to self-determination**, the second to a more **indirect** but still existing **"moral commitment"** that Germany, above all under Chancellor Schmidt has increasingly felt **towards the Palestinians.**(82) It was the second essential which led to the vehement outbursts by Israeli Prime Minister Begin in which he also accused the West German Chancellor of "callous disregard of the Jews slaughtered in World War II".(83)

Schmidt's argument can be summarized as follows: The Germans caused the Holocaust; hence their direct moral commitment to the Jewish People. The Holocaust led (voluntarily or not) to the present situation of the Palestinians. Hence, Germany's indirect moral made Israel's creation possible, or accelerated at least the establishment of the state. This, in turn, commitment to the Palestinian People.

The second essential deals with self-determination which the West German government supports in general and the German people in particular. Realistic or not, the government can thus keep the issue of German reunification alive. In a way, West Germany's support of the Palestinian right to self-determination (since 1974 publicly; the first EC member to do so) is part and parcel of German internal policy. If this were not the case, the West German government would delegitimize its claim of applying this principle to its own people.

It can be argued, however, and even Israeli "doves" do so, that the EC does not as emphatically support the right to self-determination of other peoples where it seems to be less opportune. "What about the Kurds, the Armenians, the Basques, the Scots, the peoples of Biafra, Katanga and Eritrea?" asked Abba Eban, one of Israel's most prominent Labor Party (opposition) moderates.(84)

Conversely, it is this same policy which has also prevented West Germany from recognizing the PLO as the "sole legitimate" representative of the Palestinian People." Thus, it has continually frustrated the PLO." It is up to the Palestinian People to choose its own representatives", runs the argument.(85) Without democratically held elections there can be no single, self-appointed representative.

c) Relations with Israel

Relations with Israel went from bad to worse in 1980/81. Growing public resentment toward Israel was reflected in the polls (see above). There were those who viewd Israel as "America's crazy ally",(86) and by critizing Israel they could simultaneously strike out at the United States - and President Reagan. More American-minded commentators wanted to "save Israel in spite of herself" or, as George Ball put it," to prevent Israel from making a grave mistake, for her own sake."(87) The crisis had been brewing up for quite a while, long before Begin and Schmidt.

From his country's perspective, Yochanan Meroz, Jerusalem's outgoing ambassador in Germany, characterized Bonn's growing estrangement from Israel during the 1970's and early 80's:(88) It allegedly began in the early 1970's with the political cooperation of the EC in foreign policy, especially in ME issues. The exclusively bilateral relations marked by Germany's moral commitment to the Jewish People became more and more multilateral. In other words, the original political mixture was diluted. In addition to that, EC countries like France, Italy and later Britain who were "clearly pro-Arab"(89) increasingly influenced Bonn's ME policy. The "more pro-Israel" members, the Netherlands, Luxembourg and since 1973 Denmark, were not able to set the tone. This was mainly done by Paris.

Germany's political left, the Young Socialists (= Social Democratic youth organization) also turned to the problems of the Third World and "discovered the Palestinian issue in refugee camps."(90) When Willy Brandt became Chancellor, both West Germany's "Ostpolitik" and its "Third World Policy" tended - at Israel's expense - to take the position of the Soviet Union more and more into consideration. The decline in German-Israeli relations could be observed for the first time during Brandt's 1973 visit to Israel. He no longer spoke of "a special relationship" but of "a normal relationship against a special background".(91)

Meroz's interpretation, whatever its shortcomings and biases, has the advantage of placing last year's eruptions in a wider perspective of what I call structures and cycles.

On 17 November 1980, Israel's FM Shamir arrived in Bonn for political talks.(92) Surprisingly, the Saudi FM, Prince Faisal, had come a week before. Bonn could thus easily avoid any optic one-sidedness. Whereas Foreign Ministers Genscher and Faisal had agreed on most political and economic issues(93) the talks between Chancellor Schmidt, Genscher and Shamir did not eliminate existing "differences" of opinion, despite the "good atmosphere of the meetings.(94) Shamir invited Genscher to Israel and the latter accepted "gladly".(95) This in itself was an achievement because the September 1979 visit of then Foreign Minister Dayan had annoyed the German side. Dayan had referred openly to a worsening of Israeli-German relations and had argued with his hosts about Palestinian self-determination - again publicly.

The "good atmosphere" of the Shamir talks had been far from expected. After all, Israeli reactions to the electoral gains of Genscher's Free Democratic Party had been less than enthusiastic. Genscher was allegedly "more in sympathy with the Arab countries than with the Jewish State."(96) A few days before, a leak to the weekly "Der Spiegel" had strained additionally the personal atmosphere between Begin and Schmidt. The Chancellor was reported to have called Israel's prime minister a "danger to peace".(97) Bonn's government spokesman denied this characterization but there were few commentators who doubted the authenticity of Schmidt's remark.(98)

Moreover, the German government had considered Begin a lame duck Prime Minister(99) and was fostering relations with Israel's opposition leader Shimon Peres. He was officially invited by Helmut Schmidt.(100)

Begin's counter attack, opened on 3 May 1981, was prepared by Shamir.(101) Begin's anger was raised not only by Schmidt's remarks on Palestinian self-determination and their right "to organize themselves in a state-like way"(102) but also, and to a greater degree (because of his Holocaust consciousness, by the Chancellor's low-key profile on Germany's commitment to the Jewish people and his explicit emphasis of the moral commitment to the Palestinians. On his flight back from Ryadh Schmidt declared that "German foreign policy in the 1990's cannot be overshadowed by Auschwitz".(103)

Following his return he then described in a TV interview on 30 April 1981 Germany's indirect guilt vis-à-vis the Palestinians. He also mentioned the suffering of many European peoples caused by Nazi Germany but save an "et cetera" omitted any reference to Jewish suffering.(104) This, as it were, was the straw that broke the camel's back. It enraged Begin(105) and, in addition to that, provided him with a golden opportunity to step up his election campaign, mobilize Israeli public opinion and practically paralyze opposition at home.

Schmidt obviously realized the mistake he had made by emphasizing Germany's **indirect** moral committment to the Palestinians more strongly than her **direct** one to the Jews. A few days after Begin's all-out-attack Schmidt distributed a speech he had held at a synagogue in Cologne in 1978. In this instance he had unequivocally confessed Germany's **direct** moral committment to the Jewish People. He had found similar words at the Birkenau concentration camp in 1977: "We, today's Germans, are not personally guilty. But we do have the political heritage of those who are guilty; hence our responsibility."(107)

Begin, however, had not only attacked the German Chancellor but the German People as a whole. And this outweighed and neutralized any possible internal criticism from Schmidt's opponents. The gist of what Begin had to say about Schmidt and the German People can be summarized as follows:(108) Schmidt does not know Jewish and Palestinian-Arab history. If he did he would not have said that Palestinians fled from the West Bank. Or perhaps lucrative petrol and arms deals with Saudi Arabia influenced his memory. How could Schmidt in 1981 talk in terms of a German obligation to the Arabs without mentioning the German obligation to the People of Israel? an obligation for this and all future generations? "It is naked arrogance and imprudence to tell my generation, the generation of the Holocaust as well as of the Jewish renaissance, that the German People is guilty vis-à-vis the Arabs." He then incorrectly accused Schmidt of having been present at the 20 July 1944 hanging of the resistance fighters against Hitler. Schmidt and Giscard are "greedy because they only see two things: How to sell arms as expensive as possible and how to buy oil as cheap as possible ... No memory, no heart, no principles and no humanity." Schmidt upholds the principle of Palestinian self-determination only because Saudi petro-dollars support the PLO. He does not concern himself with Israel's eventual liquidation. "He also served in the army which encircled towns until the 'Einsatzgruppen' (= liquidation squads) could finish their job."

In an interview on Israeli radio Begin elaborated his points and characterized his attitude towards the German People like this: "I have never forgiven the German People as a whole. I shall never forgive. They are all guilty. As long as Hitler brought victories they hailed him. Later, with the beginning of his downfall they turned away a bit. I will not shake hands with any German who fought in the War." And he added that only protocol and his obligations as Prime Minister forced him to do so from time to time.(109)

In the same interview Begin again referred to Schmidt's role during the War: "He has never broken his oath of allegiance to his leader Adolf Hitler. And he served at the eastern front. I do not know what he did with the Jews at the eastern front. Nobody can know. The Jews were mainly liquidated at the eastern front. I do not know whether he was in Brest (Litowsk; where Begin's parents perished in the Holocaust; M.W.) ... I only know that he served in the Army ... which did not kill the Jews directly but encircled the towns ... until the 'Einsatzgruppen' finished their job."(110)

A few weeks later he took up the reparations and restitution issue and claimed that only $ 800 million had been paid.(111) He thus triggered a pseudo-historical debate about the exact amount paid to Israelis, German and other Diaspora Jews.(112) The figure most often quoted in the German media was 70 billion Deutschmark. German officials referred to 63,249 billion Deutschmark (Federal Bureau of Statistics) or 27 billion Deutschmark to Israeli citizens and their state treasury (German Embassy at Tel-Aviv). Israeli officials then reduced this figure to 27 billion DM. Teddy Preuss reckoned up 22,15 billion DM.(113)

But Begin by no means had a monopoly on anti-German feelings as an issue of the Israeli election campaign. The easing of import restrictions initiated by Israel's Finance Minister Aridor was criticed by the Labor Party opposition in an election advertisement. The alleged reason: They would favor German industry.(114) It was insinuated that this very industry supported the German-Saudi arms deal. This, however, was not said openly in the election advertisement.

Immediately after Begin's "Mohammed Ali styled" attack on Schmidt(115) other Israeli politicians followed suit, first and foremost opposition leader Shimon Peres. He questioned the "sincerity" of Schmidt's "socialist convictions". "The spirit of Socialism does not manifest itself by utilitarian calculations but by moral obligations ... True Socialism is measured by the attitude towards the Jewish People," he continued.(116)

The President of the State of Israel, generally "above" party politics, also critized Schmidt – though more mildly. President Navon held that Schmidt's remarks were caused "either by ignorance or, even worse, by deliberate falsification." They showed a dismal "brutalization of feelings with regard to Nazi crimes against the Jewish People."(117)

The Israeli public obviously approved of Begin's style as well as the substance of his statements. Whereas in March 1981 only 19 % intended to vote "Likud" (the list led by Begin), by May and early June, before the raid on the nuclear reactor in Iraq, there were 31 %. After the beginning of the Lebanese missile crisis and Begin's attack on Schmidt and Giscard there were 37 %.(118) Still, the labor Alignment was ahead by a single percentage point, compared with a twenty point lead in March 1981.(119) In the same months, 25 % of the Jewish Israeli public wanted Peres for Prime Minister (17 % Begin); in (early) May, 31 %(!) favored Begin and only 19 % Peres; and in early June 1981, 33 % preferred Begin, 17 % Peres.(120) Most likely, Begin was "credited" with the May 1981 "success".(121)

A PORI poll conducted for "Bayerischer Rundfunk" (Bavarian Broadcasting Station) showed that 50 % of the Israeli public approved of Begin's attack on Schmidt, 32 % disapproved and 18 % were undecided. (122) On the other hand, 43 % thought that today's Germany was different (than Nazi Germany), 28 % denied this, 20 % saw partial differences and 9 % had no opinion.(123)

A Gallup poll conducted for the German weekly "Der Stern" on 8 and 9 May 1981 showed that 3 % of the Israeli public thought that Germany was, in fact, "entitled" to send tanks to Saudi Arabia, 93 % rejected the sale, 4 % were undecided. Moreover, 76 % of the Israelis claimed that "due to German crimes against the Jewish People during the Third Reich" Germany was obliged to show "special consideration" to Israel's political problems. 13 % saw no necessity for particular considerations and 11 % had no opinion.(124)

Public, publicized and political reactions in the Federal Republic of Germany were unanimous in condemning Begin(125). Even the Chairman of the German-Israel Association, Erik Blumenfeld (Christian Democratic Party) blamed Begin.(126) It is worth mentioning that the attacks by Peres and Navon as well as practically the whole Israeli press, even the moderate papers ("Haaretz") – in other words Israeli public, publicized and political opinion (marginal groups not taken into consideration) - were hardly referred to in German counter-arguments.

With few exceptions, it was a highly personalized debate which the German government and especially Helmut Schmidt tried to cool off. The Chancellor warned against "exaggerated polemics," urged further reconciliation between the two countries and avoided personal remarks concerning Begin.(127) On the other hand, opposition leader Helmut Kohl calling Begin's diatribe "unacceptable" reproached the Chancellor with having continually put off a visit to Israel.(128) (He had been invited by former Israeli PM Rabin in the summer of 1975.) Heiner Geissler, the Secretary of Kohl's CDU (Christian Democrats) disapproved of Begin's style but called some of Schmidt's statements "hostile" to Israel, statements which "disregarded and ignored Israel's situation". As to the PLO, Geissler said, the Chancellor should have stipulated an abandonment of "terrorist assaults" and recognition of Israel's right to exist.(129)

Jürgen Möllemann (Free Democrats), who was elected Chairman of the German-Arab Association in November 1981 and had repeatedly met with Arafat, demanded that German-Arab relations be expanded and that the PLO be included in the negotiating process.(130) FM Genscher, chairman of the Free Democrats, reassured outgoing ambassador Meroz that Israel could "count on" Germany.(131)

Emotions gradually cooled an **diplomatic** business between the two countries continued to normalize.

The long-term damage, however, can hardly be guessed at right now (fall 1984). But given the above-mentioned political structures and cycles on both sides it seems safe to assume that an additional estrangement is most likely to occur.(132)

Last but not least, the return to relative normalcy (a kind of special normalcy) on the diplomatic level was achieved by two outgoing ambassadors, Klaus Schütz and Yochanan Meroz, both of whom seemed to remind the political community of the respective countries of "another Germany/Israel. Farewell articles in the papers were more than just routine courtesies. In each country, the press insinuated that the official representative was, in fact, "much better" than his government.(133)

The successors, Dr. Niels Hansen and Yitzhak Ben-Ari, tried very hard to foster the recovering patient, i.e. relations between Germany and Israel. In Israel, Hansen looked forward to finding something which he could no longer find in his own country: Motivation, a positive attitude towards the state, a sense of duty toward the community.(134) Ben-Ari stressed the positive effects of transnational contacts (on the sub-governmental level) between Germany and Israel over the years and declared his willingness to help solve existing problems.(135)

Diplomatic niceties aside, the two ambassadors realized that an understanding between their respective governments was unlikely in the near future. On the sub-governmental level, however, there might be soothing factors. Considering the opinion cycles and structures, this perspective, too, remains open to doubt.

Even tourism, a mainly (though not exclusively) unpolitical area, was effected by Begin's eruption. In the first half of 1981 about 80,000 German visitors came to Israel, 11 % more than during the same period in the previous year. But after June 1981, the growth rate rapidly declined.(136) The "main target" of Israel's tourism industry(137) did not live up to expectations.

Diplomatic normalcy was also furthered by Bernhard Vogel's visit to Israel in June 1981. The Prime Minister of Rhineland-Palatinate, a member of the national main opposition party CDU and the first high-level politician from Germany to come to Israel following the war of the words criticized Schmidt's Middle Eastern and Israel policy but unequivocally rejected the form and substance of Begin's attack on the Chancellor.(138)

The outcome of the **Maydanek trial** in July 1981 led to renewed tensions in German-Israeli relations. In Israel, both the government and opposition condemned the sentences which they considered too mild.(199) In the same month, the German condemnation of **Israel's air raid on Beirut** was clearcut but expected, almost a "routine" ritual. Consequently, the PLO representative in Bonn (accredited by the Arab League office) demanded German actions rather than words.

He indirectly hinted at the oil weapon.(140) The following day, the government spokesman, reflecting a tougher stance, called Israel's actions in Lebanon "unacceptable", claiming they constituted the danger of enlarging the conflict.(141)

Nevertheless, July 1981 also brought about a certain improvement in relations: Ben-Ari stated that the invitation to the Chancellor to visit Israel was still valid(142) and Ezer Weizman (one of Begin's outspoken adversaries within Israel!) met with Schmidt.(143) After their talk Israel's former defence minister labeled Schmidt a "friend of Israel" but conceded that "Germany has got problems" (which he did not specify).(144)

Information from the German-Israel Association in August allegedly led Begin to believe that Schmidt(!) might apologize.(145) In September 1981, Foreign Ministers Genscher and Shamir met at the UN and the latter again extended an invitation to Genscher to visit Israel. The German FM indicated his willingness to come in early 1982.(146)

At Sadat's funeral service Schmidt and Begin stood close to one another and there were speculations that more than just hand shaking passed between them. Reports from Cairo said that they had had a "very friendly talk".(147) Israel's government spokesman referred to whatever had really happened as a "correct step" on the way to reconciliation. His counterpart in Bonn would neither confirm or deny the reports, but insisted that "the Chancellor is most interested in having good relations with Israel". He added that Schmidt had sent a congratulatory telegram on the occasion of Begin's new term of office as Prime Minister.(148) A few days later, it was officially announced that FM Genscher would visit Israel in February 1982.(149) But nobody at Israel's Ben-Gurion airport was to see Mr. Genscher until April 1982. (150)

In early November 1981, Annemarie Renger, vice-president of the Bundestag and chairwoman of the German-Israeli parliamentarian group, returned from Israel where she had spoken with Begin, Shamir, Burg (Minister of the Interior) and opposition leader Peres.(151) Mrs. Renger is a long-time friend of Israel and belongs to the right wing of the Social Democratic Party (SPD), Germany's major government party. But like some other friends of Israel within the SPD, she personifies the contra-cyclical tendency of Israel and her supporters.

The very same Mrs. Renger was among the wholehearted supporters of the NATO double-track decision and warned her colleagues in the SPD not to identify one-sidedly with the Peace Movement. Election results favoring the oppositional CDU showed that some of them tended to over-estimate the political potential of this movement, she added.(152)

Mrs. Renger, together with Georg Leber (until 1978 Minister of defence) and Herbert Wehner (parliamentary leader of the SPD), two other traditional friends of Israel, supported theses of an essay on the "Identity and Future of the SPD". Here, the renowned political science professor Richard Löwenthal, himself a Social Democrat, redommended an end to party chairman Willy Brandt's strategy of integrating "the marginal groups of drop-outs", i.e. ecologists.(153) Löwenthal explicitly excluded the Peace Movement from the "drop-out" groups,(154) but the critical remarks concerning ecologists indicated the anti-cyclical trend of the essay and of those who supported it by their signature. Significantly, Mrs. Renger was most active in organizing the write-in campaign.

It is also more than just symbolically significant that "Aktion Sühnezeichen", founded by the Protestant Church to actively "repent" for Nazi crimes in Israel and with Jews, has turned its main energy to the Peace Movement. In fact, the 10 October 1981 Bonn Peace Rally was co-initiated by this organization.(155)

d) Bonn's Iranian Connection

When former U.S. President Jimmy Carter welcomed the hostages released by the Iranian authorities in West Germany he explicitly referred to the important contribution of Germany's Teheran ambassador Ritzel as well as FM Genscher and thanked them for their help.

At his farewell dinner America's outgoing ambassador in Bonn, Walter Stoessel, again expressed the gratitude of his government and people. (156) Although Kurt Becker, the government's spokesman, declined to give specifis about German efforts the picture was soon quite clear. (157) Ritzel, knowing Sadek Tabbatabai, the brother-in-law of Ayatollah Khomeini's son Ahmad, used him as a go-between. Tabbatabai had studied biochemistry at Aachen's Technical University and had later worked as a lecturer at Bochum's Ruhr University. Shortly after the takeover of the American embassy at Teheran, Tabbatabai and Minister of State Wischnewski, then Chancellor Schmidt's righthand man and well known for his excellent connections with the Arab World - first and foremost Algeria(!) - held talks on the fate of the hostages. The Algerian channel was later extended by FM Genscher's visit to Algiers and Chancellor Schmidt's meeting with Algeria's president Shadli at the funeral ceremonies for Yugoslavia's Tito in Belgrade. There, FM

Genscher also met secretely with Tabbatabai (March 1980). The ill-fated U.S. rescue mission on 24 April led to a temporary interruption of the German-Iranian contacts. In May 1980, however, they were resumed when the Iranian envoy participated in an international conference of the Friedrich-Ebert-Foundation (linked with the Social Democratic Party) in Bonn.

In July, at a meeting in Oslo of the Socialist International, Willy Brandt and Wischnewski sounded out Iran's FM Qotzbadeh about negotiations on the release of the hostages. In the same month Wischnewski flew to the U.S. where he was made familiar with American ideas on a possible solution. Finally, in September 1980, the Iranians responded favorably to Genscher's and Ritzel's readiness to act as go-betweens. Teheran authorities were allegedly impressed by the fact that Genscher had not paid any official visit to the ousted Shah. On 16 and 18 September 1980, Deputy Secretary of State Warren Christopher met secretely with Tabbatabai at FM Genscher's private house near Bonn. The outbreak of the Iran-Iraq war led to a breakdown of the original timetable but did not prevent the ensuing final phase in which Algeria played the key role. Again Wischnewski's contacts to this country might have been pivotal.(158)

By late 1981, however, German-Iranian relations had deteriorated. Much to Teheran's displeasure, officials in Bonn redoubled their criticism of human rights violations in Iran.

The Iranian ambassador in Bonn attacked Minister of Justice, Jürgen Schmude, for his remarks concerning Teheran's judicial practice and the executions that were taking place there. Additionally, Iran's representative accused the Social Democratic Party of having formed an alliance with "Terrorism in Iran".(159) - In 1983 the repayment of the political debt took place: Tabbatabai had been caught by custom officials when he had tried to smuggle enormous quantities of opium via Düsseldorf Airport. Before his conviction by a German court he had fled from the country. The role of the German foreign ministry was dubious.(160)

On the **micro-economic level** Iran demonstrated what "recycling" could lead to. Possessing 25.01 % of Krupp Corporation Iran is therefore able to veto any decision arrived at by the board of this enterprise. The Krupp management had originally planned to restructure steel production. According to these plans about 5,000 workers would have lost their jobs and to this Ahmad Zadeh, the Iranian representative on the board - and not the German Metal's Union delegate - objected. Islam stresses the importance of the destiny of man rather than economic necessities, declared Ahmad Zadeh. He then explained that his government would be led by these considerations in any future decision concerning Krupp. Adding mockery to insult he remarked that the Union's representative, the vice-president of IG Metall (the biggest single union in the world) Mr. Judith, must have been "quite angry about being overtaken from the left. Mr. Judith countered promptly and claimed that "at home Iran doesn't give a damn about workers' rights". Said Zadeh: "Workers' participation in Iran means more than just being a member of the board."(161)

4) GERMANS TO THE GULF?

"Germans to the Front?", i.e. to the Persian Gulf, the influential weekly "Die Zeit" asked in early October 1980.(162) Five months later "Der Spiegel", at least as influential, exchanged the question mark for an exclamation mark: |U.S.| "Pressure on Bonn: The Germans to the front!"(163) In 1980/81, however, the Germans remained where they had been stationed before.

Responding to U.S. demands that European allies increase their defence efforts in order to facilitate additional American naval redeployment from the Atlantic and Mediterannean to the Indian Ocean, the "Federal Security Council" (the West German equivalent to the U.S. National Security Council) decided on 19 June 1980 to expand the operating radius of the German navy beyond the 61st parallel.(164) This decision was to ensure the defence of North Sea oil and gas as well as a vital supply route from America to Europe. Wheras the American move was directly linked to the Afghanistan/Iran double crisis, the German reaction was only indirectly connected.

The question of a global German defence orientation (within NATO) quickly became an issue in the fall 1980 national elections campaign. The oppositional CDU/CSU openly favored this line. "Hawks" like Alfred Dregger and "doves" like Walther Leisler Kiep, the CDU/CSU candidate for the Foreign Ministry portfolio, differed only as far as nuances were concerned. Whereas Dregger argued for a principal extension of NATO's North Atlantic regional committments to the South Atlantic and Indian Ocean, Kiep wanted similar moves "in an extreme case" only.(165) He could, in fact, envisage "extreme situations" where German naval units would operate "in the Mid and South Atlantic as well as at the Cape of Good Hope".(166) In the Gulf region he did not perceive any necessity for German involvement because of America's strength in this region. But in general, Kiep was thinking in terms of additional regional tasks for the Bundeswehr in order to enable France, Britain and the U.S. to operate outside of NATO.(167) Franz Josef Strauß, the CDU/CSU candidate for the Chancellorship, also rejected a geographic redefinition of NATO's tasks. Instead, he recommended a "division of labor" between its members. "Maritime powers" - in other words the United States but also Britain and France - should play an increasingly important role regarding the defence of Western interests in the Gulf region, the Middle East and Africa while the Bundeswehr would be charged with new operations in NATO's traditional region.(168)

The outbreak of the Iran-Iraq war as well as the dispute over the "international fleet" (see above) aroused the fear in Germany that direct involvement of her soldiers beyond NATO limits was much more than just an academic question.

The debate as such provided the Social Democratic Party with a golden opportunity to turn "Friedenspolitik" (peace policy) into an issue in the election campaign which had been dominated by economic questions hardly favorable to the incumbent SPD and Free Democrats (FDP).

Five days before the polling-stations opened, Chancellor Helmut Schmidt wrote an open letter to this "Liebe Mitbürgerinnen und Mitbürger" (dear female and male fellow-citizens). Here he categorically rejected "security guaranties for Near and Middle Eastern states" or the deployment of "German soldiers in the Middle East, the South Atlantic or the Cape of Good Hope".(169) It is worth mentioning that this obvious political approach and the invisible but practiced Schmidt-Giscard line on the ME, including security guaranties, contradicted each other. In his open letter the Chancellor called security guaranties and German troops deployment "life-endangering nonsense".(170) He also pointed to the West German constitution ("Grundgesetz") which forbids such operations and asked his fellow-citizens to vote SPD in order to enable him to "continue the course of prudence and reasonableness. For the sake of our Fatherland." Middle Eastern developments enabled the Chancellor to characterize his rivals as warmongers.

As Schmidt's letter indicated, there were also constitutional problems involved. Article 115a of the West German Constitution ("Grundgesetz") allows the employment of troops only if and when the "territory of the Federal Republic is attacked by force or if such an attack is immanent ("in case of defence"). Article 87a(4), too, emphasizes the "case of defence", i.e. an "immanent danger to the existence of the Federal Republic, or the free and democratic order of one of its states". Would a stoppage of oil from the Middle East, would a blockade of the Strait of Hormuz constitute an "immanent danger" for the existence of the Federal Republic or its free and democratic order?

According to "Der Spiegel", constitutional experts of West Germany's Foreign as well as Defence Ministries were rather skeptical of the constitutionality of the employment of the Bundeswehr in such a case.(172) It would require a constitutional amendment, stated the memorandum dated 17 December 1980.(173)

Moreover, the top commanders of the German navy were also quite reluctant to expand their operational field. "Der Spiegel" reported them as claiming that quantitative as well as qualitative gaps would have to be bridged.(174)

The Commander-in-Chief ("Generalinspekteur") of the Bundeswehr, Jürgen Brandt, flatly rejected the idea of sending German soldiers to the Gulf. The pursuit of the interests of the Western World and the military defence of the NATO area are "two completely different things for the Federal Republic of Germany", contended the commander.(175)

On 5 November 1980, the federal cabinet charged the Foreign Ministry with reviewing this subject. It anticipated - correctly, as the following months would prove - that President Reagan might step up American pressure for increased military burden sharing, including Bundeswehr operations in the Persian Gulf.(176)

Like Carter's previous administration,(177) Reagan's expectations went beyond host nation support for the American Rapid Deployment Force. As a consequence of additional U.S. military obligations "due to Afghanistan and the destabilization of the Middle East" Germany should be expected to share some of the burden, "expecially in the maritime sector".(178)

The new administration obviously remained dissatisfied with FM Genscher's position expressed at the end of his visit to Washington, D.C., in early March 1981. Genscher had clarified Bonn's attitude towards her contribution to security in the Persian Gulf region: The German government welcomed the idea of host nation support.(179) Any reference to increased efforts on the port of the Bundesmarine (navy) was conspicuously absent. The account of two parliamentarians, both security experts, was more informative as to German-American differences of opinion. Jürgen Möllemann (Free Democrats; government party) and Alois Mertes (Christian Democrats; opposition)(180) made diverging observations during their Washington talks on U.S. arms limitation policies but made converging observations on U.S. expectations of European efforts for the security of the Gulf region. France, Britain and West Germany should not content themselves with financial support but should also participate militarily. Möllemann and Mertes rejected the notion of any military involvement but favored additional financial contributions in order "to secure energy sources at the Gulf."(181) Mertes, security spokesman of the CDU/CSU parliamentary group, clearly signalled opposition approval of the government position in this issue. (182) Gone were the days when Kiep had spoken of the German navy operating globally.

Another possibility of Bundeswehr deployment in the ME was brushed aside more easily. There were rumours in October 1981 that the Federal Republic would participate in the multinational Sinai peace keeping force. Bonn's ambassador in Cairo, Hans-Joachim Hille, declared unequivocally: "The German constitution does not allow the German army to take part in operations abroad".(183)

The issue was soon forgotten later in 1981, at least with respect to public discussion and concern. The constitution provided a safe shield for all political parties to emphasize "soft" policy issues. This line was also adopted by the oppositional CDU/CSU which had failed with Strauß's "hard" line in the 5 October 1980 general elections.

III. THE ARMS DEAL WITH SAUDI ARABIA

A) THE SPD-FDP COALITION 1981/82

1) The Disclosure

The public debate on this issue was opened by "Der Spiegel". On 5 January, in its first 1981 issue, the weekly asked: "German tanks to Saudi Arabia?"(184) Officially, it remained a non-issue, at least for a while. Bonn's spokesman repeatedly insisted that they had not received any precise requests from the Saudi government, but rather vague indications from West German manufacturers.(185)

What did the Saudis plan to buy? Here, too, there were conflicting reports. Saudi FM Feisal allegedly told Chancellor Schmidt that his country would like to purchase "all kinds of West German weapons, small and large. Heckler & Koch machine-guns and above all Lepard 2 tanks."(186) Initially, newsmen wrote in terms of 300 Leopard 2 tanks, 1,000 "Marder" armored personnel carriers, self-propelled guns and other weapons systems.(187) An unnamed "high-ranking government official" was reported to have said that the Saudis desired "three-thousand candles."(188) The "candles" he referred to were Leopards 2, "Marders" and the "Gepard" anti-aircraft vehicles. Other versions cited with 1,500 vehicles such as Marders and Gepards: 155 mm howitzers were also on the alleged Saudi list.(189) In April 1981, on the eve of Schmidt's visit to Ryadh, "Der Spiegel" implied that it had the authoritative figures: "Only" 150 Leopard 2 and "not more than" 1,500 other vehicles (Gepard, Marder).(190) It was evident, that the Saudi deal would be a precedent. Other "large orders" from Egypt,(191) Libya, the United Arab Emirates and Kuwait were expected.(192)

One disclosure followed another, the allegations snowballing. On 10 February 1981, the Israeli daily "Haaretz", usually quoting reliable sources, claimed that the Saudis had also asked West Germany if they could purchase 100 Tornado fighter planes, a German-British-Italian co-production.(193) If realized this would be a one billion U.S. dollar deal with each of the producing countries receiving about 300 million $. A spokesman for the British Ministry of Defence denied any knowledge of such a deal or negotiations concerning it. There was no official Saudi request, she added, but on the other hand, Britain would be happy if potential buyers expressed interest in the Tornado and it could well be that Saudi Arabia would be interested in the Tornado.(194)

The country's news agency denied reports that Saudi Arabia was attempting to buy Tornado planes, on 23 February 1981. It quoted the Defence and Aviation Ministry in Riyadh as saying that the report was fabricated "by the radio of the Zionist enemy."(195)

On 21 February 1981, however, the "Frankfurter Allgemeine Zeitung" informed its readers of London's request for German approval of the Tornado deal. Four days later, on 25 February 1981, the West German cabinet discussed the issue without any intention of making final decision on it.(196)

In mid-March Jürgen Möllemann (FDP), who often functions as the German contact for Arab politicians, announced that Riyadh was no longer interested in purchasing Tornados, be it in Germany or in Britain.(197) In mid-April, however, British FM Lord Carrington and Chancellor Schmidt reportedly discussed Saudi interest in the Tornado. (198) This talk took place shortly after Mrs. Thatcher's visit to the Kingdom and shortly before Schmidt's own trip there. The Saudi purchase was lucrative, indeed, because the Tornado program was a financial troubleshooter for the West German government. Even in June 1981, the very continuation of the production was endangered.(199) Despite all financial and political problems the Tornado was officially inaugurated by the Bundeswehr on 16 February 1982.

2) The Decision Process

a) The Governmental Level

The history of the arms deal had begun in 1975 when the Saudis first signaled their interest in buying 600 "Marder" armoured tanks.(200) The West German goverment then refused to consider the request and reminded the would-be partner that the Federal Republic did not send weapons into "areas of tension".(201)

In June 1980 King Khalid visited the Federal Republic of Germany. The Saudi request was put forward once more, this time vigorously and by the King personally.(202) This, of course, made things rather difficult for the Germans. At that time Chancellor Schmidt asked his host to delay his request for a while. The election to the "Bundestag", the West German national parliament, was to take place on 5 October 1981 and before this date the federal government was obviously and understandably unwilling to decide on such a delicate issue involving hard policy options.(203)

"Shortly after" election day the Saudis repeated their request, and in mid-November 1981 Saudi foreign minister Prince Faysal met with the reelected chancellor. Now, it seemed, chances would be better.(204)

Contrary to the line of argument vis-à-vis- the U.S., where the Saudis had generally emphasized the overall importance of the Arab-Israeli conflict and minimized the global American-Soviet confrontation, Faysal tried to win over Schmidt by stressing the immanent danger to the Arabian Peninsula caused by steady Soviet penetration. The Russian invasion of Afghanistan constituted as much a mortal danger to Saudi oil as to vital European interests. Soviet-South Yemeni and Soviet-Syrian cooperation made Saudi armament more urgent than ever. The Arab-Israeli front was now of "secondary importance".

Chancellor Schmidt and his Foreign Minister Genscher (FDP) would like to have strengthened German-Saudi ties by meeting these requests but they faced stiff opposition from their own respective parties, less so from the parliamentary opposition (CDU/CSU). At the same time, Schmidt wanted to "consider Israel's interests", as he told the Bundestag.(205) In fact, he had to square the circle.

On the one hand, there was the pro-Israel lobby of the SPD and FDP, on the other hand many parliamentarians refused global commitments entered upon by exporting arms. Another group rejected the very idea of it on moral grounds.

Moreover, German governments have traditionally been limited in their arms export policies by self-imposed restrictions. These forbid sales to "areas of tension".

Schmidt had clearly encountered the limits of his personal and institutional power and had to find a way to say "no" to the Saudis without endangering economic and political ties with this country; in other words he had to square the circle again.

On 27 April 1981 Schmidt arrived in Ryadh where King Khalid tried to convince the Chancellor by reminding him that Germany had been the first supplier of arms to his country - "in the 1930s".(206)

Somehow, the Chancellor did square the circle. He did not and could not promise the delivery of the desired hardware "right now".(207) Thus, the Saudis and Schmidt could hope to drive their game home. The former still hoped to obtain the weapons,(208) the latter to win the approval of the Bundestag(209) (parliament) and the West German public. As to the last point, Prime Minister Begin's diatribe against Schmidt served the Chancellor's case very well.

In February 1981, before Begin's historical attacks, only 29 % of the **West German public** supported the idea of delivering tanks to Saudi Arabia, 49 % were opposed and 22 % undecided. On 8 and 9 May 1981, immediately after Begin's speech, 52 % favored the deal, 33 % were against, and 15 % undecided.(210) Contrary to this poll conducted by the Institut für Demoskopie Allensbach, the EMNID institute at Bielefeld found that as early as February 1981, 57 % favored the "delivery of 300 tanks to Saudi Arabia", 41 % were against.(211)

The hopes of the Saudis also materialized, at least partly. In early October 1981 in Qatar, FM Genscher had declared that Germany would not send arms "to Israel or other Near Eastern States".(212) On 12 October 1981, "Der Spiegel" reported that, responding to a British request, West Germany would approve of selling the Saudis PzH 155-1 tank howitzers.(213) This was denied by government spokesman Kurt Becker, but he confirmed that 155 mm field howitzers, a German-British-Italian co-production (45 % of the value of the weapon produces by German firms, mainly "Rheinmetall", Düsseldorf, would be sent.(214)

These would be sent gy Great Britain, government spokesman Becker informed the press.(215) FM Genscher referred to this as "a schizophrenic situation".(216) Schmidt, reportedly, considered it "logical". After all, Germany had lost two World Wars and were responsible for the crimes of the Nazi regime. Therefore, "others deliver what we do not."(217)

The Saudis were to agree not to resell the weapons or to send them to one of Israel's neighbouring states.(218) The German government spokesman categorically denied allegations by "Der Spiegel" claiming that this would be the beginning of the Leopard 2 deal.(219) In March 1982, Mrs. Renger was "absolutely sure" that the tank deal with the

Saudis would not materialize.(220) On 28 October 1981, Crown Prince Fahd" dropped in on his friend Helmut Schmidt and wanted to ask how he was."(221) In early November 1981, it was officially confirmed that the Saudis would get "almost 100" 155 mm filed howitzers, a deal worth 150 million Deutschmark, 45 % of it going to West German firms.(222)

The Saudi arms deal was complicated not only by Germany's special problems with Israel but also, and in fact primarily, by judicial restrictions, moral principles and earlier government decisions not to export weapons to **"areas of tension"**.(223) Article 26(1) of the West German **Constitution ("Grundgesetz")** forbids any action endangering the peaceful coexistence of peoples or making possible preparations for offensive wars.

Article 26(2) states that "arms destined for warfare may only be produced, transferred or circulated with government permission. Details are regulated by Federal Law."

This Federal Weapons' Control Law "Gesetz über die Kontrolle von Kriegswaffen", April 20, 1961; with amendments and decrees of May 1968, July 1969) refers mainly to heavy weapons listed separately ("Kriegswaffenliste", an annex to this law). They include, among others, tanks, planes and ships. The export of light weapons is dealt with by the Foreign Trade Law ("Außenwirtschaftsgesetz", April 28, 1961) with its more liberal guidelines.

These judicial restrictions which were, of course, a direct result of Germany's past and therefore normative did not encompass political reality. Between 1962 and 1964/65 Germany had secretly sent arms worth about 150 million Deutschmarks to Israel.(224) The normative and judicial aspects had thus been neutralized by the normative and political aspects of Germany's moral commitment to Israel. The deal was disclosed in October 1964 and entailed much diplomatic trouble for the Federal government. Thereupon the CDU/CSU/FDP coalition decided on February 14, 1965 not to export arms to "areas of tension" (whatever that may be ...).(295) The SPD/FDP coalition specified this principle on June 16, 1971. The cabinet agreed to allow deliveries to NATO partners as long as the "final destination" of the weapons was known. The concept of "areas of tension" was not clarified, however. Table I (page 71) proves that this moral and political purity was not taken literally but rather liberally. West Germany became one of the world's biggest arms exporters and the list of recipient countries included "areas of tension" as well.

The easiest way to circumvent restrictive arms export controls was (and is) by **co-production with NATO partners** less srupulous in their dealings, such as France, Italy and Britain. (After all, these countries had not provoked World War II). Moreover, foreign firms were authorized to build **German weapons under licence** and the producing country exported the final product, which, in fact, was German.

Co-production with NATO partners made sense not only as far as the circumvention od arms export controls was concerned but also regarding other economic and military considerations: cheaper development, exchange of know-how and standardization of NATO equipment. For example: anti-tank weapons such as the "Milan" missile (co-production of "Messerschmidt-Bölkow-Blohm", Munich and "Aérospatiale", Paris;

Table I: Middle Eastern Recipients of West German Arms 1978-1982
(Million Current US Dollars)

Recipient Asian Middle East:	Million $
Bahrain	20
Egypt	260
Iran	120
Iraq	240
Jordan	5
Kuwait	40
Lebanon	5
Saudi Arabia	550
Syria	70
United Arab Emirates	110
N. Yemen	10
North African Middle East:	
Algeria	370
Libya	430
Morocco	20
Sudan	330
Tunisia	20
Total Middle East	2600
World Total of West German Arms Exports	5600
% Middle East of World Total	46.4

their roof-enterprise being "Euromissile Dynamics Group"), the "Hot" and "Roland" missile.(228) The "Arianne" satellite is also produced, among others, by Germany and France (see France). The "Alpha-Jet" is another example of French-German co-production.(229) The "Tornado" jet is built by Germany, Britain and Italy.(230)

Several non-NATO countries build German weapons under licence: Argentina produces the "TAM" otherwise known as the "Marder".(231) In fact at first, Helmut Schmidt tried to divert Saudi attention and interest in this product to the Latin American address(232) Pakistan ("area of tension" as far as India is concerned) has received "Marder"/TAM by this route.(233)

The Leopard 1 tank is built under licence by the Italian firm "Oto Melara". In 1978, SIPRI and in February 1981, the "International Defence Review" claimed that Libya had ordered 200 of them - and then passed the model on to the Soviet Union for "control".(234)

At the same time, these EC partners are competitors as well. Former French President Giscard d'Estaing was far from pleased when he learned of the possible Saudi-German tank deal.(235)

It is difficult to reconstruct circumstances surrounding and reasons for the fact that the prospective Saudi arms deal was leaked to "Der Spiegel" in late 1980 (or even earlier). But it seems safe to assume that this had much more (or at least as much) to do with Chile than with Saudi Arabia.

At that time, the West German government had planned to sell Chile six submarines, previously ordered by the Shah of Iran. The Khomeyni regime was not interested in buying them and Germany was forced to look for other potential clients. India wanted to purchase "three or four", Chile two.(236) "Clandestinely"(237) the Federal Security Council agreed but the decision-makers had underestimated Social Democratic resentment toward Pinochet and his authoritarian rule.(238) The Chancellor then realized that he could not possibly expect to win the support of his party for the Chilean as well as the Saudi deal. Having to chose, he obviously preferred the latter. He let it be known that he was willing to "reconsider" the Chile decision(239) and conceded that there were other criteria involved than those he had originally departed from. "I am able to learn and willing to compromise".(240) In other words, he aimed at a quid pro quo: You agree to the Saudi export, I freeze the Chile deal.(241)

Interpreted in purely Machiavellian terms one could offer two interpretations: 1) The leak originated from a source close to the Chancellor in order to save the more important of the two transactions. 2) The leak originated from a source opposing the Chancellor's position: in order to add another issue to the first, thus torpeding both.

Whatever the truth, timing and circumstances clearly point to the Latin American connection. Moreover, the controversy, the politically sophisticated means by which it was fought out and the involvement of supporters and opponents alike prove that **the very essence of Germany's post-World War II foreign policy was at stake.**(243) **The question was**: Has (West) Germany developed into a "normal" international political actor or has it remained in the shadow of the National Socialist past? If one tended to support the first assumption

Germany was clearly entitled to "normal" foreign policy behavior - including arms exports (whatever their moral aspects). If, however, one tended to emphasize moral obligations derived from the past, Machiavellian foreign policy actions, such as submarines to Chile and tanks to the Saudis, were unacceptable. It goes without saying that such a controversy transcends traditional party boundaries.

It seems that Chancellor Schmidt was himself ambivalent. On the one hand he wanted "normal" foreign policy, on the other he belonged to a generation too reminiscent of the past in order to be able to pursue such a line unhesitantly. Personally, the Chancellor was morally (not only historically) well aware of the Nazi crimes - and if not, Mr. Begin would and did remind him.

In other words, Schmidt's unability to push the Saudi deal through may have been caused by this dilemma which, in turn, led to an ever increasing loss of prestige in general. It facilitated all-out attacks against the Chancellor in many political areas from coalition, dissident and opposition politicians and undermined his authority which reached an all-time ebb in early 1982. (In fact, he had ceased to be the key man long before he lost power.) To solve his dilemma Schmidt (and reportedly, Genscher, too) thought in terms of compensating Israel by sending her German arms as well. He made this suggestion to Israeli opposition leader Shimon Peres during their Bonn talk in January 1981.(243) Peres publicly announced that Israel would, in fact, apply for German arms, should the Saudis get them.(244)

The debate concerning the essence of Germany's foreign policy necessarily led to **reconsideration of the existing arms export restrictions**.

SPD and FDP members of parliament had asked for such a reconsideration at the end of the outgoing Bundestag in 1980.(245) They demanded that the legislature be consulted on prospective arms exports and wanted to limit the exclusive decision making power of the "Bundessicherheitsrat" (Federal Security Council) to which only the Chancellor and the Foreign, Defence, Economics and Finance Ministers belonged. Had it not been for the Chilean and Saudi deals the debate would never have been triggered off.(246) The Bundessicherheitsrat and separate "working groups" of the SPD and FDP (each one consisting of supporters and opponents of the transfers) discussed the aspects of the two controversies in particular as well as the essence of Germany's arms exports and their foreign policy implications in general.

In March 1982, it became evident that the executive would retain the upper hand in the decision-making process(247), but it had to compromise on the scope of future arms exports. In other words, West Germany's foreign policy behavior will remain slightly "unnormal" for the time being.(248)

Generally speaking German arms will only be sent to NATO countries or countries with a similar status (Spain, for instance). Exceptions are possible if the executive government deems them necessary for "vital foreign and security interests" of the Federal Republic or its allies. Additionally, the "internal situation" within the recipient country will be scrutinized. The concept of "areas of tension" has been dropped for the internal decision-making process but will be used vis-à-vis the outside world, explained the Chancellor.(249) Moreover, licences and production facilities are to be dealt with more restrictively. As far as co-productions with Bonn's allies are concerned, "consultations" are to be held in order to ensure the realization of Germany's arms export guidelines.(250)

Originally, coalition legislatures wanted to achieve much more participation in the decision-making process. Here they had to compromise. The chairmen of all three parliamentary groups as well as their respective experts for security problems will get advance information regarding prospective arms deals.

Annemarie Renger interpreted the new guidelines optimistically - from her point of view - and did not expect the weapons to be delivered. (251) Dissatisfied unnamed members of the left wing of the SPD fraction as well as disappointed and also unnamed Free Democrats grudgingly conceded that the traditional export restrictions had been liberalized. In the end, the new guidelines allowed for the export of the tanks to the Saudis, they explained.(252) This, however, was in contradiction to Chancellor Schmidt's remarks in September 1981. At that time, he told a delegation of the "American Jewish Commitee" that Saudi Arabia would not get West German weapons.(253) The Chancellor kept his promise. In May 1982 he announced officially that Saudi Arabia would not get the weapons it had asked for.(254) The Chancellor had been defeated by his party, finally.

b) The Social Democratic Party

The controversy about the liberalization of arms export guidelines in general and its Middle Eastern dimension in particular came at a very unfortunate time for the **Social Democratic Party**. The October 1980 general elections had strengthened the coalition parties, but the Free Democrats were the only true winners whereas the Social Democrats had practically stagnated. Consequently, the FDP was able to strongly assert its position in the coalition agreement. This, in turn, augmented SPD frustrations. The left wing of the party criticized what it considered too far-reaching accomodation of FDP principles. The debate reached to the very essence of the SPD/FDP coalition with the purists favoring purist opposition rather than government positions which necessitated the abandonment of Social Democratic principles. Economic policy, the NATO two-track decision, workers' participation, energy policy, the neglect of rank and file wishes within the party, these were the issue which almost led to a split in the SPD.(255) Obviously, these controversies would have constituted more than a full-time job for any crisis-manager. But in addition to this list there was also the Saudi connection.

The establishment of the "Working Group Arms Export Policy" in February 1981 was part and parcel of the crisis-management package deal adopted by the executive committee of the SPD.(256) Ultimately, it represented an attempt to institutionalize the divergent opinions within the SPD.

As far as most of the issues were concerned one could easily distinguish between the left and right wing of the party. But the Saudi deal was an exeption to this rule. Left and right wingers had formed an antagonistic alliance. Thus, right-wingers of the SPD like Hans Apel (Minister of Defence), Gerhard Jahn (former Minister of Justice, then "Geschäftsführer" (coordinator) of the SPD Bundestag fraction) and Annemarie Renger, deputy chairman of the Bundestag and known for her contra-cyclical positions on nuclear energy, the two-track decision of NATO and her pro-U.S. stand,(257) found themselves fighting side by side with prominent left-wingers such as Oscar Lafontaine (Mayor of Saarbrücken)(258). Manfred **Coppik** (who left the SPD in early 1982 in order to found a "democratic and truly socialist party"); Klaus **Thüsing**, Karl-Heinz **Hansen** (who had characterized the Chancellor's behavior vis-à-vis disarmament and arms export affairs as "political swinishness"(259), the **Young Socialists** who had expressed their solidarity with Hansen's remarks(260), Freimut **Duve** (Hamburg, Karsten **Voigt** (former chairman of the Young Socialists), Norbert **Gansel** (Kiel, one of the few leftists in the SPD trying to harmonize his general convictions with a pro-Israel involvement; in spite of Mr. Begin's remarks, surely an honest effort; the chairman of the Young Socialists **Piecyk** and the spokesman of the anti-nuke and peace movement within the SPD Erhard **Eppler**.

But the left wing of the SPD was not united in its opposition to the Saudi deal. The "feudal desert kingdom does have a certain exotic attraction even for orthodox SPD left-wingers", stated "Der Spiegel", a generally reliable source as far as anti-leftist tendencies are concerned.(261) Gerhard Schröder, once chairman of the Young Socialists ("Jusos") would have liked to agree to send Leopard 2 to the Saudis "to prove that we support the Arab cause in the Middle East conflict against the reactionary Camp David Agreement between Israel and Egypt."(262) Even so, the SPD left has remained basically opposed to liberalizing arms export guidelines; not because of its (mainly non existant) affiliations with Israel but because of its objections on moral grounds.

Other prominent SPD politicians opposed to delivering arms to Ryadh were Hans Koschnick (Mayor of Bremen, former vice-chairman of the party) and Herbert Wehner (chairman of the Bundestag parliamentary group of the SPD and long-time friend of Israel who did not want Germany to be "drawn into the so called holy war against Israel"(263), and finally party chairman Willy Brandt.(264)

In fact, those opposed to Germany's all time largest arms export opportunity were very condifent. Mrs. Renger thought that most of her colleagues of the SPD Bundestag fraction "see things as I do"(265) and Karsten Voigt boasted vis-à-vis the Chancellor: "Helmut, you cannot have both the two-track decision (of NATO, M.W.) and arms exports."(266) Considering Begin's diatribes against the whole German people, this was quite a diplomatic success for Israel - "in spite of herself".

SPD **supporters** of arms exports to the desert kingdom consisted of the following: First and foremost Chancellor **Helmut Schmidt** (right-wing of the SPD), Minister of Finance Hans **Matthöfer** (right wing), Erwin **Horn** (deputy chairman of the Bundestag Defence committee, right wing) and also some (but few) left wingers like Gerhard **Schröder** who wanted to punish "reactionary" Israel (see above).(267)

The most genuine argument supporting the lucrative transaction was developed by SPD Vice Chairman Hans-Jürgen **Wischnewski** (also belonging to the right wing): Saudi Arabia could not be considered an "area of tension".(268) Besides, 60 billion Deutschmark were at stake and jobs had to be secured.(269) Given the unemployment figures as well as the traditional sociological base of SPD voters, this was a tempting perspective.

Contrary to this rather simplistic and completely one-sided approach, Chancellor Schmidt recognized and formulated the political and moral dimension as much as the dilemma of the decision. It would be too simplistic to reduce the question to "oil or morals" when trying to resolve the problem of securing future energy supplies. Schmidt had to attempt to harmonize pragmatic actions with moral standards.(270)

c) The Free Democratic Party

The **Free Democratic Party (FDP)** was also divided. Party chairman and Foreign Minister Hans-Dietrich **Genscher** originally supported a general liberalization of the guidelines in general and the Saudi deal in particular. Conceding that Saudi Arabia was politically and militarily involved in the Arab-Israeli conflict he nevertheless refused to call the kingdom an "area of tension".(271) For all that, the Foreign Minister, until October 1982 well known for his tactical excellence, made his approval of the export of Leopard II tanks conditional on SPD consent.(272) In March 1981, after having met formidable resistance within his own parliamentary group, Genscher tried to play down his basically affirmative approach without endangering later consent.(273) In May 1981, at the FDP party convention he asked the delegates not to bind him over this issue before consultations within the cabinet and coalition.(274) Finally, in October 1981, he declared in Qatar(!): "We do not deliver weapons to Israel or any other country in the Near East."(275) After month-long deliberations he had obviously come to the conclusion that the embattled government wing of the SPD/FDP coalition should rather concentrate on its main theatres of "war", i.e. the realization of the NATO two-track proposal as well as the cabinet's economic austerity program.(276)

The Free Democrat Minister of Economy, Count Lambsdorff, also favored government approval of the tank sale.(277) Helmut Schäfer, the foreign policy spokesman of the FDP parliamentary group, likewise tended to give a green light to the Leopard II delivery. He dismissed the sincerity of moral arguments opposing it on the grounds that Israel, cooperating with South Africa, supplied the Guatemala government as well as Salvadoran guerillas with weapons.(278)

The most ardent FDP politician in favor of the Saudi demand was Jürgen W. **Möllemann**, security spokesman of his parliamentary group and as much a well known supporter of "the Arab cause" as a harsh critic of Israel's policy.(279) Admitting that Israel's security and Germany's "historical responsibility" had to be taken into consideration he nevertheless supported arms exports to the Arabs. Ultimately, he claimed, external threats to the moderate but not because they were leftists. True, critics of this deal (and the two-track proposal of NATO) like Helga **Schuchardt** and Ingrid **Matthäus-Maier** (chairman of the Bundestag Finance Committee) or Mr. **Strässer**, the chairman of the "Young Democrats" (affiliated with and supported by the FDP)(280) belonged to the left-of-center Free Democrats,(281) but Hildegard Hamm-Brücher (State Secretary, Foreign Ministry) or Detlef **Kleinert**, a long-time supporter of Israel in Germany's parliament, and Burkhard **Hirsch**, chairman of the North Rhine Westfalian FDP and member of the Bundestag, were, like Möllemann, right wingers.(282)

Mrs. Hamm-Brücher, though definitely not left, was undoubtedly guided by a pro-Israel sentiment. Even without the tank export West Germany's Middle East policy had become unbalanced, "dubious" and too pro-Arab, she told FM Genscher at a session of a rebellious FDP Bundestag group where leftists and rightists - for different reasons - united. (283) Mrs. Hamm-Brücher did, in fact, jeopardize her post as Secretary of State in Genscher's foreign ministry but she was willing to run this risk, she said.(284)

Dissenters called this link "blackmail".(285)

Saudis would not help Israel either. In face of worldwide Soviet power politics and expansionism it would be anachronistic to hold to the principle of not sending arms to areas of tension.(286) Internally, however, Möllemann was less balanced as far as the Arab and Israeli position was concerned. In FDP parliamentary group sessions he reportedly tried to label all opponents of the arms transfer as "leftist dreamers" or "Israel lobbyists".(287) Moreover, he pointed to the link between arms exports and economic co-operation.(288)

Genscher could "not follow her intellectually,"(289) but this debate probably led him to change his course later on, at least tactically and then strategically. After all, he wanted to secure the support of his party for the main issues (see above).

In March 1981, a committee was created to consider guidelines for German arms exports. It consisted of supporters (Schäfer, Möllemann) and opposers (Hirsch, Hamm-Brücher, Schuchardt) alike.(290)

Contrary to the Social Democrats, the Free Democrats were practically unanimous in rejecting the job-market argument for a revision or upholding of existing arms export rules.(291)

d) The Christian Democrats (CDU/CSU)

The **Christian Democratic/Christian Social (CDU/CSU)** opposition was divided, too. Supporters of easing arms export regulations in general and delivery to the Saudis in particular, however, set the tone. Opposition leader Helmut **Kohl** did, in fact, reject Mr. Wischnewski's (SPD) and, originally, Mr. Genscher's (FM, FDP) analytically adventurous denial that Saudi Arabia was not an area of tension. But in face of the Soviet invasion of Afghanistan it would be wise to help friends living in an area of tension, he stated in January.(292) Kohl's line remained consistent. In April, a few days before the Chancellor was due to travel to Ryadh, he recommended that the Saudi request be "thoroughly and benevolently considered". Future actions would have to be coordinated with the U.S., Israel and Egypt.(293) Here, he implicitly criticized the Chancellor who had declared that the German decision would be made "without outside interference".(294) By this Helmut Schmidt was thinking mainly of Israel.(295)

In recommending the delivery of the tanks to the Middle East Mr. Kohl emphasized German economic interests.(296) In April he was more outspoken than in January when he had referred more to the strategic aspects.

Rainer **Barzel**, chairman of the Bundestag Foreign Relations Committee, was an implicit supporter of the Saudi deal. In September 1981, he explicitly reproached the government with having spoiled Germany's relations with both sides. Because of Bonn's unwillingness to supply the kingdom with arms it recalled its ambassador in late May 1981.(297)

Alois **Mertes**, foreign policy and security spokesman of the CDU/CSU Bundestag fraction, held his Washington talks at the same time as Jürgen Möllemann (FDP). Summing up his impressions in late March 1981 he came to the same conclusions as his Free Democratic colleague: United States would support the delivery of Leopard 2 tanks and interpret this step as a contribution to a stabilization of the Middle East as well as to a Western division of labor.(298)

Walter **Leisler-Kiep**, like Kohl and Mertes generally belonging more to the soft-line and liberal wing of the Christian Democrats, also favored the sale.(299)

Alfred **Dregger**, chairman of the Hesse CDU, a hard-liner and one of the first West German politicians to "discover" the strategic importance of Oman (in late 1980), wanted to fulfill Saudi demands. This would be part and parcel of an all-Western approach in the Middle East. Besides, German depended on the Saudis with regard to two important areas. First, on the flow of oil; second, on credits from this country. After all, Saudi Arabia had become Germany's number one creditor.(300)

The more hard-lined **CSU** was also unequivocal in its support. Chairman Strauß okayed the deal.(301) Friedrich **Zimmermann**, his party's Bundestag spokesman, urged that arms be sent to those places where German "vital interests" were served. Apart from the weapons, Germany should seek an agreement with the Saudis concerning, among other things, guarantees for oil supplies and industrial construction projects. Zimmermann undoubtedly had understood very well not only the macro-economic but also the micro-economic (enterprise level) cycles. Social Democratic supporters of the arms sale wanted to serve their "clients" (workers) as much as the CSU (industry: see below). Two interesting modifications were suggested by Zimmermann. Like Turkey, Saudi Arabia should get the Leopard 1 and not the Leopard 2. Thus, logistic cooperation in the region could be achieved more easily. He was sure to win Israeli approval for an approach strengthening the West as a whole.(302) According to Franz Alt, a CDU critic of Zimmermann and the delivery of the tanks, the CSU politician suggested that Israel, too, be supplied with German weapons.(303)

Similar to Möllemann (FDP), Zimmermann explained that the "Holy War" declared by Crown Prince Fahd after Israel's Jerusalem Law in 1980 only meant "intellectual controversy".(304)

Basically, the supporters argued pragmatically and spoke in terms of a **Realpolitik** guided as much by consideration of "national interest" (as they perceived them, of course) as economic motivations. The moral dimension played a minor role, if at all.(305)

At this the more radical (in the literal sense of the word: roots) Christian Democrats took offence. Heiner **Geissler**, general secretary of the CDU and close to the "Sozialausschüsse", the social policy-oriented left-wing of the party, argued on moral grounds. Reconciliation with the Jewish People had been one of the cornerstones of the history of the CDU. The Federal Republic's first Chancellor, Willy Brandt, had knelt at the Warsaw Ghetto memorial, and the second Social Democratic Chancellor would bend to "Israel's Arab enemies and their oil."(306) Geissler no longer wanted to give the impression that the CDU would unanimously favor the arms transfer to the Kingdom. Prior to this, mostly outsiders like Franz Alt, a well-known moderator of a political TV program ("Report") and a member of the CDU called his party "hypocritical". On the one hand, it referred to Christian values and origins, on the other, it supported arms exports to "the rightist dictatorship in Chile and to one of Israel's enemies." "Are there no more Christians in the CDU ...?" he asked.(307)

Among the few more prominent CDU politicians rather critical of the deal were **Bernard Vogel**, Prime Minister of Rhineland-Palatinate, Kurt **Biedenkopf**, the CDU's number one in North-Rhine Westfalia, Germany's biggest "Land" (state),(308) and Manfred Wörner, defence expert, long-time chairman of the Bundestag Defence Committee and since late 1980 deputy speaker of the CDU/CSU Bundestag fraction. In late April 1981, he demanded that Israel's interests be considered.(309)

Whereas Geissler wanted to open an internal debate on the issue as late as early May 1981, the majority of the CDU/CSU insisted - one way or another - on a decision at last.(310) After all, they knew what the Chancellor would have liked; and this was their preference, too.

e) Industry

Tough **pressure** had been exerted on the federal government to liberalize German arms export guidelines and to agree to send weapons to the Saudis.

In a TV interview after his return from Ryadh, Chancellor Schmidt disclosed that German **industrialists**, not government ministers, had encouraged the Saudis to expand cooperation with the Federal Republic to the arms sector.(311) In face of certain indicators, these remarks could hardly be dismissed as relief actions by Schmidt. In 1980 as much as 1981 the Düsseldorf based enterprise "Rheinmetall" (40 % of its turn-over arms production)(312) had been suspected of having illegally exported weapons to Argentina, Paraguay, South Africa and Saudi Arabia.(313) Rheinmetall, however, claimed that all these exports had been okayed by the federal agencies in charge of arms exports. (314) In 1981, the executive board claimed to know the source of the "indiscretions": SPD left wingers had leaked judicial investigations on Rheinmetall activities to the press.(315)

The Munich based "Krauss-Maffei", producer of the Leopard tank, had, in fact, had "preliminary contacts" with the Saudis long before government officials were involved.(316) In February 1981, shortly after public debate on the tanks deal had begun (5 January, 1981) Krauss-Maffei made it known that negotiations had been "ended."(317) These negotiations had been agreed to by the Bonn government but without any mandate, it was explained.(318) On 4 November 1981, Mr. Haas and Rötzel of the arms producing branch of Krauss-Maffei wanted to know whether or not the time was right to apply for an export licence for 71 anti-aircraft vehicles ("Flakpanzer"; "Gepard") and 151 Leopard 2.(319) Initiatives and activities of German industrialists interested in arms exports were also reported as far as Malaysia was concerned. More and more, they pressed the Bonn government to liberalize the existing restrictions.(320) Even the "Frankfurter Allgemeine Zeitung", generally friendly towards and close to industrial circles ran a headline reading: "Arms industry presses Bonn".(321) Indeed, all these "preliminary contacts" did create additional pressure, raised expectations within German industry as well as prospective buyers of German arms and made it more difficult for the Bonn government to resist.

"Messerschmitt-Bölkow-Blohm" (Ottobrunn, near Munich), co-producer of the "Tornado" fighter plane, the "Roland" and "Milan" missiles, acted more discretely than Krauss-Maffei. Its chairman, however, Professor Gero Madelung, made it unequivocally clear that the aeronautics industry was financially dependent on exports in order to "maintain its abilities".(322)

Hellmuth Buddenberg of British Petrol (Germany) stressed the Federal Republic's dependence on oil producing countries and favored supporting "security interests" of such a country. He expected difficulties for future commercial ties "if we do not consider Saudi wishes".(323)

Harald Peipers, member of the construction enterprise "Hochtief" (Essen), expected far-reaching damages to the Federal Republic should the Saudis not get German weapons because of the "wrong internal considerations".(324) Of course, the construction industry would have much to lose (see economic cycles).

Last but not least, the "Bundesverband der Deutschen Industrie" (BDI; German's Association of Industrialists), repeatedly demanded that Bonn send arms to the Saudis. German-Saudi relations would depend on this deal, declared Professor Rolf Rodenstock, President of the BDI at the end of a tour which brought him and other members of an official delegation of the association to Saudi Arabia and the United Arab Emirates.(325) Yes, Bonn was "somewhat obliged" to support the Saudis militarily.(326) The industrialists had received the impression in Saudi Arabia that economic relations could not be isolated from the political dimension, wrote the director of BDI's foreign trade department Mr. Steves in his report on the visit. Sheikh Yamani, he added, would discuss long-term cooperation in the "oil sector" only if the German side would suggest "something unique" as far as "technology" was concerned.(327)

"The Saudis repeatedly signaled to us that friendship had to be felt", another unnamed member of the BDI delegation remarked.(328)

Few were the voices of leading businessman which were more careful or even reluctant to send German arms to the Middle East. Surprisingly, the chairman of the German "Near and Middle East Association", Hans-Otto Thierbach, also a member of the board of the "Deutsche Bank" (Germany's biggest) argued that a country's security depended not exclusively on weapons but also on other "equipment".(329) Clearly, he wanted to have the cake (contracts) and eat it, too (no weapons and the political problems this would cause).

In June, i.e. after the delay of the decision, he did, however, press Bonn to finally make up its mind. Again he reminded German industrialists that the export of consumer goods had been neglected as compared with investment goods.(330)

Otto Wolff von Amerongen, President of the "Deutscher Industrie- und Handelstag" (Chamber of Commerce), originally favored "restraint" in arms exports and allued to Germany's past. Nevertheless, "friendly countries" should not be "put off with unconvincing arguments" such as the concept of "areas of tension".(331) In April, he still could not see any link between arms exports and oil deliveries as well as contracts.(332) In April 1981, he also wrote that in spite of non-existing "ambitions" for arms exports West Germany should not "offend friendly countries".(333)

The worries of the German industrialists were, at least partly, a reaction to Saudi warnings. Mohammad Nouri Ibrahim, Ryadh's ambassador in Bonn, had stated as early as in January 1981 that he could not understand the excited discussion of Social and Free Democrats. After all, Chancellor Helmut Schmidt had definitely promised the arms to King Khalid. If the Federal Republic did not abide by her agreement the diplomat predicted "unpleasant consequences".(334)

After Schmidt's visit to the Kingdom and the postponement of the decision optimism was artificially created. Count Lambsdorff, Minister of the Economy, expected an "enormous volume of contracts" to be awarded by the Saudis but modified his hope by stating that German exporters would have "to work hard".(335)

In late May 1981 Ibrahim was recalled to Ryadh and at his farewell dinner he complained of Germany's unwillingness to provide his country with "what we need for our security". He reminded the audience that "friendship is a two-way street".(336) The new ambassador was arrived in May 1982!

The Saudis increasingly showed preference to higher U.S. interest rates on the capital market and in early June 1981 they were unwilling to grant credits to Germany on terms as favorable as in the past.(337)

f) Trade Unions

Diverging reports referring to the position of **workers** and **unions**, were to be found. On the one hand, rank and file workers' councils openly demanded a liberalization of arms export guidelines in general and delivery to the Saudis in particular.(338) Horst Grunenberg, SPD Bundestag parliamentarian from Bremerhaven, said he had met with "anti-

Semitic emotions" in several plants. The gist of the argument was as follows: Should the Social Democrats reject lucrative contracts because of Israeli pressure their windows would be the first to be smashed and then those of the Jews.(339)

IG Metall, the metal workers' union (the biggest single union in the world), however, has consistently rejected arms exports to non-NATO states.(340) Eugen Loderer, the chairman of IG Metall, warned that additional arms exports would create an unwelcome dependence on even more sales of this kind and asked the government not to give in to pressures.(341)

g) Jewish Influence

Jewish spokesmen, generally establishment-oriented, reacted differently. Whereas Werner Nachmann, number one of "Zentralrat der Juden in Deutschland" (West Germany's top Jewish organization) would not reject the Saudi deal out of hand, Heinz Galinski, President of Berlin's Jewish Community (Germany's "biggest" with about 7,000 members) dismissed the idea categorically.(342)

Nachum Goldmann, honorary President of the World Jewish Congress, the "enfant terrible" as far as inner-Zionist criticism of Israel's policy (past and present) is concerned and highly esteemed by Chancellor Schmidt was also part of the Jewish input to the decision-making process. Having talked to Schmidt, Genscher and Kohl, he advised German politicians to handle the problem "very carefully." Moreover, he welcomed Bonn's tendency to wait until after the Israeli elections (30 June 1981). Considering France's and Britain's determination to outbid Germany in any weapons deal and the prospect that the Saudis would turn to alternative suppliers, Goldmann recommended "certain compensations" for Israel, "perhaps certain weapons".(343) In other words, he supported the original Schmidt-Genscher-Zimmermann-Peres line. (Goldmann forgot to mention Austrian keenness to replace Germany as Saudi Arabia's new supplier of tanks.)(344)

The Jewish connection went far beyond Germany. A delegation of the **American Jewish Committee** met with Chancellor Schmidt in September 1981 and was reassured that Germany would not send weapons to the Saudis.(345)

3) LESS VISIBLE ACTIONS

The Saudis were also interested in reducing their dependence on the United States by introducing missiles destined for anti-aircraft purposes developed by the Munich enterprise "Otrag" (see also Libya).(346) Negotiations started in the summer of 1980 with General Harald Wust, until 1978 West Germany's Chief of Staff ("Generalinspekteur der Bundeswehr"), acting as got-between for the Frankfurt-based firm "Meaplan".

"Meaplan" is a subsidiary company of "Intertec" which is owned equally by the West German businessman Klaus-Dietrich Nickel and Prince Nawwaf ibn 'Abd al-'Aziz (the Saudi Minister of the Interior). On 22 May 1979, Intertec and Otrag signed an agreement authorizing the former to buy Otrag including all its technical know-how and to sell it to third parties. This was done despite Bonn's unequivocal admonition on 31 August 1977 that Otrag would not be allowed to export missile devices. Nevertheless "Project Delta", was then pressed for hard by Meaplan. It is worth mentioning that "Polensky & Zöllner" (one of West Germany's biggest construction! enterprises) as well as AEG-Telefunken representatives participated in the 20 June 1980 meeting at the Meaplan office. Having enough troubles with the Leopard 2 deal, the Bonn government was less than enthusiastic about these activities and tried to bloc further Otrag undertakings which, in any case, were more disquieting with regard to German-Libyan relations (see German arms to Libya).

Behind the scenes, Germany and Saudi Arabia did, in fact, quietly **realize** at least some less spectacular but not unimportant **security efforts.**

West Germany's **anti-terror squad "GSG 9"** began to support Saudi forces in charge of internal security after the November 1979 incident at Mecca's Great Mosque.(347) The commander of GSG 9, Ulrich Wegener had reportedly come to the kingdom repeatedly.(348)

According to "Arab News" (Jidda), the Saudi part of Jubail served as a base not only for American-made minesweepers but also for German-made **torpedo boats.**(349)

Moreover, during the 1981 debate nobody referred to the unspecified number of **"Marder" armoured personnel carriers** ordered by the Saudis in 1977.(350)

There had been much ado during 1981/82 about the Leopard 2 and the supplementary deals. Little was published on the above mentioned details which also belonged to the package of German arms exports. Almost nothing was noticed publicly on the following actions and transactions. Nevertheless, it was possible to find out these data in 1981/82 already - if there was a will. Here is a list of some of these activities with a number of Middle Eastern States.

Algeria: After Chancellor Schmidt's visit to Algeria and Morocco in January 1981, deputy government spokesman Lothar Rühl reassured journalists that the Federal Republic would not export arms to North Africa.(351) On the sub- and non-governmental level, however, the "Fritz Werner" enterprise (West Berlin) reportedly provided Algeria with know-how for the "most modern weapons" (whatever that may be).(352)

Bahrein: "Type TNC-45 fast patrol boats were ordered in 1980.(353) In 1980 the Bahrein-Qatar row over the Huwar islands had already cropped up. Again, tensions were visible.(354)

Egypt: Some Egyptian tanks operate with optical night devices originally delivered to Britain from Germany.(355) Defence Minister Ghazala considered the Leopard 2 tank too expensive.(356) On 26 October 1981, Egypt and Germany signed and agreement on nuclear energy cooperation. Two 2,000 megawatt reactors are to be constructed.(357)

They are destined to produce electric energy, the "sensitive areas" of nuclear cooperation having been excluded.(358) - The activities of the Munich-based private enterprise "Otrag" in Libya aroused Egyptian suspicions as well as dissatisfaction (see Libya).(359)

Iran: Revolutionary Iran has profited from a weapons factory ordered by and delivered to the ousted Shah by "Fritz Werner". At the time this enterprise was worth two billion Deutschmarks.(360)

Iraq: Iraq signed an agreement with Brazil, not yet aligned with the nonproliferation treaty countries with respect to supplying uranium and exchanging technology.(361) Brazil and West Germany also cooperate in the nuclear sector.(362) There is no reason to believe that the Brazilians would not extend their acquired knowledge to their Iraqi colleagues.

Besides, Israel's intelligence and espionage agency "Mossad" reportedly learned that Iraqi delegations were touring nuclear installations not only in France, Italy and Sweden but also in West Germany.(363) In May 1981, shortly before Israel's raid on the Iraqi reactor, Bonn and Baghdad allegedly signed an agreement on nuclear cooperation. According to unnamed "diplomatic sources" referred to by the Israeli daily "Haaretz", Bonn officials were anxious to not publicize the arrangement providing for an exchange of experts working on nuclear energy. Moreover, it was claimed that Bonn had planned to send nuclear fuel but that pressure from U.S. led to a revocation.(364) - Via France Iraq continuously received "Milan" and "Hot" anti-tank missiles (see cooperation with France). The "Roland" missile arrived in Iraq the same way.(365) - According to U.S. intelligence sources, West Germany sent military supplies to Iraq during the war with Iran, only small quantities.(366) - Israel's Prime Minister Begin, not exactly a reliable and unbiased source, claimed that Bonn delivered 1,200 tank transporters to Baghdad.(367) - Optical night devices made in Germany are also popular with Iraq.(368)

The climax was reached in April 1981 when Iraq, quasi-officially, signalled her interest in buying West German arms and in May 1981 Deputy Prime Minister Ramadhan officially confirmed the intention during his Bonn visit.(369)

Israel: As far as "visible politics" is concerned, little has been observed about the military dimension of German-Israeli relations. Below the surface, however, despite Begin's diatribes against the West German Chancellor, there may still be some actions worth reporting.

In the early 1970s, as Minister of Defence, Helmut Schmidt had obviously enabled Israeli experts to have access to German arms construction and planning sites.(370) After Begin's second anti-Schmidt round, in spring 1982, Israeli opposition leader Shimon Peres, himself an ex-Minister of Defence (1974-1977), defended the German Chancellor publicly (for the first time) and mentioned the latter's "merits" (from the Israeli point of view) as much as his "sympathetic behavior" during his tenure of office as minister of defence.(371) Even now there were "things" in the military field between Israel and Germany one would rather not publicly talk about, Peres insinuated.(372)

Kuwait: This country reportedly received an unspecified number of fast patrol boats.(373)

Libya: As in the case of the Leopard 1 tank, Libya's Qadhadhafi reportedly wanted to buy **Leopard 2 tanks** via Italy. But the West German government refused: Its position on arms exports was known, it said. (374) No further consideration was given to this request. In view of Libya's interest in Austrian "Kürassier" tanks signalled during Qadhadhfi's visit to Vienna in February 1982, the Leopard 2 request is not at all unlikely.

On the sub-governmental level of military affairs between Libya and the Federal Republic of Germany, the activities of the Munich-based "**Otrag**" (Orbital Transport und Raketen AG, one of the few private rocket companies in the world) clearly dominated the news.

In January 1981, Franz Wukasch, technical director of Otrag, disclosed his company's plans for launching an unmanned, single-stage low-cost rocket "for the suborbital region". In 1982, it was hoped "to test a three-stage rocket with a package of 48 propulsion jets."(375)

The go-ahead for the launching of the low-cost missiles was planned for late February/early March 1981 in Libya. On 1 March 1981 the first missile was, in fact, launched in the Lybian Sahara(376) - much to the displeasure of Egypt and Morocco and the United States. These countries asked the Bonn government to intervene and prevent further tests.(377)

Bonn, too, was unhappy about these activities which caused additional troubles for Germany's Middle Eastern policy and couls, as unnamed "officials" claimed,(378) indeed, be used militarily. This, however, was categorically denied by Otrag's Franz Wukasch who called the nuclear dimension referred to by Morocco "complete nonsense" and "totally made up".(379) The company stressed the exclusively commercial aspect of its tests.(380) The Arms Control Office of the "West European Union" sided with the Munich enterprise emphasizing the non-military character of the missiles.(381) U.S. intelligence and space agency officials, in turn, asserted that the rocket could be intended to have a military application.(382) Fred Weimar, a businessman who had been active on behalf of Otrag in Zaire in the late 1970s, put things straight by explaining that "We are not children any more. It is very easy, indeed, to transform these missiles for military purposes."(384) Besides, the Amercian observers were disquieted by the fact that Otrag's tests were conducted under Libyan military officers connected with this country's atomic energy program.(385)

Regardless of the military or non-military capabilities of these missiles, the political damage to Bonn was evident. Officially, the West German government contended at first, there was little it could do to restrict Otrag because it was a private firm and its Libyan activities were said to be supported in large part from a subsidiary on the Italian island of Sardinia.(386) "It is outside control and yet still embedded in the Federal Republic; it would appear the company is both inside and outside Germany," said deputy government spokesman Lothar Rühl.(387)

Karl-Heinz Hansen of the SPD left-wing and well known for his principal objection to arms exports demanded in the Bundestag that Otrag's income tax privileges be cancelled.(388) (The company was, in fact, also set up as a tax dodge for investors who could write off their involvement as a loss, considering the fact that the firm had made no money.(389) The Secretary of State of the ministry of the Economy, Martin Grüner, replied rather evasively that new regulations would drastically reduce activities of companies such as Otrag.(390) But behind the scenes the government, first and foremost Chancellor Schmidt, must have pressed very hard for Otrag to retreat from Libya.(391) In early November 1981, Wukasch announced that his company had ended its Libyan involvement(392) and expressed his desire for future cooperation with Bonn. The political preconditions had to be improved, he explained.(393)

Unnamed "military sources" in London contended that Otrag had withdrawn because its managers were afraid of Israeli reprisals.(394)

Morocco: This country, too, was not supposed to get West German arms (see Algeria), but according to SIPRI 10 Do-L8D-2 Transport planes had probably been ordered in 1979.(395)

PLO: This organization did, of course, not receive German weapons by government consent. But here, too, the sub-governmental level is worth considering. In March 1981, members of the "Palestine Liberation Front" (PLF; rejection front within the PLO, not represented at the executive committee, the "cabinet", of the PLO) tried to reach Israel unobserved by means of a motor-propelled glider and then to attack targets in upper Galilee.(396)

As it later turned out, the glider was made in West Germany.(397) Syrian "businessmen" had bought it from the two constructors and distributors Fritz Schweiger and Eberhard Jehle at their small production site in Seeg (Bavaria).(398)

Military training of West German neo-Nazis and leftist terrorists by the PLO has been mentioned already (see Relations with the PLO).

Sudan: Judging from Sudan's problems with Libya, Chad and Ethiopia, but also from her internal structure (South versus North), one could hardly claim that this country was not an area of tension. Nevertheless Sudan was able to order 20 Bo-105C helicopters in 1977, ten of which were delivered in 1979 and another 10 in 1980.(399)

Sudan herself produces weapons with "Fritz Werner" (West-Berlin) know-how.(400)

In early 1981 brigadier-general el-Bakri disclosed in the Egyptian weekly "Mayo" that Sudan had reached an agreement with the U.S., Great Britain, France and the Federal Republic of Germany on the delivery of "modern weapons and military hardware". He refused, however, to give any additional details.(401) The timing had, of course, much to do with the crisis in Chad, but here, again, the principle of not exporting arms to areas of tension was ridiculed by Germany itself.

Syria: A confrontation state against Israel, and because of her latent tensions with Iraq and Jordan as well as of her involvement in Lebanon, Syria, too, falls short of being a non-tension area.

But an undisclosed number of AS-34 Kormoran air-to-ship missiles (Euromissile; cooperation) had been ordered in 1977 without having been delivered up to now.(402)

Unnamed "military sources in London" told the "Haaretz" correspondent in Britain that the Munich-based missile enterprise "Otrag" (see Saudi Arabia and Libya) had signed an agreement with the Syrian government providing for satellite launching sites.(403) Otrag's Frank Wukasch denied these reports (four months later!) and accused "hostile intelligence agencies" of spreading these rumours.(404) Via France (co-production) Syria has been receiving the anti-tank missiles (see above).

Tunisia: Clearly a friendly country and a pro-Western one, too, but evidently not without tensions. The January 1980 Gafsa incident which saw Libya try to stage a takeover attempt illustrates this description which, in turn, proves the necessity (from the West-German perspective, that is) to support the Bourguiba run state.

In April 1980 (Gafsa!), 3 Lürsen Type 57M fast patrol boats were ordered in the Federal Republic of Germany.(405) They were expected to be delivered in 1981/82 and were listed by the International Institute of Strategic Studies among the "major identified arms agreements" between July 1980 and June 1981.(406)

Turkey: As a NATO member this Middle Eastern country cannot be compared with other states in this region. Suffice it to say that a military assistance grant agreed upon in November 1980 included 70 Leopard 1 tanks, 2,500 Milan anti-tank missiles and the renovation of 200 M-48 tanks.(407) This transaction, too, was listed among the "major identified arms agreements" between July 1980 and June 1981 by the International Institute of Strategic Studies.

United Arab Emirates: 6 Jaguar-2 Class fast patrol boats had been ordered in 1977, two of which were delivered in 1979 and another two in 1980. Four Type TNC-45 fast patrol boats were ordered in 1979 and not yet delivered. 20 Leopard 1 tanks were ordered by the U.A.E. in Italy which produces this German tank under licence.(408)

B) EPILOGUE: THE CDU/CSU-FDP COALITION, 1982-1985

It had seemed in late May 1982 that the debate on the German-Saudi Arabian arms deal was over. The new guidelines for the export of German weapons as well as Chancellor Schmidt's public announcement had set the stage. But the actors on that stage, at least on the stage in Bonn, had changed by October 1982.

The coalition of Social Democrats and Free Democrats had broken apart, and Schmidt had to resign following a no-confidence-vote.(409) Helmut Kohl of the CDU/CSU became Chancellor with FDP leader Hans-Dietrich Genscher serving as his Foreign Minister. The FDP had switched its allegiance to the CDU/CSU.

The new coalition partners set out to effect a "turn" in West Germany's political course, first and foremost in economic policy ("Wende"). In the domain of foreign policy, "continuity" was declared the order of the day.

1) FLOW OF EVENTS

"Continuity" was proclaimed the most important foreign policy goal coalition, but the question what was "continuity" meant in terms of the German-Saudi Arabian arms deal.

Chancellor **Kohl** claimed that he had inherited this unresolved problem. (410) The Social Democrats, first and foremost Hans-Jürgen **Wischnewski**, one of Ex-Chancellor Schmidt's closest associates and former chief of the chancellor's office ("Kanzleramtsminister"), contended that a negative decision on the deal had already been made by the former coalition.(411)

Foreign Minister Genscher had been requested to inform the Saudis unequivocally of the position of the SPD-FDP government.(412) Thus the SPD leadership seemed to have found another opportunity to blame Herr Genscher, whom they (correctly) considered to be one of the architects of the October 1982 "Wende", i.e. the downfall of the SPD-led government. Both domestic and foreign policy issues were, once again, intertwined in this affair.

The new CDU/CSU-led government and the FDP as its junior partner countered that the documentary evidence left by the former government was far from unequivocal and a decision had yet to be made.(413)

The weekly "Der Spiegel" which has been most critical of the new coalition (and which had also not treated the former one gently) reported on 11 April 1983 that the arms deal with Saudi Arabia had been chosen as the political issue to initiate the turn in course ("Wende"). (414) The London-based "Middle East Economic Digest" wrote in July 1983(415) that Kohl's election victory in March 1983(416) raised "In some commentators' minds the possibility" that Bonn would "re-think its ban on the export of weapons to countries outside NATO." On the other hand, it quoted an unnamed "top-level German official in Bonn" as telling the weekly." I doubt very much ... that the Saudis will get what they want. It is, however, difficult to predict ..."(417) This statement was in clear contradiction to the information "Der Spiegel" had received from "a Kohl confidant" in April 1983 who had purportedly proclaimed: "They will get the Leo."(418)

These were speculations but a number of actions had in fact been undertaken. In May 1983, Saudi Defence Minister Prince Sultan had come to take a cure in the Federal Republic. During his stay he called on Kohl at his private home near Ludwigshafen. According to "Der Spiegel" the Saudi minister came away with the impression that his country would get the desired weapons with the exception of the Leopard 2 tank.(419) According to the "Frankfurter Allgemeine Zeitung" the two politicians had "talked" about the tank deal and the Chancellor's approach was apparently favorable.(420)

In any case, Hans-Heinz Griesmeier, the chairman of the board of "Krauss-Maffei", the main producer of the Leopard tank, confirmed in June 1983 that "technical contacts" with the Saudis had been established.(421) Prospects for government permission to export the tank seemed bright.

In October 1983 Chancellor Kohl arrived in Saudi Arabia for a state visit.(422) At the close of his stay Kohl confirmed that the possibility of providing the tanks was raised in his talks with King Fahd, but no agreement was reached. In fact, a non-commital compromise had been achieved. Other weapons which the Saudis had asked for were offered and a delegation from the Kingdom was to journey to the Federal Republic in late 1983 to "identify weapons that could be bought."(423) The communiqué published at the end of the visit emphasized that the planned talks would involve only the delivery of German armaments "suitable for defense."(424) King Fahd explained that "friendship between out two countries does not depend on arms deliveries"(425) but Foreign Minister Faisal did not conceal a certain disgruntlement.(426)

The delegation of Saudi Arabian experts arrived in early December 1983 and paid visits to enterprise such as Krauss-Maffei, Messerschmidt-Bölkow-Blohm, Siemens, Iveco, Magirus, AEG-Telefunken, Standard Electric Lorenz, Dynamit Nobel, Thyssen and Henschel.(427)

Any weapon except the "Leo"s; this seemed to be the formula. Simultaneously, the West German government declared Israel an "area of tension" (and therefore ineligable to receive German arms), whereas Saudi Arabia was not placed on that list.(428)

In early January 1984, Jürgen Möllemann (FDP), President of the German-Arab Association and since October 1982 Minister of State at the Foreign Office, told business leaders that Bonn was waiting for Saudi Arabia to present its arms shopping list.(429)

In late January 1984 Chancellor Kohl flew to Israel for a meeting with his Israeli counterpart, Prime Minister Shamir, who was less drastic than his predecessor but nontheless unequivocal in his opposition to the export of German arms to Saudi Arabia.

Chancellor Kohl had repeatedly stressed that the final decision would be made in Bonn uninfluenced by any outside party.(430) This, did, in fact, sound familiar and indicated "continuity" between Schmidt and Kohl both in terms of substance as well as terminology.

Approximately one year later, in February 1985, however, it was leaked to "Der Spiegel" that Genscher had been "taken by surprise" when he learned of Kohl's promise to consult with Israel before making any decision on arms deliveries to Saudi Arabia. This promise had been reportedly made during Kohl's visit to Israel and was interpreted by Genscher as creating dependence on Israel in this issue.(431)

The government's policy was at best contradictory, even on the visible level. On 9 February 1984 Kohl reiterated to the Bundestag that his government was willing to sell arms to Saudi Arabia except for the Leopard 2 tank but would, on the other hand, insist on "guarantees" that these arms not be used against Israel.(432) A few days later Möllemann elaborated three principles for the prospective transactions: First, no sale of the Leopard 2 tanks. Second, Saudi assurances that the weapons would not ultimately be delivered to a third party. Third, an assurance that all arms provided would be used only to defend Saudi territory.(433)

"The Kingdom of Saudi Arabia rejects any conditions or restrictions to be imposed on it which deny it the legitimate right to defend itself and Arab territory," an unnamed "Saudi official" told his country's press agency.(434)

Bonn's policy lay in shambles. It now appeared, that both the Saudis and the Israelis were outraged or, at least, angered. This was a new development, as the negotiations between the Kingdom and the former German government had annoyed only Israel.

In early March 1984, the Bonn correspondent for "Haaretz" reported that an arms agreement was impending after all and a Saudi delegation would arrive in Germany to sign it. Anti-aircraft weapons and armoured vehicles were allegedly on the list.(435) At the same time Chancellor Kohl stated once again that the Leopard 2 tank would not be delivered.(436)

In April 1984 the Saudis were reported to have accepted Bonn's conditions for the delivery of the Leopard 2. In return, they wanted to test two of these tanks in their desert.(437)

Things seemed to be running more smoothly again, and in July 1984 a German delegation secretly flew to the Kingdom. It was headed by Andreas Meyer-Landrut, Undersecretary ("Staatssekretär") at the Foreign Ministry. He was accompanied by Chancellor Kohl's foreign policy adviser Horst Teltschik as well as by high-ranking officials from the Defence and Economics Ministries.(438) The two delegations were in agreement concerning both weaponry and basic political principles, including the recognition of the right of all states in the region to exist.(439)

As with the events related in the previous paragraph we have the leaks published in "Der Spiegel" to rely upon. The weekly contended that the guiding principles mentioned earlier were supplemented by another which had been unacceptable to the Saudis from the very beginning: The stipulation was that the Kingdom would not only recognize the right of all Middle Eastern states to exist, i.e. to recognize Israel's right to exist implicitly, but also to recognize this particular right explicitly.(440) Did Bonn expect to solve the particular problem by putting aside "the" main stumbling block of Middle Eastern politics? Now the Saudis were reluctant to sign the arms deal which had been agreed upon earlier.(441) Both the principal stumbling block and the particular problem remained. As Franz Josef Strauß, CSU chairman and Bavarian Minister President, a politician who had always favored arms exports to both the Saudis and Israel summarized it: Bonn had succeeded in alienating both the Arabs and the Israelis.(442) The public articulation of this perception together with persistent Israeli criticism and repeated pronouncements by West German politicians on an issue which was obviously not "moving" indicate that the leaks published by "Der Spiegel" were not based on phantasy.

Behind the scenes the encless cross-talks continued well into early 1985 with no end in sight. It seemed in early March that the Saudis were attempting to regain the position arrived at in the summer of 1984: the right to purchase not further specified "German weapons" to be used for defensive purposes only (thus implicitly writing off the Leopard 2 tank for the time being).(443)

Nevertheless, the Free Democrats continued to bloc the deal, whereas Strauss kept pressing for its completion. (See below: The political parties).

In March 1985 West German Ambassador Hansen stated in Israel that the Leopard 2 would not be sold to Saudi Arabia.(444) A few days later it was reported, that the Saudis had decided to give up the Leopard 2 and would instead receive British "Challenger" tanks.(445)

a) Compensation for Israel?

As under the previous coalition suggestions were put forward to square the circle by selling arms not only to Saudi Arabia but to Israel as well.(446) In 1978 Israel had signaled its interest in buying or, preferably, producing the 120 mm Leopard 2 cannon but this demand had been rejected by Bonn. This canon, produced by "Rheinmetall" in Düsseldorf was not for sale, it was said.(447) In July 1983, however, the new West German government seemed to have indicated to Israel that it might be able to buy this cannon.(448) At the same time, Frank Bär, member of the board of "Rheinmetall", announced that his company would be willing to deliver weapons not only to member states of the NATO alliance but to other countries as well, provided the government permitted the sales.(449)

But if Bonn had hoped to be able to soothe Israeli opposition to the sale of arms to Saudi Arabia by suggesting this exchange deal it had miscalculated the Israeli reaction. Jerusalem's ambassador to Bonn, Yitzhak Ben-Ari, denied reports that his government might be willing to compromise on the issue and excluded the possibility of "buying" Israeli aquiescence with compensations.(450)

b) The Snowball Effect: German Weapons to other Arab States

Even before the deal with Saudi Arabia could be concluded other Arab states hinted that they, too, would be interested in buying West German arms. Among these states which have made their intention public are the Sudan(451), Kuwait, Bahrain, Qatar, the United Arab Emirates and Oman.(452) Syria appeared interested as well and Franz Josef Strauss' visit to Damascus (February 1984) was interpreted as a tour to promote such a deal.(453) It was also in February 1984, i.e. shortly after Chancellor Kohl's return from Israel, that Krauss-Maffei was reported to be "considering an Egyptian request to develop a new battle tank." No contract had been signed, but the Bonn government was "notified of the plan."(454) Critics feared that these tanks would end up in Saudi Arabia or Iraq.(455) The speculations were neither confirmed nor denied and West German Defence Minister Manfred Wörner flew to Cairo in March of 1985. The press only mentioned Egypt's interest in buying or building the Leopard 2 tank.(456) The Minister had prepared the press for low-profile and unspectacular results, and Egyptian production of the Leopard 2 tank under licence seemed far from likely.(457) Meanwhile rumours were floating about that Saudi Arabia might get the tank through Turkey, which would construct it under licence.(458) Both fiction and reality provided food for speculation. Clearly, all these fictions and realities added insult to injury of Bonn's foreign policy. In the meantime the West German government had become an active participant in this war of press leaks. It disclosed its knowledge of Israel's arms exports to Iran and accused the Jewish State of thus prolonging the Gulf War.(459)

c) A Pre-Emptive Israeli Strike against Saudi "Leopards"?

Chancellor Kohl's visit to Israel produced another variation, the Israeli-German war of nerves. Matityahu Shmuelevitch, director-general of Prime Minister Shamir's office, indicated in a newspaper interview the possibility of a pre-emptive Israeli strike against Saudi Arabian Leopard 2 tanks, should these weapons be delivered. This implication was not only criticized by the main opposition party in Israel, the Labor Party, but also categorically denied by Shamir himself.(460)

d) "Tornado" Planes for Saudi Arabia?

In 1981 and 1982 speculations about the possible sale of "Tornado" fighter aircraft to Saudi Arabia had been denied.(461)

In July 1984 "British Aerospace" confirmed that Saudi Arabia had "expressed interest in buying" 40 Tornados built by a British-German-Italian consortium." Any suggestion that they (i.e. the Saudis; M.W.) are about to buy is totally untrue", added a British Aerospace official.(462)

The original agreement signed by the governments of the three co-producers had included the clause that all three governments to approve exports to countries which did not belong to the NATO alliance. In May 1983, however, Bonn gave in to British and Italian demands to cancel this clause. Now each government could decide individually on this issue.(463) Israel's reaction remained low-profile, publicly at least.

2) Economic Aspects(464)

a) The Macro-Economic Level

Although German exports to and imports from Saudi Arabia fell in 1983 and 1984(465) but the Kingdom nevertheless remained an important economic partner of the Federal Republic of Germany.

Moreover, the Saudis granted financial credits to the Federal Republic both in 1982 and 1983.(466) The credits to FR Germany between 1980 and 1982 totaled about 20 billion Deutschmark, a figure cited by government spokesman Peter Boenisch(467) and by Chancellor Kohl himself.(468) By mentioning this fact Kohl tried make German openness to Saudi arms demands more plausible. Boenisch also mentioned "guarantees" which had been given by Saudi Arabia to deliver oil to West Germany. In other words: A quid pro quo was expected from Bonn, and it was willing to live up to these expectations and obligations.

b) The Micro-Economic Level

On the sub-governmental, micro-economic level arms-producing West German companies continued to be active world-wide.(469)

Clearly, these firms were the avant-garde of prospective arms deals to be agreed to or tolerated by the government.

Thus, **Krauss-Maffei** seemed to have initiated the Egyptian demands before they were forwarded to the West German government.(470) Until March 1985, these contacts have not led to any concrete deals.(471)

Activities undertaken by other firms were more successful, some deals even being carried out without the knowledge or consent of the West German government. Here are some examples which have come to light for the period surveyed in this section:

Another Munich-based company, **Messerschmitt-Bölkow-Blohm** (MBB) had been sounding out Saudi Arabian interest in buying its helicopters and informed the chief of Chancellor Kohl's office, Waldemar Schreckenberger, about Saudi Arabian intentions to present a "list of wishes". German restrictions should not be harsher than French or British rules, pleaded Sepp Hort of MBB.(472) On 1 August 1984 MBB confirmed that it had supplied Iraq with six helicopters with "luxury equipment for carrying members of the government."(473) According to MBB spokesman, Udo Vierheilig, "there were no problems arising from the weapons control law."(474) Three days later it turned out that the members of the Iraqi government must have renounced the "luxury equipment" in favor of guns. Moreover, the number of helicopters delivered rose to twenty-four. But: They were supplied by the Spanish "Casa" enterprise which had built them under licence from MBB.(475) Somewhat earlier MBB had opened a London office that critics charged would be used to further evade West German controls on arms-sales.(476)

Four managers of **"Rheinmetall"**, the manufacturer of the famed Leopard 2 gun, were indicted for having circumvented West German arms-sales restrictions by arranging for Rheinmetall and its subsidiaries to send weapons to Argentina, South Africa and Saudi Arabia.(477)

In September 1983, there were rumours that Saudi Arabia would buy 24.5 % of "Rheinmetall".(478) There has not yet been any confirmation of this.

Shortly before Kohl's trip to Israel it became known that the foreign ministry had not objected to deliveries of bullet-proof vests to Syria by the Fulda-based firm **"Mehler"**.(479) The Reagan administration reportedly reacted angrily,(480) and in the end effectively vetoed the deal.(481)

The export to Iraq equipment that could be adapted to chemical weaponry by the Frankfurt-based **Karl Kolb** Gmbh also infuriated the US administration in the summer of 1984.(482) Iraq is believed to have employed nerve-gas produced by Kolb's Samarra (Iraq) partner for months in its war with Iran.(483)

1984 was undoubtedly a year in which these companies were most active. After all, they expected backing from their new government. But this backing proved less enthusiastic than expected. The political implications seemed to be too far-reaching for the coalition in Bonn.

3) Bureaucratic Politics

The new coalition was far from united on the issue of arms exports to areas of tension in general and to Saudi Arabia in particular. Infighting within and among the different governmental agencies and between the politicians, in other words: "bureaucratic politics" was the order of the day. There were built-in contradictions between politicians and policies.

Whereas Chancellor **Kohl** supported the proposed deal with the Saudis, his Vice-Chancellor, Foreign Minister **Genscher** (FDP), was opposed. (484) It must be remembered, however, that in 1980/81 Genscher had originally supported the deal. He had changed his mind because of stiff opposition within his own party. Manfred **Wörner**, the Minister of Defence (CDU), proved generally more cautious.(485)

Within the foreign ministry there were two undersecretaries of state, Jürgen **Möllemann** (FDP), chairman of the German-Arab Association, who favored the deal, and Alois **Mertes** (CDU), who spoke repeatedly at conferences of the German-Israel Association(486) and who was opposed to changing arms-sales restrictions.(487) In October 1983 he told reporters that Israel's security interests would have to be taken into consideration should Saudi Arabia get West German weapons. This remark angered Saudi officials.(488) It was claimed by "Der Spiegel" in February 1985 that Mertes had succeeded in pushing through the demand that Saudi Arabia recognize Israel's right to exist before receiving German weapons.(489) The career diplomats of the foreign ministry, especially the Near Eastern desk also reportedly rejected the liberalization of arms exports.(490)

Mertes and the diplomats could win the day more easily in late 1984/ early 1985 after Möllemann had been forced to face two obstacles: Foreign Minister Genscher's more cautios approach, and a political controversy of his own making.

a) The Rise and Fall of Jürgen Möllemann

With the new coalition taking over in October 1982 Möllemann's star seemed to rise higher and higher: He first became undersecretary in the foreign ministry. Then, in April 1983, he succeeded Burkhard Hirsch as chairman of the FDP in North-Rhine Westfalia, West Germany's most populous federal state and the strongest party branch. Hirsch had been a supporter of the old SPD/FDP coalition and of Israel. Now, it seemed, the new FDP line would take over completely, both in the domestic and foreign policy domains.(491) In January 1984, a few days before Kohl's departure for Israel, Möllemann felt strong enough to re-emphasize his "pro-Arab" line in a public speech. This, in turn, rather than polluted before the Chancellor's departure for the Jewish State.(492)

In the following months opinion polls predicted a disaster for the North-Rhine Westfalian FDP both in the forthcoming elections to the European Parliament as well as in local elections. Both predictions turned out to be correct.

The day after the debacle at the polls for the European Parliament, on 18 June 1984, "Der Spiegel" published a story on Möllemann which caused a devastating blow to the rising star. Möllemann, "Der Spiegel" wrote, had used his political posts for private gain.(493) The politician protested and denied(494) the story but "Der Spiegel" came out with new details which put Möllemann in an ever more akward position.(495) He became so confused as to commit his gravest mistake: Möllemann stated he would not exclude the possibility of a "Zionist conspiracy" aimed at disturbing German-Saudi Arabian cooperation, especially of course, with regard to military affairs.(496) Arab emissaries on the other hand seemed to let him down or, at least, not to support him any more: "We consider this case an internal (German) affair," declared Emile el-Kik, of the office of the Arab League in Bonn.(497)

On 8 October 1984 Möllemann stepped down as the FDP candidate heading the party list for the elections to the North-Rhine Westfalian State legislature scheduled for 12 May 1985.

4) The Political Parties

a) CDU/CSU

As far as visible politics were concerned it seemed that the main thrust for a revision of the arms export guidelines as well as the delivery of weapons to Saudi Arabia originated in the Bavarian CSU.

Until the March 1983 general elections the coalition partners were absorbed with the question of their own survival as a coalition. It was unclear whether or not the FDP would return to the Bundestag and be able to form a coalition with the CDU/CSU. On the other hand, an absolute majority of the CDU/CSU seemed unlikely. In the end the FDP did make a comeback and the CDU/CSU emerged as by far the strongest party.

The negotiations for a renewed CDU/CSU-FDP coalition followed. Strauss and the CSU pressed for general liberalization of arms export guidelines.(498) In the end Strauss and his party had to give in and in the coalition agreement there was no mention of foreign policy matters at all.(499) The chairman of the CSU had argued for changes in other foreign policy issues as well, whereas Foreign Minister Genscher (FDP) favored "continuity". He was supported by Chancellor Kohl, and it was agreed that the chairman of the CDU (Kohl), FDP (Genscher) and CSU (Strauss) would meet again to discuss foreign policy matters.(500) Originally this meeting was to have taken place before Kohl's speech outlining the new government's policies to the Bundestag but this was not the case. Other discussions of the three chairmen planned for later dates were postponed as well. Strauss and the CSU had lost an important battle.(501)

Nevertheless, Strauss continued his efforts to promote the German Saudi Arabian arms deal in particular and arms sales in general until the end of the period surveyed in this section, i.e. until March 1985.(502)

Despite his stands Strauss was criticized less harshly during his trip to Israel than Chancellor Kohl had been on his visit. Although encountering opposition to his policies in the Jewish State, Strauss was treated with respect and to few verbal attacks.(503) The reasons were quite obvious: The CSU politician did not try to brush aside "History" as awkwardly as Kohl had appeared to do more by style than by substance. Moreover, Strauss had played a key role in the 1950s and 1960s in a German-Israeli arms deal. This had not been forgotten. After all, Strauss' counterpart on the Israeli side of this deal, Shimon Peres, had in the meantime become Prime Minister. Finally, Strauss presented a consistent policy line by emphasizing simultaneously his proven(!) friendship towards Israel, his criticism of certain policies and his interests.(504) Even his efforts to promote German-Syrian relations did not constitute an obstacle for his success in Israel in February 1985. (505) His own government was more angry with him, it seemed and spokesman Boenisch reiterated that the Leopard 2 tank would not be delivered to Saudi Arabia.(506)

It should be mentioned that other CSU politicians also actively supported the export of German arms, including the Leopard 2 tank, to the Kingdom.(507)

In the CDU only one politician pushed hard for changes in the arms export guidelines: Werner Marx, a CDU foreign policy expert spoke in favor of such modifications in early 1983, shortly after the Bundestag elections.(508) In view of Genscher's (new) position on the issue this was totally unrealistic.

b) The Free Democratic Party (FDP)

Jürgen Möllemann bore the banner of those in the FDP who supported the delivery of arms to the Saudis (and other countries outside NATO) in general and the export of the Leopard 2 tank in particular.(509)

The left wing of the FDP had always been known for its objection in principal to liberalization of arms export guidelines and deliveries to the Kingdom. These politicians continued to pursue their traditional line even after the "Wende". The most outspoken left wingers were Baum, Helmut Schäfer, Hirsch (who was to be replaced by Möllemann in North-Rhine Westfalia!), Hildegard Hamm-Brücher, and Olaf Feldmann.(510) But right wingers like Gallus and Gattermann also rejected liberalization of the guidelines.(511) Genscher, too, belonged to the majority of the parliamentary faction which opposed basic changes in in Germany's arms export policy.(512)

c) The Social Democratic Party (SPD)

For the SPD this issue did not pose any problem. As the major coalition partner they had rejected the deal, and as the major opposition party they could even more easily disallow considerations other than their ideological principles.(513) Even Hans-Jürgen Wischnewski (who was called "Ben-Wisch" because of his "pro-Arab" line) was more than cautious and explained that the Federal Republic could use "other possibilities" to strengthen Saudi Arabia's "security and stability". (514)

In order to embarrass Chancellor Kohl on the occasion of his visit, Israel's main opposition party (Labor) officially thanked the SPD for its consistent rejection of the Saudi Arabian deal.(515)

d) The Greens

The Greens were completely opposed to liberalizing arms-sales policy in general and to exporting weapons to Saudi Arabia in particular.(516) Since the Greens formed part of the West German "Peace Movement" this position came as no surprise.

In December 1984 a group of Green parliamentarians flew to the Middle East. Their itinerary included Israel, where it could be observed how the Greend combined a basically "anti-Israel" policy with opposition to the Saudi arms deal. Again, this opposition was dictated by reasons of principal, not by a particular leaning towards Israel. A description of this trip and its aftermath would go beyond the scope of this study.

5) Interest Groups

a) Trade Unions

The trade unions had gone at arm's length on the issue of the Saudi deal while the SPD-FDP coalition was in power, and continued to keep their distance after the "Wende" as well. Even the metal workers' union (IG Metall), which was directly concerned, remained opposed to the export of German arms to Saudi Arabia. The delivery of weapons would not serve to improve the overall employment situation in Germany nor in this particular industry, it was argued.(517) The statement by the IG Metall chairman, Hans Mayr, came in response to the claim by Franz Josef Strauss that arms exports would, in fact, create jobs.

b) The Protestant Church

As far as I can see, the Catholic church remained silent on the issue, but the Protestant Church repeated its opposition.(518) They stressed the Israeli problem even more than the general issue, i.e. arms exports to the Third World.

c) German Jews

The dilemma of German Jews will be dealt with in the Appendix. Suffice it to say that one of the members of Helmut Kohl's entourage in Israel was the highest-ranking representative of German Jewry, Werner Nachmann. But even he could not prevent the negative reaction to the Chancellor's performance in Israel. Moreover, Nachmann tried to convince members of West Germany's Jewish communities that the visit of the Chancellor had been more successful than generally perceived by Israelis and Jews.(519) Nachmann's approach was low-keyed whereas the chairman of Berlin's Jewish community, Heinz Galinski, was more critical, also publicly.

Despite the basically low-profiled response of organized Jewry "pro-Arab business sources in West Germany" were quoted by the ("pro-Arab" - if the simplifying generalization may be accepted) "Middle East Economic Digest" to be skeptical if Kohl could get away with his stand and added: "The pro-Jewish lobby is once again baying."(520) The "pro-Jewish lobby" may have been "baying": the Jewish lobby was not.

6) The American Connection

Three versions circulated as to Washington's evaluation of the prospective German-Saudi Arabian arms deal: According to the first, the Reagan Administration supported the deal. The second version cast Washington as opposed and the third spoke of non-interference. Whatever the truth may have been, there can be no doubt whatsoever that the Israeli government was determined to carry its fight against the deal to Washington. Besides, Prime Minister Shamir did not even try to conceal these efforts. Shortly after he had failed to convince Chancellor Kohl in Israel ro renounce the deal he told reporters that the American attitude would be decisive. Shamir added that his government had already contacted Washington and asked the administration to use its "influence" with Germany.(521) As could be expected, Saudi Arabia was infuriated by this outside interference and by the fact that Chancellor Kohl consulted President Reagan.(522)

The first version was to be found in the papers, for instance, in August of 1983. Daniel Dagan, the "Haaretz" correspondent in Bonn had heard that West Germany's Defence Minister Manfred Wörner had obtained the approval of the Reagan administration during his visit to Washington in July of that year.(523) A few days before Kohl left for Israel the papers reported again that the U.S. Administration had "encouraged" West Germany to pursue the deal and to deliver weapons, including the Leopard 2 tank.(524)

The second version was to be found in "Der Spiegel", which wrote that the Reagan Administration had reproached Bonn for making profits while the United States would have to bear the burden in case of military confrontation.(525) The leader of the Social Democratic parliamentary faction in the Bundestag, Hans-Jochen Vogel, told the press that he had registered "grave concern" about German arms exports to Saudi Arabia at the White House and at the Pentagon.(526) A modification of this second version described a change of mind at the White HOuse which had been the object of pressures from US manufacturers and the Jewish lobby.(527) At the very same time, in March 1984, during Kohl's talks with President Reagan, other journalists contended that the "official American position" considered the German deliveries of weapons an internal matter of the West German government. It would be up to Bonn to decide, they reported.(528) In other words, nobody knew for sure.

Alois Mertes (CDU), Undersecretary in the Foreign Ministry, offered an interpretation of his own which, on the one hand, avoided describing the actual problem and, still on the other hand, hit the mark. He missed the point when he emphasized that the Reagan Administration perceived Saudi Arabia's role in the Gulf region as positively as did the French, British, Italian and West German governments. He was completely off target when he simply left the issue of arms exports unmentioned. But he did hit the mark by drawing attention to the fact that the Jewish lobby mustered formidable support on Capitol Hill.(529) The Jewish and pro-Israel lobbies were active, indeed. The "American Israel Public Affairs Committee" (AIPAC) published in its "Near East Report" that sixty-nine Representatives had publicly opposed the proposed sale of West German weapons to Saudi Arabia. Their letter, sent on February 3, 1984, to Chancellor Kohl, urged Bonn not to become "a merchant of arms and destruction" in the Middle East and cited Germany's "past painful association with the Jewish people" and "special obligations" to Israel.(530)

The Jewish community of the United States organized an advertising campaign during Kohl's March 1984 visit to Washington in which they appealed to the Chancellor to renounce the arms deal with Saudi Arabia.(531) In Washington, the Chancellor met with representatives of the Jewish community but neither side was able to convince the other.(532) In late March 1984 Kohl met again with Edgar M. Bronfman, the President of the World Jewish Congress (who was accompanied by Werner Nachmann and the Secretary General of the organized German Jewish community, Alexander Ginsburg). Basically, nothing was changed by the meeting.(533) Nevertheless, Bronfman told the Jewish weekly "Allgemeine" that he was "impressed" by Kohl's "openness" and his friendship towards Israel and the Jewish People.(534) Edward Koch, the Mayor of New York City also used his visit to Germany to criticize the prospective arms deal(535) and the Canadian Jewish community did not remain idle either.(536)

C) THE PAST AS PRESENT: THE SHADOWS OF THE HOLOCAUST

It may be recalled that former Chancellor Schmidt declared during his return flight from Saudi Arabia that West Germany's foreign policy could no longer be overshadowed by Auschwitz.(537) He was obviously wrong. The counter-arguments against the German-Saudi arms deal, which came from Israel, Jewish organizations, and the United States government arose less from the military challenge such weapons (and the Leopard 2 tank in particular) would pose. It was an open secret that American-made "Abrams" tanks equipped with the 120 mm gun produced by "Rheinmetall"(538) were available to the Saudis. It was precisely this gun which made the Leopard 2 tank so attractive.

Helmut Schmidt was not alone in rejecting the Auschwitz connection which was put forward in Jewish-Israeli-American counter-arguments. "The undersecretary in the Foreign Ministry (Möllemann? Mertes?) was also quoted as rejecting such associations out of hand.(539) Continuity in style, formulation and substance between the SPD-FDP coalition on the one hand and the CDU/CSU-FDP coalition on the other hand can be seen in the angry remarks by Kohl's government spokesman Peter Boenisch in Israel: The terrible events of Auschwitz should not be exploited as political issues, he said, adding that Bonn had extended sufficient aid to Israel when Israel was in need and that the charges levelled against Bonn by Israel were neither fair nor justified.(540) Auschwitz could not be allowed to determine daily policy matters, he explained.(541)

Even Alois Mertes, who accompanied the Chancellor to Israel and was beyond suspicion as to his commitment and friendship towards the Jewish State, declared that Bonn cannot allow the past to affect present West German interests and that the sale of arms to the Saudis was in his country's interest.(542)

Even this well-informed, balanced, highly intelligent and historically-minded politician misconstrued Bonn's foreign policy realities which, ironically, were more strongly influenced by the past in 1984 and 1985 than in previous years. Kohl's visit to Israel was to be the "first installment" of Germany's encounter with its past: The commemoration of the allied landing at the Normandy was celebrated in June 1984 without German participation - much to Bonn's dismay. Italy's Foreign Minister Andreotti called Germany's desire for reunification "Pan-Germanism" (September 1984). At the same time, the Soviet bloc, most especially the USSR and Poland proceeded to remind West Germany of the past more frequently than in the years before. Like the Israelis, West Germans began to think that "the world" was against them, and Israeli observers of the West German political scene could and would not conceal a certain satisfaction.(543)

In late 1984 the decision on how to commemorate the fortieth anniversary of VE Day (May 8) could not be further postponed. The Bonn government handled this issue akwardly and proved to be much more touchy with regard to the past than it had tried to make believe in Israel in January 1984. Now the Chancellor was troubled by the possibility that President Reagan might, during his state visit to Germany, choose that day to visit the site of the former concentration camp at Dachau, near Munich. In the end, the visit was cut short to circumvent the dilemma.(544) Reagan's visit was scheduled to end before May 8, 1985.

The West German media inundated their audiences with broadcasts about the recent past, including German as well as Allied war crimes such as the bombardment of Dresden in February 1945.

A revived interest in 19th and 20th century German history could be observed in general. Whole series of new books, some of excellent quality, were published - and bought by the public.

"Nobody can steal away from history", said Franz Josef Strauss after his February 1985 visit to Israel (and also before).(545) Elisabeth Weichmann, the widow of Herbert Weichmann, a Jew who had left Nazi-Germany to return to West Germany after the war to become the mayor of Hamburg later on, offered an even more convincing argument: After the Second World War, she said, Germans were forced by the outside world to come to terms with ("bewältigen") the past. Now, for the first time, they were doing so. This, she added, would be much more difficult but, at the same time more successful and more rewarding.(546)

The debate over the export of West German arms to Saudi Arabia represents part of this process.

APPENDIX

WITHOUT IDENTITY AND FUTURE? GERMAN JEWS BETWEEN DIASPORA AND ISRAEL

Once upon a time ... There once was a German Jewry, and a German Judaism, but no longer. Jewish museums such as that planned in Frankfurt am Main, the reconstruction of the Rashi House in Worms or of the former Jewish quarter of this city, even the building of new synagogues (usually much too large for the local community), all of this cannot cover up the demise of Jewry and Judaism in Germany.

True, Germany at least the Federal Republic of Germany has not been "cleansed" of Jews as the Nazis intended. (The German Democratic Republic, where an estimated 650 Jews are still living, offers a somewhat different picture.) In quantitative terms, however, the approximately 28,000 Jews officially registered in the Federal Republic do not constitute a significant factor within Germany (West Germany, that is), nor within the context of worldwide Jewry.

This statement is true not only for the Federal Republic of Germany, but for all western and eastern european states as well with the exceptions of France, Great Britain and the Soviet Union, insofar as the latter can be considered a european state.

This situation, undoubtedly a result of the Holocaust, makes it appear worthwhile to examine the position of the Jews in the Federal Republic in the larger european context. Indeed, it seems to me that it is necessary to study them within the framework of the tensions between Judaism in the Diaspora on the one hand and Israel on the other. Because of the differing political conditions in the Western democracies and the communist states, especially the Soviet Union, it is only proper to compare the situation of the Jews in Germany with that of Jews in the Western Diaspora. Nearly all of the problems of the Jews in Germany prove upon closer consideration to be the problems of Jews and Judaism in the Diaspora. Since and because of the existence of the Jewish state, Israel, the Jews of the Diaspora have been forced to redefine their identity. A great deal has been written about the Jewish citizens of the Federal Republic of Germany, and they themselves have hardly been inactive in terms of publications. The majority of these presentations and self-portraits have been impressionistic and based on subjective value judgements. I would therefore like to attempt a more systematic and, if not "objective", at least a more detached approach, predominantly analytic and descriptive in nature. Within the confines of this essay it is, of course, not possible to attempt more than an approach, a rudimentary analysis.

I shall proceed in three steps: first, a demographic sketch of the German Jews; second, a description of the self-image and the behavior of the Jewish community in the context of the non-Jewish environment; third, and most important, a look into the relationship between Diaspora Jews in general and German Jews in particular on the one hand and the Jewish state of Israel on the other.

As far as possible the relevant developments are to be weighted with regard to the chronological factors involved. The question must be posed whether the conditions to be described are structural in nature, therefore of long duration and not easily susceptible to change, or whether they are subject to fluctuations or cycles, or are merely short term phenomena concerning individual events or persons.

I. The demographic situation

A brief look at the regional distribution of the Jews throughout the world demonstrations the decline in importance of the German, as well as the european Jewish community.

A consensus of estimates for 1980 shows approx. 13 million Jews worldwide. Of these, roughly 6 million or 46 % were living in North America, 6,5 million or 50 % in North and South America together. Israel accounted for 3,2 million or 25 % and Europe 3 million or 23 %.

1,1 million Jews or nearly 9 % were living in western Europe, 1,9 million or 14 % in eastern Europe (including the Balkan states, the asiatic parts of the Soviet Union and Turkey). About 28,000 were registered in the Federal Republic of Germany in 1980 or 2 % of the world total. With 535,000 Jews in 1980 France has the largest Jewish community in western Europe, followed by Great Britain with 390,000. The Jewish communities in Belgium, Italy, the Netherlands and Sweden are only insignificantly larger or smaller than in West Germany. The remaining nations in western Europe can be ignored with regard to their Jews.

A brief comparison with the demographic distribution of the world's Jews in 1939 (before the machinery of mass destruction of both Jews and non-Jews began its work) documents the basic structural change brought about by the Holocaust and the founding of the state of Israel.

In 1939 58 % of all Jews were living in Europe (including the entire USSR). 33 % were in North and South America, and a mere 3 % in the Palestine of that era.

The center of focus of Jewish life has shifted from Europe to Israel and North America. In the process, Europe lost more than half of its proportion of the world Jewish population.(1) The percentage of German Jews declined from 3 % of the total in 1933 to the aforementioned. 2 % of 1980.(2) Even at that time, the proportion of German Jews was quantitatively insignificant.

It may be parenthetically mentioned that the Jews of North Africa and the Middle East were drawn into the maelstrom of the Arab-Zionist conflict. There, too, little remains of the once large and proud Jewish communities.(3)

In other words: the demographic structure of Judaism today is bipolar, with the Diaspora on the one hand and Israel on the other. This structural and quantitative shift poses a question which is entirely new in qualitative terms and yet at the same time more than two thousand years old: Should or can Jews remain outside the Jewish community and still survive as Jews, both materially and spiritually?

Let us first take a closer look at the facts concerning the Jews in Germany today. On July 1, 1982, the Zentralrat der Juden in Deutschland (the Jewish Central Council in Germany) counted 28,272 members of synagogues in the Federal Republic and in West Berlin.(4) An additional approx. 5,000 nonregistered Jews (not members of congregations) can be estimated. Berlin's community is the largest with 6,500 members, followed by Frankfurt am Main with 4,800, Munich with 4,000, Hamburg with 1,400 and Cologne with 1,300 members. 5,400 Jews live in Bavaria, 3,600 in North Rhine Westphalia (excluding Cologne) and 2,000 in Baden Württemberg. All other West German states counted significantly less than 1,000 Jews.

As they were before the war, German Jews tend to be city dwellers, which is also characteristic of both Jews living in the Diaspora and in Israel. As before the Holocaust, the tension between those Jews born and raised in Germany and the so-called eastern-european Jews determines the internal structure of the congregations. In contrast to that earlier period, however, it is the eastern-european born survivers of the Holocaust and their descendents who are now numerically dominant. The Jews living in Germany today are therefore predominantly of non-German origin. This is to be considered a descriptive statement and in no case as a value judgement.

An important structural change has taken place in Berlin, where approx. 2,500 Jews from the Soviet Union have chosen to settle, rather than in Israel.(5) Thus it can be said of nearly 50 % of the Jews in West Berlin that, at the earliest, the second generation can be considered as German Jews.

Among the Jewish communities of Western Europe, a similar structural change has taken place only in France, where 45 % of the Jews living there at present are of French descent. 39 % are from Algeria, Morocco or Tunesia (a result of decolonization) and 7 % have immigrated from other states.(6) One qualitative result of the described quantitative structures consists of the danger of an almost exclusive preoccupation with one's own group. The smaller the community, the greater the tendency of view everything from the specific perspective of the particular group.

A recognizable trend towards mixed marriages is likely to further shrink the size of the German Jewish community and the Diaspora communities in general.(7) Although I am not aware of the existence of specific statistics for Germany, they are not likely to be significantly different from those to other countries in Western Europe. In Scandinavia approx. 50 % of all Jews marry non-Jews.(8) The same is true of Jews in France who are not active in the congregation, and the percentage of mixed marriages among active members is still 35 %.(9) In the US only 5 % of Jewish marriages in 1948 were mixed. Today it is approx. 30 %.(10)

The stronger the sense of collective Jewish identity, as expressed by a willingness to participate in the affairs of the congregation, the weaker the tendency towards mixed marriages. This sense of community identity can be of a religious or of a social nature, or a combination of the two. It is, in any case, strengthened by group pressures. A Jew who marries a non-Jew is looked upon as something akin to a traitor to his own long-suffering people. A common preventive measure against mixed marriages is the voluntary withdrawal into the ghetto.

Certainly less superficial and more substantial possibilities exist to secure the continuity and survival of Jewish life and the Jewish people. A more intensive cultivation of Jewish customs and culture would be one possibility, but this involves considerable difficulties for reasons which I shall explain later.

From a Zionist point of view, this difficulty on the part of both the German Jews and all those living in the Diaspora is not entirely unwelcome, since both antisemitism and the trend towards assimilation strengthen the argument that Jews as such can have a future only within the context of the Jewish state. For the Zionist it is axiomatic that Jews in the Diaspora can reckon with assimilation at best, and at worst with antisemitism, which, in the Zionist view, is more likely to be the case. Both, so the argument goes, would in the end lead to the demise of Judaism. (The question of Israel's Jewish identity cannot be taken up in this essay.)

On the other hand, it is this very trend towards assimilation, as documented by the increase in mixed marriages, that indicates a benevolent attitude on the part of the non-Jewish environment and a sense of well-being among the Jews in this setting. Such feelings among Jewish individuals are, however, hardly compatible with the priorities of the Jewish community at large which, like any other collective, wishes to survive as a collective.

II. Self-image and behavior

Three factors are of structural importance in relation to the self-image and the behavior of German Jews since 1945; first, the perspective distinguishing only between victims on the one hand and persecutors on the other. This perspective is simplified, but not falsified by the opposition Jew vs. non-Jew, which culminates in a "We-They" view of the world. Second, the change in biological and political generations must be discussed. Third, the change in the internal structure of the Jewish communities is to be discussed.

The "Jew" being discussed here is not the individualist, the Jew cutting across the grain of community opinion. He is also not the largely or totally integrated Jew who feels at home in a Germany, who identifies himself with the country, or one of its parties, or maybe only one of the political fringe-groups. He is also not the deeply religious Diaspora Jew or the Zionist about it. It is, to borrow a term from Max Weber, the "ideal-type" of community Jew to whom we are referring, to whom the above-mentioned characteristics do not apply. It is this "ideal-type" which I shall now attempt to describe.(11)

Either directly or indirectly, every Jewish survivor of the Holocaust has had to confront the question: "Why did I survive but not the others?" Independent of the numerous rational explanations for the survival of some of the concentration camp inmates as well as those whose fate was more fortunate, there always remains a residue of what is known as "survival guilt". As Jew, the survivor belonged to the persecuted collective. Independently of whether they had once lived within the grasp of the executioners or not, as Jews they belonged to the group of the victims and thus to the realm of goodness and light. The others, the non-Jews were per se assigned to the realm of evil and darkness, whether they had been among the executioners, their lackeys or not.

The sense of insecurity produced by the "survival guilt" was at least partially compensated by the sense of moral security in belonging by birth to the forces of good. To overstate the case: every Jew, whether a former concentration camp inmate or not, was able to "count" Auschwitz among his moral "assets". This is true not only for the Auschwitz generation, but also for their children and possibly the next generations as well, as we are dealing here with historical structures.

I am not claiming that this applies to the attitude and conduct of every individual Jew. I am describing structural conditions and these alone.

These structural conditions apply to Jews in Israel, to those in the Diaspora and most especially to the Jews in Germany, as they are living in the territory once ruled by the executioners.

Directly or indirectly, not only the Germans, but the Allies as well had made themselves guilty. The Allies had shown reluctance to take in even the persecuted Jews, had (for political reasons understandable both in general terms and in terms of regional politics)(12) been unwilling to permit immigration to Palestine or had done nothing to destroy the Nazi machinery of destruction.(13) Therefore the we-the-victims vs. they-the-persecutors perspective structurally is characteristic for all Jews, not only for the German Jews. This picture presents itself in sharper contrast to the Jews living in the contrary where the "Endlösung" (the "final solution") was attempted, but it is structurally not different from the perspective held by Jews the world over.

This attitude is especially decisive for German Jewish behavior in the political arena, where the elected or self-appointed spokesmen of the local Jewry present themselves in the role of schoolmasters distributing marks to the non-Jewish environment. Early in 1983 a leading representative of German Jewry stated his belief that the young democracy of the Federal Republic was capable of making progress in the area of human rights but at the same time criticized those whom he labeled as "German moral watchdogs" (he was referring to the "representatives of the Christian churches") who had not hesitated to draw comparisons between the Nazi concentration camps and Israel's conduct/conflict in Lebanon.(14)

The best-selling author Lea Fleischmann might also be mentioned in this context. In her book **This is not My Country. A Young Jew Leaves the Federal Republic** she writes: "When I was a child the world contained two kinds of people: Jews and Nazis."(15) The we-the-good vs. they-the-evil perspective cannot be any more clearly demonstrated, and the entire book confirms the picture.

The same is true for Henryk Broder's point of view. Before immigrating to Israel, the well-known journalist fired a final salvo at his former friends of the left, claiming that they remained "the children of their parents" and had, as he put it, "inherited" their racism.(16) Broder, born in 1946, counts the collective trauma of Auschwitz on the credit side of his individual historical-political ledger. "Auschwitz", he explained in **Der Spiegel**, "grows stronger in the Jewish consciousness the farther it receeds in time."(19) Auschwitz has become a political argument. As such it is subject to inflation and is certain to become politically worthless in the long run. When the once unique descends to the level of the daily routine, the emotional response soon becomes blunted.

The non-Jewish contemporaries of the first Jewish past-Auschwitz generation bear an amount of guilt equal to the suffering borne by the latter in the concentration camps, namely none. The we-the-victims vs. they-the-persecutors perspective is founded on both sociologically and historically invalid concepts of national character. The Nazi "final solution" demonstrated, (and this is its historical "lesson") that the human being - not just "the German" - is capable of sinking to the depths of the killer machine. Political biology is an invalid approach to the problems; political-historical anthropology is the more proper route. What is more, it is exactly this brand of what I call political biology which was employed by the Nazis as their instrument between 1933 and 1945. The conduct of Lea Fleischmann and Henryk Broder also demonstrates the change in both biological and political generations among the German Jews. I define a political generation as a group molded by political events taking place when they are between the ages of 17 and 25.(18) Fleischmann and Broder belong to the political generation of the German, european, and worldwide student revolts of the late 1960s and early 1970s. Their behavior, terminology and publications identify them as members of the "1968 generation".(19) Broder himself and Lea Fleischmann are anything but "ideal types" of the Jewish community. Nevertheless, they have immigrated to Israel. Furthermore the term political generation does not mean that all its members are identical in their conduct and opinions. Lastly it is precisely the most extreme form of the type which exhibits essential characteristics.

In France, Bernhard-Henry Lévy, born in 1949, in no way represents the ideal type of the congregation Jew, but he is an obvious representative of the Jewish 1968 generation. His controversial book **"L'Idéologie française** is a critical barrage against his non-Jewish environment. Lévy identifies Chauvinism, xenophobia, the cults of sport and youth, the glorification of technology, progress and order, antisemitism and anticapitalism, contempt for America and democracy, as the building blocks of the edifice of French ideology.(20) Apart from significant differences in Niveau between Fleischmann and Broder on the one hand and Lévy as an internationally recognized representative of the New Philosophy, the structural phenomenon is the same: the appearance of a Jewish 1968 generation. There is nothing specificly German Jewish here the adjective Jewish being understood as an ethnic rather than as a religious term.

The change in the internal structure of the Jewish community has not yet produced any basic changes in behavior. The Russian Jews have only been in Germany for a few years. In France, the democraphic shift in favor of the Jews of north african origin has resulted in a stronger movement towards the religious values of the collective community, the Jews of Algeria, Morocco and Tunesia tending to be more conscious of tradition.(21) In addition, these groups were not targets of the "classical" French antisemitism of the 19th century (the Dreyfus affair, for example), nor of 20th century antisemitism (Vichy and the Jews). It is thus only in this one Jewish community (albeit the largest in western Europe) that signs of a beginning release from the psychological bonds of the Holocaust are to be found. This, by the way, also applies to the Jews of Israel, where the proportion of the population of oriental origin is steadily increasing and today makes up approx. half of the total.(22) One can only speculate as to the future consequences in terms of self-image and behavior.

Political events sometimes result in political trends, or at the least contribute to them.

The unfortunate attacks on Jewish institutions and persons in recent years demonstrate the interlocking effects of political structures, trends and events. These attacks are, of course, almost exclusively the result of the conflict between Israel, its Arab neighbors and the Palestinians. But their effects are of significance not only for Jews in Germany but in all of Western Europe. They bring back memories of the pogroms and the fear of antisemitism. Criticism of Israel, even biting criticism is certainly not automatically to be equated with antisemitism (even if the opposite claim is often made). Many Jews, however, marked as they are by the historical structures described above draw exactly this conclusion. This political trend, the Jewish fear of what is seen as renewed antisemitism, will possibly reinforce already existing structures and may become for the past-Auschwitz generation a sort of substitute for what the previous generation experienced in the Holocaust.

On the other hand, inflationary use of the accusation of antisemitism against the non-Jewish environment may anger even the most well-disposed non-Jews into keeping their distance from the Jewish community and thus unwittingly reinforce the trend to itself-ghettoization among those Jews who have not already broken with their community or who are unwilling to maintain the accusation of antisemitism because it is contradicted by their individual experience.

It must, of course, be admitted that the attacks on Jewish institutions and persons show evidence of political, ideological and operational connections to militant antisemitic groups in Western Europe. One need only follow the daily newspaper reports or take a look at the latest reports from the German Verfassungsschutz (the agency responsible for internal security) to be informed of the collaboration between european right-wing terrorist groups such as the "Wehrsportgruppe Hoffmann" (a neonazi organization) and the el-Fatah branch of the PLO.(23)

III. The Diaspora and Israel. Or: The Double Dilemma of the German Jews

Before the Holocaust the legitimacy of the Zionist movement was a proposition of considerable doubt for the world's Jews. It remained a minority movement in constant need of self-justification. This thesis is given statistical support by the way in which Jews forced into exile during the past century chose to vote with their feet. The majority immigrated not to Palestine but to the United States.

Zionist ideologues escaped their legitimacy dilemma by declaring themselves the incorporation of the general will of the Jewish people. The following statement by Mosche Beilinson, one of the pioneers of socialist Zionism, sounds like an echo of Rousseau: "We are of the opinion that Zionism is the answer to the needs of the Jewish people and we therefore consider the Zionist movement to be truely democratic, totally independent of whether Zionist though is embraced by the majority of the people or not."(24) In other words: quantity is not quality, the volonté de tous is not the volonté générale.

After the Holocaust it was no longer necessary for Zionism to justify itself to the Jews of the Diaspora. It was widely accepted among Jews that events had proven the Zionist interpretation of history.(25) Now, in addition to bearing his share or survival guilt, the Diaspora Jew had to justify living outside of Israel. For German Jews there was a further dilemma in living in the homeland of the genocidal murderers. The German Jew was forced to not only justify his existence as such, but his existence in Germany, and this not only to himself, but to the remaining Jews in the Diaspora as well as in Israel. This was no easy burden if one was prepared to accept the historical and ideological premises which, as polls demonstrate, were accepted by Jews the world over.(26) I do not count myself among the historians and political scientists who assume the mantel of both prosecutor and judge, and therefore do not consider it my task to judge this development for good or evil. My task is to describe what happened and why. The question must thus be asked why these Diaspora Jews did not immigrate to Israel. The disarming answer of one young French Jew, to whom this very question was posed after he had been heard shouting "Down with assimilation!" and "Long live Israel", was: "Israel est un pays manifique, mais on y mange mal." (Israel is a magnificent country, but the food is bad.)(27)

That the state of Israel is the embodiment of Judaism, or at least the incorporation of the Jewish general will is a proposition accepted not only by most Jews of the Diaspora, but by numerous non-Jews as well. Time and again the the adjectives "Jewish" and "Israeli" are used synonymously in news reporting on the Middle East.(28) What I term "Israelism" is presumed to be widely prevalent among Jews in the Diaspora, including, of course, Jews in Germany. This assumption is largely correct, as I shall attempt to demonstrate. There are two aspects to "Israelism". First, and more superficial, is the identification with Israel which the non-Jewish environment has come to except almost axiomatically. Although there are no direct statistics available for German Jews, polls taken among American, French and Swiss Jews show that support for Israel was unbroken until the time of the Sadat initiative and even thereafter continued to be extraordinarily strong.(29) The second and more substantial aspect of "Israelism" concerns the equation made between Israel on the one hand and Jewry and Judaism on the other. Ultimately it concerns the meaning of Jewish identity. If "identity" is understood in its original sense to mean the complete equality of two objects,(30) then to equate Judaism with Israel is to considerably restrict the former term. Independently of whether one's standpoints is pro- or anti-Zionist, or indifferent, is must be admitted that, however meaningful Zion may be for the Jewish religion and culture, it is not completely identical with Judaism. The fact alone that the Babylonian Talmud is considered more important than the Jerusalem Talmud proves the validity of the contention for the most central sphere of Judaism: the Jewish religion.

A poll of Swiss Jews taken in the autumn of 1980 showed that "support for Israel" and "combatting anti-Israeli tendencies" were given higher priorities than "support for Jewish education" or "cultivation of Jewish tradition".(31) It is safe to assume that a sampling of German Jews would produce similar results. One might thus speak of Israelis living abroad who prefer having a bad conscience but eating well in the Diaspora to living in Israel.

"Israelism" as a form of Jewish identity means the ultimate secularization of Judaism. But if God is dead, one at least has an idol.(32) Antizionist orthodoxy recognized this danger early on and fought Zionism as "blasphemous" for interfering with God's creation by attempting to alter the course of history. I offer this, too, as a descriptive observation rather than as a value judgement.

Among German Jews there does not seem to be any great interest in Jewish culture and tradition. There are more non-Jews than Jews enrolled at the College for Jewish Studies in Heidelberg. Even then the numbers are not impressive: only 22 students declaring the subject as their major, 18 as their minor in 1982.(33) Numerous synagogues experience great difficulty in assembling the Minjan, the ten men necessary for common prayer. The situation is the same in Scandinavia(34) and in the Netherlands,(35) where the Jewish communities are of comparable size to Germany's. This is not a problem, however, in the much larger French Jewish community. Although attendance at the synagogue is perfunctory among native-born Jews in France, the French Jews of north african extraction are more religiously active, more conscious of Jewish tradition, and also tend to be stronger supporters of Israel than the rest of the French Jewish community. To these Jews the folklore of Israel represents a complement to Jewish tradition and religion, but has not become a substitute, as it is for large sections of west european Jewry.(36) This includes the German Jews.

A more pronounced "Israelism" is not necessarily an inescapable consequence of the increasing secularization of the Diaspora Jews, but it does increase the tendency towards separation from the Jewish religion and community. The increasing frequency of mixed marriages confirms this. The quantitatively stronger position of the Jewish community in Great Britain qualitatively resembles the situation in Germany. Immanuel Jakobovits, the Chief Rabbi of Great Britain, was quick to recognize the danger posed by the "Israelism" to the structure of the Jewish identity in the Diaspora. In December 1976, before the Sadat initiative and long before Jewish criticism of Israel came into fashion, Jakobovits stated that the "quality of life" in the Jewish state was a more important consideration than the question of its borders and warned against imitating the exaggerated fervour of the West Bank settlers.(37) In February of 1980 he would no longer exclude the founding of a Palestinian state on the West Bank and in the Gaza Strip with East Jerusalem as its Capital as a possible solution to the Middle East conflict.(38) Such statements on the part of spokesmen for German Jews would be totally unthinkable.

The Chief Rabbi of Great Britain apparently recognized implicitly that "Israelism" means that the Jews of the Diaspora are being drawn into Israel's internal political conflicts. Following the Sadat initiative in 1977 and the resulting debate over the "correct" peace policy, Israel has become increasingly polarized. After the peace treaty with Egypt, the controversy over the settlements policy and the Palestinian question further polarized Israeli public opinion, and the War in Lebanon, (which was actually a war against the PLO) has split Israeli society more than ever before. The close relationship between persons, events, trends and structures in Israel and Jews outside Israel means that this split has spread the Diaspora communities. The result has been an unprecedented wave of criticism of Israel among Diaspora Jews. This polarization, although more likely a passing trend, may on the other hand become a permanent feature of the Diaspora. Thus far, however, there is little to be found of this among Jews in Germany, where the position of the potential critic is especially awkward. Both the hawks within Israel and the "Israelitic" Diaspora Jews would be certain to pointedly question the right of those living in the land of the Holocaust to give moral criticism of Israel.

Characteristically, the few voices of protest raised against the war in Lebanon raised among German Jews have been mainly those of individuals who do not belong to a Jewish congregation.(39) These individuals can and do avoid the reproaches directed against them simply by avoiding contact with the Jewish community.

Only when the Jews of the German congregations are able to arrive at a less encumbered relationship to Germany will they be able to face the possibilities of such reproaches with more confidence. It cannot be predicted when such a development may come about. Polarization as a result of the Sadat initiative and especially since the war in Lebanon is characteristic of the Diaspora congregations outside of Germany.

The present split within the Diaspora congregations between "Israelistic" Jews and those critical of Isreal is reminiscent of, but not identical with the devision between Zionist and anti-Zionist Jews before the Holocaust.

The majority of Jewish critics of Israel would not yet consider themselves to be anti-Zionist. Nevertheless, for the first time since the founding of the state of Israel, the question of the identity of the Diaspora Jews has been posed in a new, less "israelitic" contect.(40)

When viewed within the framework of the whole of Jewish history, this identity problem of the Diaspora over and against a Jewish entity or state turns out to be nothing new. It resembles the period of the Second Temple (from 516 B.C. to 70 A.D.) during which were two Jewish centers in addition to Zion, one in Babylon, the other in Egypt.(41) In contract to the present-day Diaspora, especially the situation in Germany, the Diaspora of that ancient period possessed an identity of its own. Judaism today has undoubtedly arrived at a historical crossroads.

There is the central question of the meaning of Jewish existence. In addition, there are the questions: Where can there be a Jewish existence? Where should there be? The 2,500 year history of the Diaspora, during which the Jews have survived as Jews in spite of everything, proves that there is no clear answer to these questions.(42)

What is now at stake is whether Jews will opt for the cosmopolitan tradition of the Diaspora or for the tradition of the Zealots in Zion. Should the final decision fall in favor of the fervent nationalists, the Jews would ultimately become what orthodoxy has sought to avoid and the Zionists have sought to attain: "kehol hagojim" - to be like other peoples. If, the Jews are indeed politically a people like all other peoples, then a further question immediately presents itself with regard to the Jewish religion, which in Judaism can hardly be separated from the realm of politics: How can the religious claim to be the chosen people of God be maintained? According to the British Chief Rabbi Jakobovits, the realization of the goals of the Zeolot idelogy would mean the end of the Jewish people and would lead to what he termed "national euthanasia".(43)

The fact that the zealous letter of the Gush Emunim are orthodox Jews does not disprove my contention. It merely proves that these zealots have not thought through all of the consequences of their conduct. Isreal's tragedy is that it may not be able to survive without the ultranationalist zealots but would have even less a chance under the bunner of cosmopolitism. It would thus be presumptuous to assign "guilt", as there are only guiltless victims in tragedies.(44)

"Israelism" especially among the Diaspora Jews in Western Europe, has brought with it not only psychological dangers, but a physical threat as well. As substitute Israelis they have become the victims of Palestinian terror and Western Europe has become a further theater of the middle eastern conflict.(45) There is a certain logic to this from the Palestinian viewpoint, which can be recognized being morally condoned.

From an Israeli Zionist perspective, from Begin's point of view, it is equally logical that such acts of terror are to be interpreted as further delegitimizing the Diaspora. It is argued that only the Israeli government, not the French, German, Italian, British or Belgian governments, is capable of protecting the Jews.(46) Following the anti-Jewish bombings in Paris, a campaign promoting immigration to Israel was thus initiated among French Jews.(47)

But the logic of the Palestinian terror and the consequences of the Israeli reaction constitute a challenge to western european governments. Responses were provoked in Israel as well. In reply to Begin's arguments, the leader of the opposition, Shimon Peres, stated that the protection of French Jews was the responsibility of the government of France, not of the government of Israel.(48)

This difference of opinion is of the greatest significance as it involves the question whether the state of Israel is responsible for the fate of the Jewish people not only in a moral sense, but in terms of practical politics as well. Peres, perhaps without realizing it, was thus casting doubt on the Zionist claim to represent the general will of the Jewish people.

Begin's point of view represents a challenge not only to the governments of the European community but ultimately also to the leadership of the Diaspora. It is thus not surprising that Alain de Rothschild and other representatives of the French Jewish community refused to gather behind Begin's shield.(49) The challenge has thus far not become acute for Germany or for the German Jews, as the Federal Republic has not yet experienced many acts of anti-Jewish terrorism.

In addition to this challenge from outside, the present Jewish leadership in Western Europe faces an opposition from within stemming in the most part from younger intellectuals. The majority are members of the political generation of 1968, including writers and journalists, many of whom are not (or are no longer) members of congregations. A quick introduction to their attitudes and opinions concerning Germany can be obtained by reading **Fremd im eigenen Land** (Stranger to One's Own Country) edited by Broder and Long.(50) Among other targets, their criticism is directed at the phenomenon of "Israelism" among German Jews, their general disinterest in religion and lack of community spirit, the lack of intellectual, spiritual and democratic legitimation among the community spokesmen, their failure to secure grass-roots support and their near obsequiousness with regard to public authorities. The sometimes aggressively anti-intellectual attitude of the Jewish congregations and their leadership is critizised as a break with Jewish tradition as a people of the Book. There is, however, also a historical anti-intellectual tradition in the european Jewish communities, especially with regard to those viewed as freethinkers. One is reminded that the Amsterdam congregation ostracized the philosopher Spinoza. Whether and how long such a small Jewish Community as the one in Germany can afford the dubious luxury of anti-intellectualism remains to be seen.

The constantly self-reflective looking-glass perspective, the limiting of one's horizon to the view from the church tower, disgusts the critics, who also direct their polemics against the we-the-victims vs. they-the-persecutors perspective. They are also able to discover less "anti-Semitism" in their environment than the leadership of the congregations.

In France, the gap between the leadership and the potential membership of the congregations has grown to the point that only a third of all Jews belong to a congregation.(51) For Germany there are not statistics available. In Great Britain approx. two thirds of all Jews are members of congregations.(52) Having learned from the non-Jewish environment that government policies can be altered or even blocked by pressure from below, the political generations of 1968 and younger are pressing the current leadership to mobilize politically. The cry is for demonstrations against, for example, the European Community's policy on the Middle East. Guy de Rothschild has countered this demand with an irrefutable argument: "One doesn't play at mass actions when one hasn't any masses."(53)

The current leadership in France and Germany is placed in further jeopardy as a result of another structural change. In France it is the constantly increasing proportion of immigrants from North Africa; in Germany there are the rising numbers of Russian Jews. Both groups are moving into leadership positions. The present Chief Rabbi of France is of north african extraction, and the oriental Jews are sure to achieve further prominent positions.

IV. Perspectives

I have thus far focused increasingly on the centrifugal forces tending away from the centers of the Jewish congregations in Germany and Western Europe. On the opposite side, six centripetal factors are operating to restrengthen the traditional Diaspora pattern.

1) The numerous attacks on Jewish institutions and persons, independent of whether the authors are Palestinians, local terrorists of the left or right fringe, or just deranged imitators.
2) The policy of the European Community towards the Middle East. Whether in fact anti-Israel or not, it is perceived to be so.(54)
3) The increased interest in personal and ethnic roots as evidenced by both Jews and non-Jews.
4) This interest in one's own heritage stimulates the study of history and an awareness among the post-Auschwitz generation that not only the Germans, but the French, English Austrians and even the Americans carry the historical burdens of past injustices. The we-the-victims vs. they-the-persecutors perspective is thus further encouraged.
5) The increased interest in religion which has been observable for some time among both non-Jews and in Israel(55) may contribute a new and at the same time ancient consciousness, namely a Jewish consciousness to the "Israelism" of the Diaspora.
6) The economic crisis both in West Germany and in Western Europe as a whole has lead to a rediscovery of Xenophobia. Once again it is nearing social acceptability and might in future be transferred to the Jewish community. The disgusting "Turkish" jokes now current in Germany make one fear the worst.(56)

It is to be concluded that Israel has become an idol for the Diaspora Jews in general and the German Jews in particular. Slowly the latter are awakening from their dreams.(57) On the other hand, Israel is, of course, not the caricature of the professional killer as portrayed by its enemies and some of its critics. In reviewing the causes and effects of the war in Lebanon, Isrealis, Diaspora Jews and non-Jews are presented with an excellent opportunity to recognize Israel for what it in fact is: a country peopled by men, but not by supermen. Is it possible that such reflections, coupled with a rethinking of established attitudes, some of which reach back nearly two thousand years, will lead to a sense of identity of the Diaspora independent of the state of Israel? Will the German Jews perhaps be included in this reawakening, thus freeing themselves from the tutelage of the previous generations, of Israel and the other Diaspora Jews and establishing their own identity?

NOTES

PART I

1 FRANKFURTER ALLGEMEINE ZEITUNG, 29 April 1981; DER SPIEGEL, 4 May 1981.

2 They were also looking for other arms such as the "Marder" and "Gepard" as well as howitzers.

3 See Francis Nicosia, "Arab Nationalism and National Socialist Germany, 1933-1939: Ideological and Strategic Incompatability", INTERNATIONAL JOURNAL OF MIDDLE EASTERN STUDIES, Vol.12 (1980), p.364. Also Josef Schröder, "Die Beziehungen der Achsenmächte zur Arabischen Welt", Manfred Funke, ed., HITLER, DEUTSCHLAND UND DIE MÄCHTE, Düsseldorf, Droste 1976, pp.372f.; Friedrich P.H. Neubert, DIE DEUTSCHE POLITIK IM PALÄSTINA-KONFLIKT 1937/38, unpublished Ph.D. thesis, University of Bonn 1977, pp.120-123. Neubert refers only to 1937/38 and does not pursue the subject until the decisive year of 1939 (decisive for our subject, not his); Fritz Grobba, MÄNNER UND MÄCHTE IM ORIENT, Göttingen etc.: Musterschmidt 1967, p.115 states that the agreed upon weapons "could not be delivered" because of the outbreak of World War II. Grobba served as Germany's ambassador (envoy) to Jidda and Bagdad and was directly involved in the decision-making process (see below); Lukasz Hirszowicz, "The Course of German Foreign Policy in the Middle East Between the World Wars", Jehuda Wallach, ed.: GERMANY AND THE MIDDLE EAST 1835-1939, Tel-Aviv, Yearbook of the Institute for German History, 1975, p.186 claims that the "arms deal remained on paper only"; in his book THE THIRD REICH AND THE ARAB EAST, London-Toronto 1966, p. Hirszowicz is somewhat more restrained: "The deal may not have been realised, for the war broke out ..."; Gerhard L. Weinberg, THE FOREIGN POLICY OF HITLER'S GERMANY, Chicago-London, Chicago University Press, 1980, p.244 still has his doubts: "It is not clear whether the promised rifles ever reached Saudi Arabia ..."

4 For a lengthy and detailed theoretical discussion of my approach which modifies Michael Brecher (ISRAEL'S FOREIGN POLICY SYSTEM, Oxford University Press, chapter 1 and DECISIONS IN ISRAEL'S FOREIGN POLICY, Oxford University Press 1974, introduction) see my monograph DIE DEBATTE ÜBER DEN KALTEN KRIEG. POLITISCHE KONJUNKTUREN HISTORISCH-POLITISCHE ANALYSEN, Leverkusen-Opladen, Leske + Budrich 1982, chapter III.

5 Here, too, I have to point to the theoretical discussion in my book, DIE DEBATTE.

6 Andreas Hillgruber, "England's place in Hitler's plans for world dominion", JOURNAL OF CONTEMPORARY HISTORY, Vol. 9, (1974), No. 1, p.8. Hillgruber mentions the more important studies proving his thesis (Klaus Hildebrand, Norbert Wiggershaus, Josef Henke, Jost Dülffer as well as his own). Pedantic bibliographical notes are be-

yond the scope of this essay. I, therefore, only mention some authors.

7   Op. cit., p.13.
8   Ibid.
9   Op. cit., p.15, Nicosia, op. cit., p.359 claims that Hitler had already changed his tactics "by the end of 1936". He contends, however, that strategically and as a matter of principle the Führer wanted to maintain "racial solidarity" with Britain (op. cit., p. 360).
10 Charles Bloch, "Die Wechselwirkung der nationalsozialistischen Innen- und Außenpolitik 1933-1939", Manfred Funke, op. cit., p.220.
11 Hirszowicz, THE THIRD REICH, 1966, p.10. As will be shown, professionals of the Auswärtiges Amt and the Military saw this clearly.
12 Haim Shamir, "Germany and the Middle East Between the Two World Wars", Wallach, ed., op. cit., pp.167-174.
13 Nicosia, op. cit., p.356 stresses that this was also the motive for Germany's refusal to actively support the Arab cause in Palestine. See especially Neubert, op. cit.; Anthony R. De Luca, "'Der Grossmufti' in Berlin: The Politics of Collaboration", INTERNATIONAL JOURNAL OF MIDDLE EASTERN STUDIES, Vol.10 (1979), pp.125-138.
14 Op. cit., p.361, also the section on "German Arms Export Policy" (pp. 361-366).
15 See Schröder, op. cit., pp. 367-369; Hirszowicz, Third Reich, pp. 13 ff.
16 Les archives secrètes du Comte Ciano, 1936-1942, quoted from Schröder, op. cit., p.367.
17 Op. cit.; Grobba, op. cit., pp.110-111; Hirszowicz, The Course, p. 186. The Arabs feared the expansion of Italian power in the Red Sea area (Weinberg, op.cit., p.247). After all, they had established themselves in Ethiopia.
18 Hirszowicz, The Course, p.186, 189.
19 Nicosia, op. cit., p.360.
20 Op. cit., p.359.
21 Weinberg, op. cit., p.248.
22 Bloch, op. cit. p.220.
23 Eliyahu Ben-Elisar, La diplomatie du Troisième Reich et les juifs, Paris 1970; also Werner Feilchenfeld/Dolf Michaelis/Ludwig Pinner, Haavara Transfer nach Palästina und Einwanderung deutscher Juden 1933-1939, Tübingen 1972; Neubert, op.cit., pp.123 ff.
24 This agreement was concluded as early as 25 August 1933 between Eliezer S. Hoofien (Anglo-Palestine Bank, run by the Jewish Agency) and the German Ministry of Economics. See Feilchenfeld/Michaelis/Pinner, op. cit.
25 Nicosia, op. cit., p.353 claims that "even the realization that Germany was directly responsible for the dramatic increase in

Jewish immigration into Palestine after 1933 did little to dampen" Arab enthusiasm for the Nazis. A closer look at the files of the Eichmann trial dealing with this aspect (Institut für Zeitgeschichte Munich) contradicts this contention which implies Arab stupidity or blindness. Neither one can be taken at face value. The Mufti of Jerusalem, Haj Amin el-Husseini, did realize what Germany's policy was all about and pressed hard for an end to Jewish emigration from Germany and thus immigration to Palestine. Eichmann was his ally. (See Institut für Zeitgeschichte, Eichmann 1301-1303, 1309-1313, 1329, 1387, 1388 for instance).

26 Bloch, op. cit., p.220.

27 "Denken wir als Herren ("masters ! M.W.) und sehen wir in diesen Völkern bestenfalls (at best, M.W.) lackierte Halbaffen, die die Knute spüren wollen" (ADAP, Serie D, Vol.7, p.172, Hitler to the commanders in chief, Obersalzberg, 22 August 1939. In other words: shortly after his approval of arms exports to the Saudis. The racial whitewashing followed more than two years later (see note 28); H. Shamir, op.cit., p.172.

28 H. Shamir, op. cit., p.172 quoting from H. R. Trevor Roper, HITLER'S SECRET CONVERSATIONS 1914-1944, New York 1953, p.512. Hitler and the Mufti met for the first time on 28 December 1941 (De Luca, op. cit., p.129).

29 H. Shamir, op. cit., p.173 also with other examples of various ideologues and politicians, pp. 172 f.

30 Ibn Saud's physician, Sheikh Madhat al-Ard, contacted the Außenpolitisches Amt (A.P.A.; Foreign Policy Office) of the NSDAP in the "fall of 1937" (Institut für Zeitgeschichte = IfZ, Munich, MA 255, Kanzlei Rosenberg, microfilm frame 3-18, Amt für Vorderasien, v.H. = von Harder, "Aktennotiz", 21 Juni 1939; note by Herr Osthus, A.P.A., commissioned by (Freiherr) von Harder to Auswärtiges Amt (AA; Foreign Office), 23 July 1938, "Saudi-Arabien", PA, AA, Pol. VII, 1605 Beziehungen zu Saudi-Arabien, p.2, here the physician is mentioned by name, whereas in the first document contacts are mentioned in general; Hirszowicz, The Third Reich, p.47: "During his stay in Baghdad (in November 1937) Sheikh Yusuf Yasin - the King's private secretary - and other confidential agents enquired of representatives of the Otto Wolff firm if they would supply the King with 15,000 rifles on credit. The representative of Ibn Saud, his personal physician, Sheikh Madhat al-Ard (a Syrian from Damascus) contacted the Außenpolitisches Amt of the NSDAP in the King's name."; Grobba had his first reported official contacts which did not deal with weapons but with diplomatic relations between the two countries in general on 5 November 1937 (ADAP, 1918-1945, Series D, (1937-1945), Vol.V, Baden-Baden 1953, pp.648-650, also PA, AA, Pol.VII, Beziehungen zu Saudi-Arabien, 1605, p. 385458-461; Neubert, op. cit., pp.105 ff. and Schröder, op. cit., p.370 also refer to this source; based on sources of the AA Nicosia, op. cit., p.364 writes that "as early as February 1937, the Saudi government had expressed an interest in purchasing German weapons, both for the Saudi armed forces and for the Arab cause in Palestine." Von Hentig (in charge of

Politische Abteilung VII, the Oriental desk of "Politische Abteilung" in the Foreign Ministry) claimed that the King's physician did, in fact, ask for weapons at the A.P.A. "more than a year before" (this note was taken by Hentig; PA, AA, Pol.VII, 1605, p.385511, also ADAP, series D, Vol.V, p.681; in other words: in November 1937 the Saudis were interested in diplomatic relations and weapons. This document, to which Nicosia refers and from which he concludes that the Saudis expressed their willingness to buy German arms "as early as February 1937", does not mention this date at all. Von Hentig explicitly talks of the first meeting at the A.P.A., which took place in the "fall of 1937".

The second document quoted by Nicosia, does, indeed, point to February 1937 (PA, AA, Handelspolitische Abteilung, Kriegsgerät, Handel mit Irak (Geheim), Bd.1, Deutsche Gesandtschaft Kairo to Auswärtiges Amt, Berlin, zu Pol. 106g, 5 February 1937) - but to weapons bought by the Kingdom and destined for the Palestinians. The Saudis wanted to act as a go-between.

31 The latest document referred to in note 30 proves this beyond any doubt. Moreover, this was no official request but an unofficial information Fritz Tietz of the German representation in Cairo had got from a "great Hebron merchant" who had been asked by the Saudi king to "order" these weapons "from Germany". Tietz passed on this information unenthusiastically. He recommended to his superiors in the ministry of propaganda (!) to "possibly pass on" this information to "German agencies being in charge of these matters (economy)". Two copies were sent to the foreign ministry.

32 Truman Smith, Major, G.2., Military Attaché (Berlin), Military Intelligence Division to Office of the Chief of Staff, Washington, D.C., Report No. 15,346, June 15, 1937, National Archives, Washington, D.C., MID 2724-36.

33 Ibid.

34 Note "Saudisch-Arabien", "Außenpolitik" quoting Universul, Bukarest, 10 July 1939, havas information via Rador, Cairo, 9 July 1939, "Die Motive für den Berliner Besuch des arabischen Königlichen Rates", 11 July 1939, PA, AA, 1605 Beziehungen zu Saudisch-Arabien.

35 Ibid.

36 Truman Smith Major, G.2, Military Attaché (Berlin) to Office of Chief of staff, Washington, D.C., Report 15,302, May 25, 1937, Subject: German Armament Sales Abroad, National Archives, MID 2724-36.

37 Hirszowicz, THE THIRD REICH, p.47; see also footnote 30.

38 Grobba to AA, Baghdad, 9 November 1937, PA, AA, 1605, Beziehungen zu Saudisch-Arabien; also ADAP, Series D, Vol.V, p.649, the whole document ibid.

39 Neubert, op. cit., pp.106 ff.; for the question of Germany's Palestinian policy see Neubert, op. cit., in general; for the preludes of. Francis R. J. Nicosia, "Weimar Germany and the Palestine Question", YEARBOOK OF THE LEO BAECK INSTITUTE, London 1979, pp.321-345.

40 See note 38; in January 1938, in a letter to Grobba, Yasin contended that it was Germany which initiated the idea of exchanging envoys (Grobba to AA, Baghdad, 20 January 1938, PA, AA, Pol. VII, 1605, p. 385475).

41 See note 38, also Grobba to AA, 20 January 1938, loc. cit.

42 As far as I know, no author has pointed to that double strategy or, at least – if it really was not a strategy – to the problem as such.

43 Grobba to AA, 20 January 1938, loc. cit.

44 For those less familiar with Saudi Arabian history it may be recalled that Ibn Saud had ousted the Hashemites, King Hussein and his son Ali, from the Hejaz in 1924/25. On 8 December 1925, King Ali who had succeeded his father, abdicated and later sought refuge in Iraq where his brother Feisal was king. Another brother, Abduallah, was Emir of Transjordan, later King of Jordan. On 8 January 1926, Ibn Saud was proclaimed King of the Hejaz and Sultan of the Nejd and Dependencies. On 18 September 1932, he assumed the title of King of Saudi Arabia.

45 Grobba to AA, Baghdad, 7 January 1938, PA, AA, Pol. VII, 1605, p. 385467. Unless indicated otherwise; the following summary is based on the same document.

46 On 23 December 1925 Jidda surrendered to Ibn Saud.

47 Grobba to AA, 7 January 1938, loc. cit., p.385468.

48 This Hashemite association, too, misperceived German priorities vis-à-vis the United Kingdom.

49 See note 47.

50 The Association also claimed responsibility for the 1935 assassination attempt on Ibn Saud which took place in Mecca (loc. cit., p. 385469).

51 Loc. cit., p. 385469 f.

52 Loc. cit., p. 385470.

53 Loc. cit., p. 385468.

54 Loc. cit., p.385470.

55 Loc. cit., pp. 385470-385472; he had asked Seif Ibn Nasir to arrange this meeting.

56 Ibn Saud died in 1953!

57 Grobba to AA, 7 January 1938, loc. cit., pp. 385472 f.

58 Cf. Nicosia, Arab Nationalism, loc. cit., pp.361 ff.

59 Grobba to AA, 7 January 1938, loc. cit., p. 385473.

60 Yasin in a letter to Grobba handed over by the Saudi chargé d'affaires in Baghdad, Grobba to AA, Baghdad, 20 January 1938, PA, AA, Pol.VII, 1605, pp. 385474 f. The letter in German translation loc.cit., annex to Grobba's letter, p. 385476, dated 1 January 1938.

61 Yasin's letter, loc. cit., p. 385476.

62 Grobba to AA, 20 January 1938, loc. cit., p. 385475.

63 Amt für Vorderasien, APA, Aktennotiz (note) v.H. (= Freiherr von Harder), Berlin 21 June 1939, betr. Saudisch-Arabien, Institut für Zeitgeschichte, Munich, MA 255 (Kanzlei Rosenberg); this document is similar to but not identical with DAS POLITISCHE TAGEBUCH ALFRED ROSENBERGS 1934/35 UND 1939/40, ed. by Hanns-Günther Seraphim, Göttingen etc., Musterschmidt, note by Rosenberg, Berlin, 8 July 1941, "About the Activities of Envoy von Hentig in the AA", pp. 191-194. The more delicate and politically more revealing details are only in the note taken by von Harder, especially the passage on Jews and Arabs as Semites (see below);
besides, Rosenberg's chronology is far from complete; he mentions contacts between the APA and the Saudis since 1938, whereas they can be traced back to the fall of 1937; the other document has often been pointed to: "Aufzeichnung des Vortragenden Legationsrats von Hentig (Pol. Abt.)", Berlin, 28 February 1939, dealing with arms deliveries to "Arabia", PA, AA, 1605, pp. 385511 f., also ADAP, Vol. V, p.681; the spicier details are also not to be found in Harder's note, Berlin, 12 June 1939, Bundesarchiv Koblenz, NS 43/52, p.76-78 but in BAK NS 43/52, pp. 87 f.

64 This is all more possible because D. C. Watt has pointed to the competition between Yasin, Quargani and Hamza (deputy foreign minister), though in a different context (quoted from Hirszowicz, THIRD REICH, p.50).

65 Aktennotiz von Harder, APA, 21 June 1939, loc. cit.

66 Loc. cit. "an enlightening and positive message" ("aufklärende positive Mitteilung"). Besides, an invitation to the Reichsparteitag of the NSDAP was extended to a "high echelon representative of the Saudi Arabian government" (Herr Osthus, APA, to AA, Pol. VII, 23 July 1938, commissioned by von Harder, APA, PA, AA, Pol. VII, Beziehungen zu Saudisch-Arabien, 1605, p. 385486.

67 ROSENBERG TAGEBUCH, loc. cit., p.191.

68 Aufzeichnung von Hentig, 28 February 1939, loc. cit.

69 Osthus, APA, 23 July 1938, loc. cit.; note von Harder, 21 June 1939, loc. cit.; Hirszowicz, THE THIRD REICH, p.48, but on page 367: "January 1938" (would that be "spring"?); von Hentig, see note 66, writes that he came in "summer" 1938; Grobba, MÄNNER UND MÄCHTE, p.107 "February 1938". In any case, on 16 March 1938 al-Hud asked the APA to fix a date for a farewell visit to that office (note von Harder, Berlin 17 March 1938, BAK, NS 43/52, po.791).

70 Von Hentig, see note 66. The APA referred to him as an "economic consultant" to the King (Osthus, APA, see note 64); Hirszowicz calls him correctly an "Adviser" (Hirszowicz. THE THIRD REICH, p.48; see also v. Harder, 21 June 1939 loc. cit., Neubert, op. cit., p.121, uncritically, refers to v. Hentig.

71 Loc. cit. In early 1939 he wanted to cooperate with Ferrostaal which was involved in the arms deal (see Grobba to W. Jäger of Ferrostaal, Jidda, 26 January 1939, PA, AA, Pol.VII, Beziehungen

zu Saudisch-Arabien, 1605, p. 385584).

72 An implied criticism of Grobba and the AA? Harder, 21 June 1939, loc. cit.; see a summary of the talk in Osthus, APA, loc. cit.; for outsiders, the passage on the natural resources of Saudi Arabia may be misleading, for, in 1939, Germany had been offered oil concessions in the el-Hasa province, but Hitler had refused. (Grobba, MÄNNER UND MÄCHTE, loc. cit., pp. 94 f.)
In view of the fact that Khalid al-Hud introduced von Hentig to Ibn Saud's son and successor, Ibn Saud, in 1954 and in view of the fact that von Hentig became a counsellor to this King, von Harder's remarks may well suggest wishful thinking (cf. von Hentig, Werner Otto, MEIN LEBEN EINE DIENSTREISE, Göttingen, Vandenhoeck & Ruprecht 1962, chapter, "Saudisch-Arabien, pp.403 ff.; the criticism of Grobba may, however, be surprising because von Hentig, op. cit., p.319 reproached the German envoy in Baghdad with "eagerly offering his services to the Party" via the APA (Rosenberg). The reason, again according to von Hentig, ibid.: Grobba "wanted to become a great Party man ("große Parteileute" referred to in the plural).

73 Von Hentig, PA, AA, 1605, 385511; they had talked 1 1/2 hours.

74 Ibid.

75 Ibid.

76 Loc. cit., pp. 385487 f.

77 Loc. cit., p. 385488; also von Harder, APA, 21 June 1939, loc. cit.; the newly installed Foreign Minister Ribbentrop was quoted xxx agreed as well (Harder, 21 June 1939, loc. cit.)

78 Von Harder, 21 June 1939, loc. cit.; blaming v. Hentig personally.

79 Reichsgruppe Industrie, Geschäftsführung (Koppke and Moherius, i.A.) to AA, von Hentig, 10 July 1939, geheim, PA, AA, Pol. VII, 1605, p. 385632.

80 Von Harder, 21 June 1939, loc. cit.

81 Grobba to foreign minister, Baghdad, 5 July 1938, PA, AA, Pol. VII, 1541, pp. 375455 f.; also ADAP, Vol.V, pp.663 f. In February 1938, the Woodhead Commission had been charged with examining the partition proposal put forward by the Peel Commission in 1937. From April to August 1938 the Woodhead Commission stayed in Palestine and published a report in November 1938. It recommended that the partition plan not be realized. The British government then dropped the idea.

82 Von Harder, via Osthus to AA, loc. cit., p. 385488. Maybe this was the al-Hud visit of "summer" 1938 referred to by von Hentig, note 28 February 1938, PA, AA, Pol. VII, 1605, p. 385511. If this was the case, then von Hentig and al-Hud had not met in February 1938. This would correspond to Neubert's, op. cit., p.121 chronology which, I find, takes this too much for granted. Besides, al-Hud was not the personal physician. It follows that Al-Hud may have talked to the APA in February 1938 and to von Hentig in the "summer" of the same year; or, al-Hud came in February and

Madhat al-Ard, the personal physician of the King, in the "summer" (July) to the APA. But Grobba, op. cit., p.107 contends that von Hentig and al-Hud met in February 1938; or, von Hentig did not remember correctly when referring to the "summer" of 1938 and al-Hud; or, al-Hud really did come twice in 1938. This seems unlikely because both AA (von Hentig) and APA (v. Harder) spoke of one visit al-Hud had paid to Berlin; or the physician did not turn up, for there are no more references to his visit.

83 V. Hentig, note, 27 August 1938, PA, AA, Pol. VII, 1605, pp. 385489-491, also ADAP, Vol. V, pp.664 f.; Hirszowicz mistakenly writes that the deputy foreign minister remained about a month in the German capital: 23 July to 27 August, Hirszowicz, THIRD REICH, p.48.

84 Von Hentig, see note 80; also the following summary and quotations of/from this meeting.

85 Ibid.; the rest of the talk was devoted to the "common adversary (note that v. Hentig did not speak of "enemy"), i.e. Jews, as well as to "cultural policy" programs (language training, media, literature).

86 Ibid.

87 Note Paul Schmitz, Cairo, 2 February 1939, "Zur politischen Situation in Saudisch-Arabien", BAK, NS 43/5, p.63.

88 This has obviously been overlooked so far. He may have also met with Ibn Saud's personal physician.

89 Note von Hentig, Berlin, 28 February 1939, PA, AA, Pol.VII, 1605, p. 385512, also ADAP, Vol. V, p.681.

90 Prüfer was not only superior to von Hentig as far as the hierarchy of the AA was concerned but also "an old friend" (von Hentig, MEIN LEBEN, p.316).

91 Von Hentig, 27 August 1938, loc. cit.

92 Cf. Nicosia, "Arab Nationalism", p.364. Canaris had met with the Mufti in the summer of 1938 while travelling incognito to Lebanon (ibid.); also Neubert, op. cit., p.120. There is no evidence, though, of anti French activities in Syria instigated by Germany (Nicosia, op. cit., p.364).

93 Von Hentig, 28 February 1939, loc. cit.

94 Ibid.; another transport was destined to reach Palestine via Iraq. Hamza was also given money for the Palestinian insurgents but it probably was not passed on (note von Hentig to the foreign minister via secretary of state and undersecretary of state, Berlin, 22 May 1939, p. 385560, also ADAP, Vol., p.461 seemed to be sure about that).

95 Ferrostaal to Halid Alhud (sic) in Jidda, 9 August 1938, PA, AA, Pol. VII, 1605, pp. 385579 f. annex to letter by W. Jäger (board of Ferrostaal) to von Hentig, Essen 19 June 1939. It dealt with the construction of a cartridge factory able to produce 10-20,000 7,9 mm kaliber cartridges per day (= eight working hours). Another offer referred to 8,000 rifles including cartridges.

96   Note Woermann (head of the "Political Department" to which the Original desk of von Hentig belonged), Berlin, 3 September 1938, PA, AA, Pol.VII, 1605, pp. 385492 f., also ADAP, Series D, Vol.V, pp. 665 f.

97   Ibid.

98   He had joined the Party only after the 1933 takeover (Hans-Adolf Jacobsen, NATIONALSOZIALISTISCHE AUßENPOLITIK 1933-1938, Frankfurt/Main-Berlin, Metzner Verlag 1968, p.63); 29 September 1938 being the day of the Munich Conference.

99   Malletke to Woermann, Berlin, 26 September 1938, PA, AA, 1605, p. 385497, also ADAP, Vol.V, p.666.

100 Gez. Woermann to Malettke, Berlin, 29 September 1938, PA, AA, 1605, pp. 385498 f., also ADAP, Vol.V, p.667.

101 Ibid.

102 See note 99.

103 It took place during the Party Rally in Nürnberg; note to von Hentig, Berlin, 26 September 1938, PA, AA, Pol.VII, 1605, pp. 385495 f. The Party Rally ended on 12 September 1938 but Woermann was in Nürnberg as early as 6 September (note von Hentig to Woermann, Berlin, 6 September 1938, PA, AA, Pol.VII, 1605, p. 385494).

104 Note von Hentig to Woermann, Berlin, 6 September 1938, PA, AA, 1605, p. 385494. On 27 Sept., he reiterated that arms to the Saudis would be, in fact, arms to England (handwritten remark on document quoted in note 95). Even the Saudi foreign minister had recommended to send (part, M.W.) of the weapons for Palestine via Iraq ("being convinced of his Master's neutrality").

105 Handwritten remarks by Woermann and von Hentig on the document quoted in note 95; on 28 September, Woermann asked von Hentig to formulate a "friendly reply" which the latter submitted the following day.

106 See note 100.

107 Ibid.

108 Copy of letter von Hentig to Malettke, APA, Berlin, 22 October 1938, PA, AA, 1605, p. 385500.

109 Note, Abteilung Ausland FL of Ferrostaal, 22 December 1938, PA, AA, 1605, pp. 385581 f., annex to letter Jäger to v. Hentig (see note 110): "We have submitted (when? December? M.W.) the following offer to Sheikh Alhud in Jidda:" This offer included:
- 8,000 "Mauser" rifles including 1,000 cartridges per rifle (= 10,196 per rifle)
- cartridge factory, 20,000 cartridges per day (8 hours) (= 30,800).

The Saudis then wanted to dump. In addition, they wanted to pay the price £ 10 per rifle cif Jidda and not fob Hamburg, by installments (5 years). For the factory they wanted a 5 years' credit.

110 Saudi Arabian Minister of Finance, Abdulla as-Suleiman, to "Halid Alhud", 28.10. 357 = 20 December 1938, PA, AA, 1605, p. 385585. This letter is an annex to the letter of W. Jäger (board of Ferrostaal) to von Hentig, 19 June 1939, loc. cit., pp. 385577 f.

111 Note, Abteilung Ausland FL, 22 December 1938, see note 109; see the position of the AA, note Schlobies (von Hentig's research assistant), Berlin 10 January 1939, PA, AA, 1605, pp. 385464-466, also ADAP, Vol.V, pp.671 f. The firm tried to mobilize the support of Grobba (see Grobba to Jäger, 26 January 1939, Jidda, PA, AA, 1605, p. 385583, annex to letter Jäger to Hentig, 19 June 1939 (see note 110).

112 Schlobies note, 10 January 1939, see note 111.

113 Grobba, MÄNNER UND MÄCHTE, p.109. Before, there had been only three permanent missions there, the British, French and Italian. The Netherlands, Turkey and Iraq were represented by permanent chargés d'affaires. The Egyptian envoy was also accredited to Baghdad and the Afghan envoy to Cairo (Hirszowicz, THIRD REICH, p.50).

114 Grobba to Jäger (board of Ferrostaal), 26 January 1939, Jidda, PA, AA, 1605, pp. 385583 f.; the competition between Germany and Italy on the micro-economic (enterprise) level has not been pointet out so far. It may also explain Italian second thoughts on the German-Saudi connection, apart from political reasons.

115 PA, AA, 1605, pp. 385522-529, also ADAP, Vol. V, pp.672-680. He was received by the King on 13 February.

116 Hirszowicz, THIRD REICH, p.52.

117 Ibid.

118 Op. cit., p.51; he has not elaborated the Italian aspect sufficiently.

119 Grobba, see note 115.

120 Ref.: von Hentig, note, 24 February 1939, PA, AA, 1605. The official may have been Schlobies, for v. Hentig was in the Near East then.

121 W. Jäger (board of Ferrostaal) to v. Hentig, Essen, 19 June 1939, PA, AA, 1605, p. 385577. The order was issued on 23 March 1939.

122 Abdelaziz al Sa'ud, to Hitler, Ryadh, 27 March 1939, PA, AA, 1605, pp. 385557 f.

123 Ibid.

124 These words were eliminated from the final version; the letter was formulated by Schlobies (von Hentig's assistant) and officially sent and signed by Woermann to Grobba, Berlin, 18 April 1939 (posted 26 April), PA, AA, 1605, p. 385548, also ADAP, Vol.VI, p.684.

125 Loc. cit., p. 385547, ADAP, p.683.

126 Hirszowicz, THIRD REICH, p.54.

127 Von Hentig, MEIN LEBEN, p.325; there, he does not mention this stopover, only Egypt and Palestine (325 ff.); Hirszowicz, THIRD REICH, p.369 notes (uncorrectly) "April" 1939.
128 Schlobies on the draft version of Woermann's letter to Grobba (see note 124/125).
129 Grobba to Woermann, Baghdad, 2 May 1939, PA, AA, 1605, also ADAP, Vol.VI, p.336, also p.334.
130 Grobba to Woermann loc. cit., 1605, pp. 385515-521, also ADAP, Vol.VI, pp.333-337.
131 Ibid.
132 Hirszowicz, THIRD REICH, p.55. Germany looked for an opportunity to strike at British communications with India from the South (ibid.); von Hentig's note of 9 June 1939 mentions this strategy (PA, AA, 1605, pp. 385565 f.)
133 See von Hentig, note 132.
134 Aufzeichnung ohne Unterschrift, "Ansprache des Führers vor den Oberbefehlshabern", 22 August 1939, ADAP, Vol.VII, p.167 (at the Obersalzberg).
135 Ibid.; see also note 27.
136 Hirszowicz, THIRD REICH, pp. 56 f.; note Woermann, Berlin, 22 May 1939, PA, AA, 1605, p. 385564.
137 Handwritten instruction by marginal note Woermann, 25 May 1939 on note von Hentig to foreign minister via secretary of state and undersecretary of state, Berlin 22 May 1939, PA, AA, 1605, also ADAP, Vol.VII, p.461 (note 4).
138 Ibid.
139 Hirszowicz, THIRD REICH, p.57. Here, the author exaggerates a bit, for in his meeting with Foreign Minister Ribbentrop al-Hud characterized Saudi-Italian relations as "correct", Turkish-Saudi as "bad" (note von Hentig, 20 June 1939, PA, AA, 1605, p. 385611, also ADAP, Vol.VII, p.571).
Al-Hud was more unequivocally as to Italian ambitions in North Africa (where he came from, after all), see note on the invitation of al-Hud to "Horcher" on 29 June 1939, PA, AA, 1605, p. 385616.
140 Op. cit., p.58. The author is right in pointing out that Italy thus indicated that the area did, in fact, belong to her spheres of interest. The 1936 commitment had been renewed by Hitler during Ciano's visit to Berlin, on 22 May 1939 (op. cit., p.58).
141 See von Hentig's note, 22 May 1949 (footnote 133), pp. 385561 f., ADAP, Vol.VII, p.462.
142 Ibid.
143 Note von Harder, 12 June 1939, Bundesarchiv Koblenz, NS 43/52, p.78; note von Harder, 21 June 1939, Institut für Zeitgeschichte, MA 255, pp.3-18.
144 Note von Hentig summarizing the talk, Berlin, 20 June 1939, PA, AA, 1605, pp. 385610, also ADAP, Vol.VII, pp. 571 f.

145 Ibid.

146 See footnote 36.

147 See note von Hentig on his meeting with Jäger, Berlin, 8 June 1939, PA, AA, 1605, pp. 385567.

148 Ibid.

149 Note v. Hentig, Berlin, 9 June 1939, PA, AA, 1605, pp. 385565 f.

150 Note von Hentig, 20 June 1939, summarizing the talk, Berlin, PA, AA, 1605, pp. 385603 f., also ADAP, Vol.VII, pp.620 f.

151 Ibid., last sentence.

152 W. Jäger to v. Hentig, Essen, 19 June 1939, PA, AA, 1605, pp. 385577 f.

153 On 20 June 1939 Grobba wrote to v. Hentig about Ibn Saud's alarmed reaction, PA, AA, 1605; as to al-Hud's similar fears cf. the unsigned note about the invitation of al-Hud to "Horcher" (then a fancy restaurant in Berlin), on 29 June 1939, PA, AA, 1605, pp. 385615-617, also note v. Hentig, 3 July 1939, PA, AA, 1605, p. 385621.

154 Sir P. Loraine (Rome) to Viscount Halifax, telegram, Rome, 21 June 1939, **Documents on British Foreign Policy 1919-1939**, Third Series, Vol.VI, London 1953, p.126. Contrary to British indifference concerning Germany's short-lived interest in Palestine and the delivery of weapons for the Palestinian insurgents via Saudi Arabia, the direct German-Saudi connection was taken more seriously. (For Britain's approach to the German-Saudi-Palestinian triangle see Nicosia, "Arab Nationalism", p.364; Biddle, Warsaw to Secretary of State, 24 March 1939, National Archives, Washington, D.C., RG 59 8 67N. 01/1495).

155 Note von Hentig on his talk with al-Hud, 3 July 1939, PA, AA, 1605, p. 385621.

156 Note von Hentig, Berlin, 6 July 1939, PA, AA, 1605, p. 385631.

157 Von Hentig note, Berlin, 22 June 1939, PA, AA, 1605, p. 385613; handwritten marginal note by v. Hentig on the note summarizing the al-Hud/Hitler talk, 30 June 1939 (the note itself (signed on 20 June 1939), PA, AA, 1605, p. 385604, also ADAP, Vol.VI, p.621).

158 Note von Hentig, Berlin 22 June 1939, PA, AA, 1605, pp. 385614f.

159 Note v. Hentig, Berlin, 3 July 1939, loc. cit., p. 385622.

160 Note von Hentig, 4 July 1939, loc. cit., p. 385623.

161 Loc. cit., pp. 385623 f.

162 Loc. cit., p. 385625.

163 Ibid.

164 Ibid.

165 See the handwritten marginal note by Woermann, 12 July 1939, loc. cit., p. 385625.

166 Note Schlobies, Berlin, 13 July 1939, loc. cit., p. 385627.
167 Nicosia, "Arab Nationalism", pp. 365 f. quoting an OKW memorandum to the AA, 11 July 1939.
168 Handwritten marginal note by Schlobies, 18 July 1939, loc. cit., p. 385636.
169 Ibid. Hirszowicz, THIRD REICH, p.58 writes 17 July. This is wrong. On his way back, al-Hud visited Berlin on 7 September 1939, PA, AA, 1605, p. 385636.
170 1. Vermerk, U.St.S. Pol., Berlin 15 July 1939, loc. cit., p. 385636 and the letter in draft form, Berlin, 17 July 1939, loc. cit., p. 385637-640.
171 Werner Otto von Hentig, MEIN LEBEN EINE DIENSTREISE, Vandenhoeck & Ruprecht, Göttingen 1962, p.403; Note 163.
172 Hirszowicz, THIRD REICH, p.59.
173 Nicosia, "Arab Nationalism", p.365.
174 Diary Rosenberg, ed. by H.-G. Seraphim, loc. cit. p.193 (note Berlin, 8 July 1941).
175 PA, AA, 1605, p. 385640.
176 Schröder, op. cit., p.373.
177 Hirszowicz, op. cit., p.68. Contrary to Schröder, Hirszowicz is able to prove his explanation by documents. **Keesings Archiv der Gegenwart** (1939) which mentions the suspension of diplomatic relations in general has no such indication for September 1939, and on 27 October 1939 (p. 4294) it refers to an implicit but "formal declaration of neutrality".
178 Grobba, MÄNNER UND MÄCHTE, p.183.
179 OKW/Wi VId, "Kurze Übersicht über die 'Wirtschaft Arabiens'", Berlin, 6 February 1941, Bundesarchiv/Militärarchiv, Freiburg/Breisgau, Wi II 1.
180 For another attempt at quantitatively weighing historical data of decision-making processes in German economic policy see my "Industrie und Handwerk im Konflikt mit staatlicher Wirtschaftspolitik?" Studien zur Politik der Arbeitsbeschaffung in Deutschland 1930-1934, Berlin, Duncker & Humblot 1977, annex I.
181 Grobba, MÄNNER UND MÄCHTE, pp.94 f.
182 Op. cit., p.95.
183 Hirszowicz, "The Course of German Foreign Policy", p.181.
184 G. L. Weinberg, THE FOREIGN POLICY, p.243; for an analysis of Germany's efforts to produce synthetic oil see W. Birkenfeld, DER SYNTHETISCHE TREIBSTOFF 1933-1945. EIN BEITRAG ZUR NATIONALSOZIALISTISCHEN WIRTSCHAFTS- UND RÜSTUNGSPOLITIK, Göttingen, Musterschmidt Verlag 1964.
185 Hirszowicz, THE THIRD REICH, p.17, does when writing that "German firms stubbornly attempted to obtain orders". Perhaps had they tried elsewhere but not in/from Saudi Arabia.

186 Aktennotiz, Berlin, 24 June 1939, BAK, NS 43/52, p.86.
187 For similar results in other foreign policy decision-making processes J. Dülffer, "Zum 'decision-making process' in der deutschen Außenpolitik 1933-1939", M. Funke, ed., op. cit., p.201.
188 Note von Harder, Berlin, 17 March 1938, BAK, NS 43/52, p.80.
189 Loc. cit., p.81.
190 Ibid.
191 Loc. cit., p.82.
192 In July 1939 Reichsgruppe Industrie received the offer of Rheinmetall Borsig but still waited for the Mauser proposal (Reichsgruppe Industrie) to von Hentig, geheim, 10 July 1939, PA, AA, Pol. VII, 1605. The Brünn based firm Ceskoslovenska Zbrojovka A.S. had not yet reacted to the demand put forward by the Reichsgruppe to submit an offer for machine-guns and armoured cars (ibid. and letter to al-Hud, 17 July 1939, loc. cit.)
193 PA, AA, Handel mit Kriegsgerät Allgemeines, vols 1-4. They were: "Steffen & Heymann" and "Mens" (3,000 rifles and 3 million cartridges "allegedly", Reichsgruppe Industrie to AA and others, 5 November 1937, loc. cit., vol.2); "Rheinisch-Westfälische Sprengstoof AG" (1,000; Wolff & Walsrode (cartridges). The list is most probably incomplete.
194 Woermann to von Hentig, Berlin, 26 September 1939, PA, AA, Pol. VII, 1605, pp. 385495 f. informing the latter about the talk he had had with v. Harder at the Party rally in Nürnberg.
195 Von Hentig to Woermann, Berlin, 6 September 1938, loc. cit.
196 Ibid.
197 See note 194.
198 A note taken by von Hentig on 20 June 1939 (three days after the al-Hud/Hitler meeting!) may well characterize and emphasize this point: Press reports coming from Rome contended that Ibn Saud had confronted Britain with an ultimatum (on what issue?). Von Hentig did not take these reports seriously, stating that "neither the character nor the situation of the King would make such an ultimatum to England possible." (PA, AA, 1605).
199 Note Schlobies, 10 January 1939, PA, AA, 1605.
200 Note von Hentig, Berlin 27 August 1938, loc. cit.; see also his handwritten marginal note of 27 September 1938 on the same document. By May 1939, he had learned his lesson in the Saudi foreign ministry (see his note to Ribbentrop, Berlin 22 May 1939, loc. cit.)
201 Note von Hentig, Berlin, 28 February 1939.
202 Note Woermann, Berlin, 3 September 1938, loc. cit.
203 Woermann to Málletke, Berlin, 29 September 1938, loc. cit.
204 Hirszowicz, THE THIRD REICH, p.58.

205 Von Hentig, MEIN LEBEN, pp.403 ff. chapter "Saudisch-Arabien" describing his experiences as Ibn Saud's jr. adviser.

206 See von Hentig, MEIN LEBEN, p.216, 319; not all of the characterizations being too pleasant.

207 Op. cit., p.319.

208 For instance his dispatch to the AA, Jidda, 18 February 1939, PA, AA, 1605; ever and again he elaborated this point.

209 Grobba to AA, Baghdad, 20 January 1938, PA, AA, 1605, p. 385475.

210 Grobba to AA, Jidda, 18 February 1939, loc. cit.

211 My formulation derived from the passage "Moral Support", ibid.

212 Ibid.

213 Von Hentig, MEIN LEBEN, pp.318 f. He referred ironically to the "Oriental experts".

214 Grobba to AA, Baghdad, 7 January 1938, PA, AA, 1605.

215 NSDAP, Stellvertreter des Führers ("Führer's" Deputy) to APA, Munich, 11 June 1934, IFZ, MA-128/4.

216 Ibid. The "Führer's" Deputy demanded that he be instructed if other APA "agents, or whatever they may be called" were active abroad.

217 Rosenberg Tagebuch, ed. by H.-G. Seraphim, loc. cit., pp.191 ff; von Harder complained about von Hentig's alleged "impudence" forbidding al-Hud to further contact the APA (note von Harder, Berlin 21 June 1939, IfZ, MA 255, pp.3-18; note von Harder, Berlin, 12 June 1939, BAK, NS 43/52.

218 H.-A. Jacobsen, NATIONALSOZIALISTISCHE AUSSENPOLITIK, p.636.

219 Von Harder via Osthus to AA, 23 July 1938, PA, AA, 1605.

220 H.-A. Jacobsen, NATIONALSOZIALISTISCHE AUSSENPOLITIK, p.155. In his painstaking analysis of the APA Jacobsen has overlooked the Saudi activities of this office (see op. cit., esp. pp.55-89).

221 Op. cit., p.56.

222 Jacobsen, op.cit., p.156 emphasizes that the agitation against "World Jewry" and "World Bolshevism" were the centerpiece of Rosenberg's ideology.

223 Hirszowicz, THE THIRD REICH, pp.54 f.

224 C. R. Browning, "Understaatssekretär Martin Luther and the Ribbentrop Foreign Office", JOURNAL OF CONTEMPORARY HISTORY, Vol. 12 (1977), p.313.

225 W. Michalka, "Die nationalsozialistische Außenpolitik im Zeichen eines 'Konzeptions-Pluralismus' - Fragestellungen und Forschungsaufgaben", M. Funke, ed. op. cit., p.60.

PART II

1. PIW, 6 April 1981, 1.7 spoke of 10.5 %.
2. For data and details cf. my essays "The European Community and the Middle East", MIDDLE EAST CONTEMPORARY SURVEY (MECS) ed. by Colin Legum et al., volumes V to VII, New York-London: Holmes & Meier 1982 to 1984.
3. MECS V, table 1. In 1980, Iraq emerged as W-German contracts' biggest and fastest growing ME market (MEED, special report "Construction and Contracting", March 1981, p.30), J. Friedemann, FAZ, 30 May 1981: "German entrepreneurs conquer (sic) Baghdad".
4. Cf. "Hochtief" (FAZ, 19 + 24 July 1981); "Philipp Holzmann" (FAZ, 26 July 1981); "Dyckerhoff" (FAZ, 5 Oct. 1981); "Zublin" (FAZ, 23 July 1981); "Boswau + Knauer" (FAZ, 24 July 1981); cf. MEED, special report, "West Germany and the Middle East, Oct 1980, pp. 7-12, 25-26 the lists of contracts Aug. 1979-July 1980, op. cit., pp. 11.38-39.
5. MEED, op. cit., pp. 17-18 pp. 38-39; FAZ 3 March + 8 Sept. 1981. In Dezember 1980, a high-level Libyan delegation visited Germany and improved relations more expected afterwards (FAZ, 30 Dec. 1980). In Feb. 1981 Krupp steel got a contract worth 1.5 billion DM (= $ 660 m., FAZ, 23 Feb. 1981).
6. MEES, 30 March 1981, p.4; FAZ, 29 July 1981.
7. Since the days of the Shah (FAZ, 28 Jan. 1981). The Iranian representations in the board of directors blocked an executive decision to streamline the enterprise by reducing the number of employees by 5,000 (FAZ, 25 June 1981). The Social Democratic weekly "Vorwärts", 18 June 1981, asked: "Safe jobs thanks to the Islamic Revolution?"
8. FAZ, 7 Oct. 1981.
9. MEES, 24 Nov. 1980, p.II; 19 Jan. 1981, p.I; Newsweek 26 Jan. 1981; R. Herlt, Die Zeit, 5 June 1981.
10. FAZ, 25 April 1981.
11. R. Herlt, Die Zeit, 5 June 1981.
12. FAZ, 1 + 2 + 3 June 1981.
13. See 11.
14. Cf. for all available polls on German-Israeli relations Michael Wolffsohn: "Deutsch-israelische Beziehungen im Spiegel der öffentlichen Meinung", **Aus Politik und Zeitgeschehen** (supplement of the West German weekly **Das Parlament**), B 46-47/84, 17 November 1984, pp.19-30.
15. Institut für Demoskopie Allensbach for "Stern" magazine, 14 May 1981, p.28. For, earlier polls cf. this institute's "Die Stimmung im Bundesgebiet" (confidential court ... of the Allensbach Institute). Between 1965 and 1967 (Six-Days War) a similar structural change could be observed: In March 1965, 24 % sided with Israel, 15 %

with Egypt. In June 1967: 55 % Israel, 6 % Egypt. Neither on 1965: 44 %, June 1967: 27 % (Allensbach, op. cit., No.47, p.2). During the 1973 war, the EMNID institute (Bielefeld) had found out that 45 % of the West German public had "no specific sympathies", 40 % sympathized with Israel" and 6 % "sympathized with the Arabs" EMNID Informationen, Nr.11/12-1973, p.8). Supporters of the Arab cause were mostly found among "young" (up to 30 years old) university graduates as well as among inhabitants of the large cities, first and foremost Hamburg, Bremen and Berlin (ibid.). Interviewees close to the Free Democratic Party and the Christian Democrats belonged to the stronger sympathizers of Israel (ibid., alos. p.9). In May 1978, a year after Begin's election victory, 51 % of the West German public attested Israel an "accomodating policy", 41 % preferred to call it "aggressive". Again, the discrepancy between large and small towns as well as between higher and lower formal education: The longer the formal education of the interviewee, the more often Israel's policy is considered "aggressive". The larger the city, the more aggressiveness attested to Israel. However: Supporters of the CDU/CSU (43 %) and the SPD (41 %) more than those close to the Free Democrats (37 %) tended to call Israel's policy "more aggressive" (EMNID Informationen, Nr.6-1978, pp.12-14, table 3). Data courtesy of EMNID Institute, cf. Wolffsohn, "Deutsch-israelische Beziehungen, loc. cit.

16 For West European public opinion polls on the actors of the Arab-Israeli Conflict cf. my articles in **Middle East Contemporary Survey**, loc. cit. and Michael Wolffsohn: Deutsch-Israelische Beziehungen: Umfragen 1952-1983, Munich: Landeszentrale für politische Bildung 1985, section A/II/1/c.

17 Kuwait Times, 11 May 1980, He was convicted but released in 1984 (cf. Wolffsohn, MECS VII).

18 C. Glenrich, FAZ, 8 July 1981.

19 SZ, 30 Oct 1981.

20 Die Welt, 12 Dec 1981.

21 FR, 12 March 1981.

22 MECS, vol. III, p.831, note 10.

23 D. Degan, Haaretz, 24 Dec 1980.

24 23 Dec 1980.

25 ndy., FAZ, 21 March 1981; wgl. (= W. G. Lerch), FAZ, 25 March 1981.

26 Verfassungsschutzbericht 1980, part E, p.13.

27 FR, 24 und 29 June 1981.

28 Wgl. (= W. G. Lerch), FAZ, 7 August 1981.

29 26 Oct. 1980, p.69, Details on clashes between Turkish extremist from right and left cf. Verfassungsschutzbericht 1980, pp.18-20, part E.

30 Summary of the Bavarian report Fin., FAZ, 6 June 1981; of the lower Saxonian one, Tgn., FAZ, 6 July 1981.

31 Tgn., FAZ, 6 July 1981.
32 Verfassungsschutzbericht 1980, p.9, part V.
33 Der Spiegel, 8 Sept 1980, p.58-76; A. Raschied, Die Zeit, 22 May 1981, he refers to app. 20,000 Grey wolves in Germany and quotes the national Turkish prosecution.
34 Tgn., FAZ, 6 July 1981.
35 According to the secretary of the Consul General (hach., FAZ, 5 Oct 1980).
36 In Hamburg (FAZ, 27 Dec 1980; Berlin), Munich, Frankfurt (FAZ, 6 Jan. 1981)
37 In Frankfurt, fh., FAZ, 16 March 1981.
38 A. Rashid, Die Zeit, 22 May 1981; SZ, 22 May 1981; FAZ, 13 June 1981. A connection with the Grey Wolves was reported. The man who had allegedly provided Agca (the would-be murderer of the pope) with a forged passport was arrested in Hamburg in February 1982 (SZ, 17 Feb 1982).
39 Cf. polls quoted in: Institute of Jewish Affairs (IJA) How Popular is Neo-Nazism in Germany? Four Public Opinion Studies, London, May 1981, exp. pp.7-8 (courtesy of the IJA).
40 Berlin and North Rhine-Westfalia but also the federal government issued decrees which rendered, the arrival and residence of family members of guest workers (cf. SZ, 5/6 Dec. 1981; J. Engert, Rheinischer Merkur (Christ und Welt, 4 Dec. 1981; Der Spiegel, cover story, 7 Dec. 1981 spoke of "closed borders for foreigners?"
41 Reu(mann), FAZ, 12 Dec 1981.
42 Ibid.
43 L. B. (ewerunge), FAZ, 6 Sept 1980.
44 hach., FAZ, 16 Sept 1980; FAZ, 6 + 11 Aug 1980.
45 FAZ, 7 + 11 Aug 1980.
46 FAZ, 16 + 19 Aug + 19 Sept 1980.
47 21 Aug 1980.
48 Ibid.
49 hach., FAZ, 16 Sept 1980.
50 hach., FAZ, 17 Sept 1980.
51 Arab News, Jidda, 28 Jan 1981.
52 Newsweek, 9 Feb 1981, p.48.
53 FAZ, 26 + 27 May 1981.
54 Saddam Hussein in an interview to "Der Spiegel", 1 June 1981, p. 146.
55 Cf. Wolffsohn, MECS, VII.
56 Verfassungsschutzbericht 1980, part I, p.12.
57 SZ, 28 Oct 1981.

58 Der Spiegel, 13 July 1981, esp. p.76.
59 Loc. cit. p.77.
60 Answer to a parliamentary inquiry by MP Dr. Dregger and others (CDU/CSU), Deutscher Bundestag, Drucksache 9/723, 7 Aug 1981, p.1. They stayed there "since 1980" (ibid.).
61 Loc. cit., p.2; FAZ, 30 Sept. 1980.
62 FAZ, 27 Dec 1980.
63 Lga, FAZ, 8 Sept 1981. Hoffmann's and Birkmann's trial was opened in 1984.
64 Der Spiegel, Nr.38/1981, pp.49-55 quoting unnamed policemen.
65 FAZ, 31 Aug 1981.
66 Ibid.
67 Ibid.
68 SZ, 30 Oct 1981.
69 D. Degan, Haaretz, 24 + 30 June + 31 July 1981. The Bavarian Minister of the Interior denied these contacts (D. Degan, Haaretz, 24 June 1981).
70 Haaretz, 30 Aug 1981.
71 Part III, p.11.
72 Verfassungsschutzbericht 1980, part V., p.5.
73 Ibid.
74 Loc. cit., part V, p.7. No definitions of "extremist" is given in the report.
75 Loc. cit., part V, p.12.
76 Ibid.
77 Loc. cit., part V, p.13.
78 Cf. FAZ, 27 Dec 1980 + 6 Jan 1981; Haaretz, 24 + 25 Dec 1980.
79 G. Krabbe, FAZ, 6 Jan 1981.
80 Ibid.; J.-P. Langellier, Le Monde, 9 Jan 1981; G. Krabbe, loc. cit.; bb (= Krabbe), FAZ, 10 Jan 1981; J. Misrahi, Haaretz, 9 Jan 1981; Haaretz, 8 Jan 1981.
81 "Guerdian" quoted from Le Monde, 5 Jan 1981; J.-P. Langellier, loc. cit.; G. Krabbe, FAZ, 6 Jan 1981.
82 Cf., Schmidt's TV interview after his visit to Saudi Arabia (IHT, 5 May 1981; NZZ, 6 May 1981).
83 IHT, 5 May 1981.
84 In a Knesset (= parliament) speech on 19 March 1980 quoted and translated from "Zur Sache", Israeli embassy, Bonn, April 1980, p.5). Eban referred to Giscard and the EC, though.
85 cKn, FAZ, 12 November 1980. My interview with two officials of the ME desk of the German Foreign Ministery, Bonn, 22 April 1981.

86 Der Spiegel, Nr.32, 3 Aug 1981. "Craziness" without any reference to the U.S. was attested by Der Spiegel on 15 June 1981 after the Baghdad raid.
87 Fk. (F. K. Fack), FAZ, 20 July 1981. As co-editor of FAZ Fack is a most serious and influential journalist.
88 G. Gillessen farewell-talk with Meroz, FAZ, 14 May 1981.
89 Ibid.
90 Ibid.
91 Ibid. By mistake, FAZ referred to the 1972 visit.
92 ckn., (= A. Nacken), FAZ, 18 Nov 1981.
93 ckn., FAZ, 12 Nov 1980.
94 ckn., FAZ, 20 Nov 1981.
95 Ibid.
96 NZZ, 11 Oct 1980. General elections were held on 5 Oct 1980.
97 Der Spiegel, 29 Sept 1980.
98 mö/hf., FR, 9 Oct 1980; R.M., NZZ, 11 Oct 1980; C.G. (enrich), FAZ, 9 Oct 1983.
99 Der Spiegel, 29 Sept 1980.
100 FR, 16 Dec 1980.
101 FR, 4 May 1981. Shamir was "shocked" by Schmidt's 30 April TV interview (without knowing the exact text).
102 R.M. NZZ, 6 May 1981.
103 Der Spiegel, 11 May 1981, p.28.
104 ARD, TV, 30 April 1981.
105 Cf. his interview to Israel Radio translated in Der Spiegel, 11 May 1981, p.29.
106 H. Herles, FAZ, 8 May 1981.
107 Der Spiegel, 11 May 1981, p.28.
108 FR, 5 May 1981; FAZ, 5 May 1981.
109 Quoted and translated from Der Spiegel, 11 May 1981, p.30. On 19 June 1981 he repeated "collective guilt" accusations against the German People (FAZ, 20 June 1981).
110 Ibid.
111 David K. Shipler, IHT, 4 June 1981.
112 Cf. Teddy Preuss, Die Zeit, 30 Oct 1981; also Jerusalem Pst, 2-8 Aug 1981.
   For a scholarly analysis cf. N. Balabkins, West German Reparations to Israel, New Brunswick, N.J.: Rutgers University Press; N. Sagi, German Reparations. A History of the Negotiations, Jerusalem: Magness Press 1980; German ed. Wiedergutmachung für Israel. Die deutschen Zahlungen und Leistungen, Stuttgart: Seewald

1981. Lily G. Feldman: The Special Relationship between West Germany and Israel, Boston-London-Sidney: Allen & Unwin 1984, p.96.

113   Ibid.; according to Sagi German ed., p.202, 56,5 billion DM altogether until 1978; her factual evidence, however, is open to criticism. For exact data cf. M. Wolffsohn: Israel: Politik, Gesellschaft, Wirtschaft, Opladen: Leske 1984, p.248.

114   The election advertisement read: "Thank you – in the name of German industry", Haaretz, 22 March 1981. Coloured TV-sets (!) were cheaper.

115   The Histadrut (= Labor) daily "Davar" quoted from bry., FAZ, 6 May 1981 criticizing only Begin's style not substance.

116   Bry., FAZ, 6 May 1981.

117   Bry., FAZ, 7 May 1981.

118   Tsyona Peled, Political Mood and Voting Intentions: Towards the 1981 Elections and Immediately after them", (Hebr.), Jerusalem: Israel Institute of Applied Social Research (IIAS), Bulletin No. 55, Aug. 1981, table 2, p.12.

119   Ibid.

120   Ibid; cf. Wolffsohn: Israel, p.51 with additional data.

121   Unfortunately, the poll did not weight the Lebanese missile crisis and the anti-German diatribes.

122   PORI institute, no date given; courtesy of Stephan Bergmann, author of a TV feature on "The Special Relationship-Israel and the Germans" broadcasted on February 14, 1982; data provided by letter of Feb. 25, 1982; cf. Wolffsohn: Deutsch-Israelische Beziehungen, pp.22 ff. for detailed polls.

123   PORI, loc. cit.

124   Der Stern, 14 May 1981, p.30.

125   FAZ, 5 May 1981, pp.1-2; the statements of opposition leader Kohl and FM Genscher in the Bundestag (parliament) cf. FAZ, 8 May 1981. FR, 5 May 1981; NZZ, 6 May 1981.

126   FR, 5 May 1981.

127   FAZ, 8 May 1981; IAT, 8 May 1981.

128   FAZ, 8 May 1981. As chancellor Kohl planned this trip as quickly as possible. It was delayed because of Begin's resignation in August 1983.

129   FAZ, 7 May 1981.

130   FAZ, 11 May 1981.

131   FAZ, 23 May 1981.

132   This was written in December 1981, before the Beirut Massacre. Cf. later polls Wolffsohn, Deutsch-Israelische Beziehungen, p.20.

133   Cf. on Meroz: G. Gillessen, FAZ, 14 May 1981; on Klaus Schütz cf. Yediot Acharonot, 18 May 1981 called Schütz "an honest friend",

who leaves behind him "many friends remembering him most positively".

134 A. Weinstein, FAZ, 25 July 1981. Dr. Hansen learned Hebrew and proved to be an exceptional ambassador for various reasons.

135 E. Mörbitz, FR, 7 July 1981; cf. also his interview to "Bayernkurier" (weekly of the CSU, the Bavarian branch of the oppositional Christian Democratic Union).

136 According to informed estimates (Haaretz, 6 Oct 1981). The recovery came in 1984 (Wolffsohn: Israel, p.251 with data).

137 Haaretz, 24 May 1981. The timing of the decision of the tourism branch to make Germany its "main target" documents a dismal miscalculation as well as ignorance on political moods and their influence on "vacation behavior". People may be indifferent to the regime of the country they visit, but are hardly willing to be insulted collectively by its leadership.

138 FAZ, 9 June 1981.

139 Haaretz, 1 July 1981.

140 FAZ, 22 July 1981.

141 Saarländischer Rundfunk, 23 July 1981, 18 hours, CMT.

142 D. Degan, Haaretz, 7 June 1981 quoting an interview with FR, 6 July 1981. Schmidt did not visit Israel until the end of his chancellorship - and later (December 1984 when this was written).

143 FR, 14 July 1981.

144 D. Degan, Haaretz, 15 July 1981. The arms deal with Saudi Arabia was undoubtedly one of the problems.

145 Haaretz, 24 Aug 1981.

146 ckn, FAZ, 13 Oct 1981. He did come.

147 Ibid.

148 Ibid.

149 M. Golac, Haaretz, 19 Oct 1981; FAZ, 20 Oct 1981.

150 Shortly before Israel began the war against the PLO.

151 ckn., FAZ, 4 Nov 1981.

152 ban. (= G. Bannas), FAZ, 26 Aug 1981.

153 SZ, 8 Dec 1981, pp.1-2; text on p.5.

154 Richard Löwenthal: Identität und Zukunft der SPD, in: Die Neue Gesellschaft (= the "theoretical" periodical of the SPD), vol. 28, Dec 1981, p.1086. Two months later, however, he extended his criticism: "I have got the impression during the détente period that most people in the Peace Movement and a not at all unsignificant number of party (SPD, M.W.) members have forgotten about the basic normative differences in the East-West Conflict." (Löwenthal in the Berlin weekly "Berliner Stimme", quoted and translated from Die Welt, 15 Feb. 1982).

155 SZ, 8 Dec. 1981, pp.1-2. It belongs to the "Peace Movement".
156 ckn, FAZ, 24 Jan. 1981.
157 See esp. Michael Naumann, Die Zeit, 30 Jan 1981; also cdkn, FAZ, 24 Jan 1981; uncomplete Newsweek, 2 Feb 1981.
158 The importance of Germany's role was confirmed by Rabbatabai himself. It was due to Germany's effort, he said, that Washington finally negotiated with the right partners in Iran and not with Bani-Sadr and Quotzbadeh (FAZ, 26 Jan 1981).
President Jimmy Carter was somewhat more restrained on West Germany's key role when he described the process in his memoirs (Jimmy Carter: **Keeping Faith. Memoirs of a President,** Totoronto et al.: Bantam Books 1982, pp.557 ff.
159 SZ, 29 Oct 1981.
160 Wolffsohn, MECS VII.
161 FR, 12 June 1981.
162 Dieter Buhl, Die Zeit, 3 Oct 1980.
163 Der Spiegel, 9 March 1981, p.19.
164 Der Spiegel, 14 July 1981, p.28.
165 Interview with Kiep, Der Spiegel, 21 July 1980, p.27.
166 Ibid. Kiep explicitly referred to navy unit and explicitly excluded the possibility of "sending Bundeswehr divisions to the Cape of Good Hope. In other words, no ground troups (ibid.).
167 Loc. cit., pp.26-27.
168 ckn., FAZ, 29 Sept 1980, summarizing a "Deutschlandfunk" interview with Strauss.
169 See FAZ, 30 Sept 1980. The letter was headlined: "We may not be drawn into foreign conflicts".
170 Ibid.
171 Ibid.
172 Der Spiegel, 9 March 1981, pp.21-22.
173 Ibid.
174 Ibid., p.22.
175 Ibid. In a lecture at Hamburg's renowned "Übersee Club".
176 Loc. cit., p.19. As to West Germany's internal political process, "Der Spiegel" is usually well informed. Knowledge about external affairs, among them the Middle East, is, limited, however. Repeatedly, the article quoted here referred to events of the past calling Egypt's President in 1967 Sadat! (see p.23).
177 See the letter of then U.S. ambassador in Bonn Walter Stoessel in April 1980 and unanswered American requests of January 1980 (FAZ, 23 March 1981).
178 Ibid.

179 ckn., FAZ, 11 March 1981.
180 Both became ministers in 1982 and worked in the foreign office.
181 C. Glenrichl, FAZ, 26 March 1981.
182 The next coalition to which he belonged kept this promise (FAZ, 15 May 1984).
183 DW, 27 Oct 1981.
184 Der Spiegel, 5 January 1981, p.19.
185 J. Vinocur, IHT, 3 April 1981; W. Hoffmann, Die Zeit, 6 March 1981, quoting government spokesman Kurt Becker, FAZ, 16 Jan 1981.
186 Der Spiegel, 5 Jan 1981, p.20.
187 See footnote 451.
188 W. Hoffmann, Die Zeit, 6 March 1981.
189 Ibid.; Der Spiegel, 27 April 1981, p.25.
190 Der Spiegel, 27 April 1981, p.25.
191 Egypt announced later that the Leopard 2 was too expensive, Defence Minister Abu Ghazala explained that his country would prefer the French AMX-32 and the British "Challenger" which was still in a developmental phase (SZ, 21 Oct. 1981).
192 SIPRI, 1981, p.194; Der Spiegel, 12 Jan 1981, p.27, wrote that Libya wanted 200 Leopard 2 and added North-Yemen to the list of potential buyers.
193 J. Melman, Haaretz, 10 Feb 1981; J. Melman, Haaretz, 11 Feb 1981, quoting a report of "Aviation Week" on the same issue. In 1984 the deal was pushed via Britain, FR Germany agreed.
194 Spokesman of the British Ministry of Defence to J. Melman, Haaretz, 11 Feb 1981.
195 IHT, 24 Feb 1981. The British Undersecretary Pattie, in charge of the Royal Air Force, had officially submitted his government's request in mid-February 1981 (FAZ, 25 Feb 1981).
196 FAZ, 25 Feb 1981. Judicial and secrecy aspects of the Tornado deal were checked (fy., FAZ, 26 Feb. 1981).
197 ban., FAZ, 19 March 1981.
198 C.G. (enrich), FAZ, 24 April 1981.
199 FAZ, 26 June 1981.
200 H. Vielain, Die Welt, 11 February 1976.
201 Kieler Nachrichten, 6 November 1976.
202 See Der Spiegel, 5 Jan 1981 which disclosed it.
203 **Der Spiegel**, 5 January 1981.
204 Ibid. The following paragraph summarizing the developments can also be found there.
205 During the debate on the federal budget, hls. (H. Herles), FAZ, 31 Jan. 1981.

206 This short historical lecture was given at a state dinner in honour of the German delegation (Der Spiegel), 4 May 1981; FAZ, 29 April 1981). See part I of this book.
207 FAZ, 29 April 1981.
208 FAZ, 30 April 1981.
209 fy., FAZ, 2 May 1981.
210 Poll conducted by Institut für Demoskopie Allensbach for "Stern" (weekly), 14 May 1981, p.29.
211 Der Spiegel 23 Feb 1981, p.32. The formulation of Allensbach was more refined. It presented the interviewee with two diverging opinions on the deal, whereas EMNID asked about yes or no. Cf. Wolffsohn, Deutsch-Israelische Beziehungen.
212 ban., FAZ, 7 Oct 1981.
213 pp. 17-19.
214 SZ, 13 Oct 1981.
215 Ibid.
216 At the Federal Security Council meeting deciding upon the matter (Der Spiegel, 12 Oct 1981).
217 Ibid.
218 Government spokesman Becker, SZ, 13 Oct 1981.
219 Ibid.
220 Die Welt, March 11, 1982. It had been "put to the files", she said.
221 SZ, 29 Oct 1981; ckn, FAZ, 29 Oct 1981. Schmidt had fallen ill before and could not participate at the North-South Summit at Cancun from where Fahd came.
222 SZ, 4 Nov 1981. This howitzer is supposed to be NATO's most modern and sophisticated artillery weapon (Ibid.). This is beyond the expertise of the author.
223 For an overview on West Germany's arms export policy see the recent essay by Joachim Krause. Die Rüstungsexport-Politik der Bundesrepublik Deutschland, **Europa Archiv**, 1981, No.12, pp.363-372 with some bibliographical references.
224 Op. cit., pp.364-365. They included 50 planes, tanks, anti-aircraft weapons, howitzers and lorries (G. Gillessen, FAZ, Feb 3, 1981).
225 G. Gillessen, FAZ, Feb 3, 1981. Mistakenly, the authors repeatedly writes 1965 insted of xxx?
226 United States Arms Control and Disarmament Agency: **World Military Expenditures and Arms Transfers 1972-1982**, Washington, D.C. April 1984, pp.95 ff.
227 FAZ, Feb 17, 1981.
228 Wolfgang Hoffmann, Die Zeit, Jan 30, 1981, p.10; partly Der Spiegel, Jan 19, 1981, p.119; FAZ, Jan 3, 1980, p.13. In 1980, the

"British Aerospace" at Stevenage joined. The new firm operated under French law (FAZ, Jan 3, 1981, p.13).

229 J. Isnard, Le Monde, Sept 24, 1980.

230 W. Hoffmann, loc. cit.

231 Ibid., Der Spiegel, Jan 12, 1981, p.27.

232 Der Spiegel, Jan 12, 1981, p.27.

233 According to SIPRI, quoted by W. Hoffmann, ibid.

234 M. Cohen, Haaretz, Feb 19, 1981, quoting "International Defence Review"; see also D. Degan, Haaretz, Aug 24, 1981. His investigations were neither confirmed nor denied by officials he had asked. SIPRI 1978 quoted from W. Hoffmann, Die Zeit, Jan 30, 1981, p.10. SIPRI spoke of 210 tanks and also mentioned the transfer to the Soviet Union via Libya. They were also "seen" in Ethiopia (Der Spiegel, 11 Aug 1980, p.29).

235 ein (= A. Weinstein, an extremely well informed journalist on military matters), FAZ, Jan 29, 1981.

236 According to Der Spiegel, Jan 26, 1981, p.44 India wanted two.

237 Theo Sommer, Die Zeit, Jan 16, 1981.

238 Whereas 54 % of the West German public were opposed to the submarine deal with Chile, 68 % of SPD voters refused. 60 % of the FDP voters and 39 % of CDU/CSU voters rejected it (EMNID poll for Der Spiegel, Feb 23, 1981, p.30). On December 12, 1980 the Vorstand of the SPD had formulated its disagreement.

239 Der Spiegel, Jan 12, 1981, p.27.

240 Der Spiegel, Jan 26, 1981, p.44.

241 Pending Chilean consent. There might be troubles, if the Latin Americans blocked. In Oct 1981 they bought two British submarines (FAZ, Oct 7, 1981). But they had obviously not withdrawn their demand because the German government was still looking for "alternative solutions" (SPD parliamentary group spokesman Terjung, quoted from SZ, March 11, 1982).

242 Norbert Gansel (left wing of the SPD), a moral purist who refused to think in terms of Realpolitik (Der Spiegel, Jan 26, 1981, p.42), was one of the few politicians clearly realizing and formulating it. He called the problem a "key-decision of German foreign policy" (Der Spiegel, March 23, 1981, p.23), see also his remarks quoted in W. Hoffmann, Die Zeit, Jan 30, 1981, p.11).

243 D. Degan, Haaretz, 20 + 27 Jan 1981.

244 ckn., FAZ, 28 Jan 1981.

245 W. Hoffmann, Die Zeit, 30 Jan 1981, p.10.

246 The guidelines of the Bundessicherheitsrat were worked out mainly by the Foreign and the Defence Ministry (see: G. Bannas (= ban.), FAZ, Oct 30, 1981).

247 The SPD Bundestag fraction did not even discuss the report and

recommendations of its "working group" (SZ, March 11, 1982). Here, the government wing of the coalition parties was unusually tough (unusual compared with its general weakness in these weeks).

248 This is by no means a normative but an exclusively analytical statement implying that purely Machiavellian aspects have been put aside by moral and historical motives.

249 SZ, March 11, 1982; R. Moniac, Die Welt, March 11, 1982; FAZ, March 11, 1982. The guidelines are to be found in: Presse- und Informationsamt der Bundesregierung: Bulletin, May 5, 1982. The cabinet decided on these guidelines on April 28, 1982.

250 Ibid.

251 R. Moniac, Die Welt, March 11, 1982.

252 SZ, March 10, 1982.

253 Der Spiegel, Oct 12, 1981, p.19. Participants of the meeting told the author of this book that Schmidt was more vague than SPIEGEL reported.

254 Sza (= Szandar), SZ, May 28, 1982. The announcement was made a week before FM Genscher's visit to Israel.

255 Cf. H. Wehner's warnings addressed to the purists widhing to sustain social democratic purism in the opposition (hls., FAZ, Feb 13, 1981), also FAZ, Feb 9, 1981).

256 Party Chairman Willy Brandt's "Five Points-Program", FAZ, Feb 13, 1981, p.1,2,7.

257 See her article condemning the "returning anti-Americanism in the Federal Republic" (FAZ, April 4, 1981). Cf. her interview with Der Spiegel, Jan 12, 1981, pp.26-27, favoring nuclear energy and consideration of the internal situation of receiver countries (later part of the new government guidelines!).

258 mtz, FAZ, Feb 18, 1981. The left wing critics of the NATO two-track decision were, in turn, praised by "Prawda" (FAZ, Jan 30, 1981).

259 In the weekly "Konkret". In the end, he was excluded from the SPD and it was expected that he would found a "democratic socialist" party in 1982.

260 For instance in Schleswig-Holstein (FAZ, Feb 17, 1981).

261 Jan 5, 1981, p.21.

262 Der Spiegel, Jan 26, 1981, p.42.

263 FAZ, Jan 28, 1981, p.2.

264 C.G., FAZ, Jan 29, 1981; D. Degan, Haaretz, Jan 28, 1981; Der Spiegel, Jan 26, 1981, p.42.

265 Interview with Der Spiegel, Jan 12, 1981, p.27.

266 Der Spiegel, Oct 12, 1981, p.19.

267 See Matthöfer's and Horn's contribution to the rather propagandistic brochure "Saudi Arabian Partner für die Bundesrepublik

Deutschland" edited by the "Nah- und Mittel-Ost-Verein" Hamburg April 1981 (just shortly before Chancellor Schmidt's official visit to Ryadh), pp.19-20, 53-54.

268   According to his "personal opinion", C.G. (enrich), FAZ, Jan 8, 1981, p.1 and p.2. Bruno Friedrich, another prominent right of center SPD politician wanted to have this concept dopped altogether. He preferred to refer to "zones of European security interests" (Der Spiegel, 26 Jan 1981, p.42).

269   Der Spiegel, 11 May 1982.

270   At the Friedrich-Ebert-Foundation of the SPD. He spoke on "Remarks on Morals, Duties and Responsibilities of Politicians". The occasion: A symposium on Immanuel Kant, see H. Herles, FAZ, 16 March 1981.

271   W. Hoffmann, Die Zeit, 30 Jan 1981, p.11. J.W., Le Monde, 13 Jan 1981 quoted Genscher slightly differently. According to his version, the FM had said that Saudi Arabia was not located in an area of tension. This point of view went even beyond Mr. Wischnewski's (SPD) analysis.

272   fy., FAZ, 12 Jan 1981; C.G. (enrich), FAZ, 27 March 1981. He wanted to prevent another debacle similar to the controversy on the delivery of submarines to Chile. Then, the Cabinet, Genscher, too, approved of the sale and the SPD parliamentary group later torpedoed it. Genscher, like Schmidt, also believed temporarily at least, that Israel could be compensated by another package of German arms as well (above on Schmidt).

273   C.G. (enrich), FAZ, 20 March 1981; C.G.; FAZ, 18 March 1981.

274   FAZ, 30 May 1981, p.2.

275   Der Spiegel, 12 Oct 1981, p.18.

276   Loc. cit., p.19. Disapprovingly, he agreed with Carsten Voigt (see under SPD).

277   C.G. (enrich), FAZ, 21 Jan 1981; see Lambsdorff's contribution to the brochure "Saudi Arabian Partner für die Bundesrepublik Deutschland", pp.13-14.

278   C.G. (enrich), FAZ, 20 March 1981. The information on guerillas was wrong. By now, one knows for sure about the cooperation between them and the PLO. Neither side tries to hide this fact.

279   He was the first establishment oriented West German politician condemning Israel's raids on Lebanon as "state terrorism" and has repeatedly - and officially! - met with Arafat. In November 1981, he was elected chairman of the German-Arab Society". He vehemently criticized Israel's bombing of the Iraqi nuclear reactor "unbelievable", "act of aggression in contradiction to international law and endangering peace"; FR, 10 June 1981). The Camp David process had reached a dead-end and the PLO would have to be included in any solution. Begin's attacks on Schmidt should not prevent Germany from deepening relations with the Arab World, Iraq especially (FAZ, 11 May 1981). He clearly reflected the interests of business circles in Iraq (see economic structures).

280 fy., FAZ, 24 Jan 1981. Clearly, with regard to this last point Möllemann was somehow anti-cyclical. The sale of tanks to the Saudis would stabilize the West in the ME (C.G., FAZ, 26 March 1981).

281 According to Der Spiegel, 2 Feb 1981, p.18.

282 C.G. (enrich), FAZ, 20 March 1981.

283 Ibid.

284 Membership in this youth organization (up to 35 years of age) is only partly identical with FDP party membership. Those who belong to the young Democrats do not have to be party members. Most of them are, however. Both Schuchardt and Matthäus-Maier left the FDP after its break with the Social Democrats in the coalition. The latter was elected to the Bundestag as a member of the SPD in March 1983, the former became a senator in the state government of Hamburg in 1983. But Schuchardt remained "independent" as far as party affiliation was concerned.

285 For their attitude see Der Spiegel, 2 Feb 1981, p.18; ckn., FAZ, 9 Feb 1981; C.G. (enrich), FAZ, 20 March 1981.

286 Hirsch had demanded that the FDP part ways with the Young Democrats (L.B(ewerunge), FAZ, 27 Jan 1981); Mrs. Hamm-Brücher and Mr. Kleinert supported the rival right-of-center "Young Liberals" still unrecognized by the FDP as "its" second let alone only organization (SZ, 16 March 1981).

287 Der Spiegel, 2 Feb 1981, p.18. In 1982 she was opposed to the coalition switch of her party but she did not leave the FDP.

288 Ibid.

289 Ibid.

290 (C.G.(enrich), FAZ, 20 March 1981. Hans-Günter Hoppe, deputy chairman of the Bundestag group of the FDP, was chairman.

291 ckn., FAZ, 28 Jan 1981.

292 fy., FAZ, 12 Jan 1981.

293 ban. (G. Bannas), FAZ, 27 April 1981.

294 FAZ, 21 April 1981.

295 See note 545, p.2.

296 See 545.

297 Ho./ban., FAZ, 19 Sept 1981, p.2.

298 C.G.(enrich), FAZ, 26 March 1981. See also Mertes' contribution to Saudi-Arabian, Partner für die Bundesrepublik Deutschland, loc. cit., pp.45-47 where he also stressed the all-Western approach and a global view.

299 See his explanations in Saudi Arabien. Partner für die Bundesrepublik Deutschland, loc. cit., pp.51-52.

300 Interview to "Deutschlandfunk" quoted from ckn., FAZ, 13 April 1981.

301 See CDU General Secretary Geissler's remarks, hls. (H. Herles), FAZ, 4 May 1981.
302 fy., FAZ, 16 Jan 1981. See also ckn., FAZ, 13 April 1981 or C. G.(enrich), FAZ, 23 Feb 1981.
303 Franz Alt's essay, Der Spiegel, 26 Jan 1981, p.46. Chancellor Schmidt, too, had the same idea; see above.
304 C.G.(enrich), FAZ, 23 Feb 1981. Möllemann passed on the knowledge he had learned from Saudi Foreign Minister Saud al-Faysal. The latter told him that the Arab word ("djihad" (Holy War) meant "great effort".
305 Again, by no means a normative statement, but an analytical one. The supporters, themselves, ever and again, stressed Realpolitik necessities.
306 hls. (H. Herles), FAZ, 4 May 1981).
307 See note 554. He reproached the SPD of abandoning its Socialist tradition while favoring arms exports.
308 W. Hoffmann, Die Zeit, 6 March 1981, p.25.
309 ban. (= G. Bannas), FAZ, 27 April 1981, p.2.
310 Ibid.
311 ARD (Chanell 1), 30 April 1981.
312 MV, FAZ, 22 Aug 1981.
313 Der Spiegel, 11 Aug 1980, pp.28-29; L.B.(ewerunge), FAZ, 2 Aug 1980; L.B., FAZ, 4 Aug 1980; MV; FAZ, 22 Aug 1981.
314 L.B., FAZ, 4 Aug 1980.
315 MV., FAZ, 22 Aug 1981. The right wing SPD Minister of Defence, however, was asked to support efforts to liberalize arms export guidelines (W. Hoffmann, Die Zeit, 30 Jan 1981, p.9).
316 fy., FAZ, 21 Feb 1981.
317 Ibid. Whatever that may mean (suspended? successfully concluded?). Hans-Heinz Griesmeier chairman of the Krauss-Maffei board added that no concrete deals had been concluded (W. Hoffmann, Die Zeit, 6 March 1981, p.25).
318 FAZ, 11 Feb 1981, p.15.
319 Copy of the letter in: Der Spiegel, 30 Nov 1981, p.26; see also SZ, 1 Dec 1981.
320 MV., FAZ, 17 Sept 1981.
321 MV./K.B., FAZ, 16 Sept 1981.
322 In a reader's letter to FAZ, 9 June 1981.
323 Interview to Der Spiegel, 27 April 1981, p.34.
324 W. Hoffmann, Die Zeit, 24 April 1981, p.21.
325 FAZ, 16 March 1981.
326 gl., FAZ, 16 March 1981.

327 fy., FAZ, 31 March 1981.
328 Der Spiegel, 16 March 1981, p.76.
329 K.B., FAZ, 23 April 1981.
330 K.B., FAZ, 11 June 1981.
331 K.B., 21 Jan 1981.
332 Hn., NZZ, 28 April 1981.
333 See his essay in: Saudi Arabien. Partner für die Bundesrepublik Deutschland, loc. cit., pp.51-52.
334 Der Spiegel, 26 Jan 1981, p.44.
335 K.B., FAZ, 30 April 1981; K.B., FAZ, 2 May 1981.
336 Der Spiegel, 1 June 1981, p.14.
337 Secretary of State (Foreign Ministry) Günther van Well realized "difficulties" because of Saudi credits (Der Spiegel, 1 June 1981, p.14); see also FAZ, 4 June 1981.
338 Workers Council of Rheinmetall (sic.), Die Zeit, 30 Jan 1981, p.10.
339 Der Spiegel, 27 April 1981, p.25.
340 W. Hoffmann, Die Zeit, 30 Jan 1981, pp.10-11.
341 FAZ, 15 Jan 1981. He also rejected the Chile deal.
342 FAZ, 27 April 1981.
343 C.G.(enrich), FAZ, 27 March 1981.
344 The Steyr company which produces the "Kürassier" tank cannot live from selling tractors, according to its President ("Generaldirektor") Hans Malzacher (M. Halpert, Haaretz, 1 March 1981, also Ko., FAZ, 4 July 1981). Since spring 1980 Austria had negotiated with the Saudis about the export of the Kürassier. In February 1981 Chancellor Bruno Kreisky agreed to the sale-pending Saudi willingness to buy (ibid.). Shortly after Schmidt's visit to Ryadh, Kreisky went there and reiterated his favorable approach declaring that Saudi Arabia was "not in a state of war" (FR, 7 May 1981; Le Monde, 7 May 1981; Ko(nitzer), FAZ, 10 May and 22 June 1981).
345 Der Spiegel, 12 Oct 1981, p.19. See note 253.
346 For this report see D. Degan, Haaretz, 22 March 1981 (with a copy of a "Meaplan" meeting, 26 June 1980; also D. Degan, Haaretz, 29 April 1981" and 11 June 1981).
347 NZZ, 30 April 1981, p.3.
348 Ibid.; FAZ, 29 April 1981, p.2.
349 Arab News (Jidda), 25 Nov 1980.
350 SIPRI, 1981, p.233.
351 ckn., FAZ, 15 Jan 1981.
352 Der Spiegel, 11 Aug 1980, p.29.

353 SIPRI, 1981, p.217.
354 In February/March 1982 it was renewed (see Kuwait Times, 6 March 1982; Arab Daily News 10 March 1981; Turkish Daily News, 10 March 1982).
355 Der Spiegel, 11 Aug 1980, p.29.
356 SZ, 21 Oct 1981. No matter what the German position on arms exports to Egypt.
357 K.B., FAZ, 27 Oct 1981.
358 Enrichment and reproduction (Wiederaufbereitung) of uranium, FAZ, 20 July 1981.
359 FAZ, 15 and 19 March 1981.
360 Der Spiegel, 11 Aug 1980, p.29.
361 Newsweek, 22 June 1981, p.14.
362 See M. Gester, FAZ, 12 Oct 1980. This deal preceded the agreement between Iraq and Brazil. It includes large reactors as well as a uranium enrichment plant and a plant for separating out plutonium from spent reacter fuel (P. Lewis, IHT, 19 June 1981).
363 Newsweek, 22 June 1981, p.14.
364 J. Melman, Haaretz, 23 June 1981. These rumours were neither confirmed nor denied, as far as I can see.
365 Kuwait Times, 16 Feb 1981.
366 NZZ, 7 Nov 1980.
367 FAZ, 11 Sept 1980.
368 J. Friedmann, FAZ, 30 May 1981.
369 K.B., FAZ, 28 April 1981; (FAZ, 29 May 1981).
370 See Der Spiegel, 11 May 1981.
371 Die Welt, 9 March 1982.
372 SZ, 9 March 1982.
373 Der Spiegel, 5 Jan 1981, p.22.
374 D. Degan, Haaretz, 24 Aug 1981, who did not specify the number of Leopard 2 tanks the Libyan desired was the only one reporting on this plan. He based his article on "informed circles" in Bonn.
375 FR, 23 Jan 1981; IHT, 19 Feb 1981; NZZ, 21 Feb 1981.
376 Haaretz, 29 March 1981; J. Vinocur, IHT, 13 March 1981; Egyptian Gazette, 21 April 1981. A second test conducted on 17 May 1981 was a failure (J. Miller, IHT, 14 Sept 1981).
377 Ibid.; K.B., FAZ, 21 March 1981; J. Miller, IHT, 14 Sept 1981, FAZ, 18 March 1981; FR, 18 March 1981; J. inocur, IHT, 13 March 1981. Egypt's FM Ali called them "a serious threat to peace in the region (FAZ, 18 March 1981) and Morocco contended that Libya contracted with Otrag to buy medium-range missiles capable of carrying nuclear warheads to any target in the ME or southern

Europe by early 1986 (J. Vinocur, IHT, 13 March 1981). An unnamed Libyan "official, however, was quoted by the West German weekly magazine "Stern" to have confirmed the capability of these missiles to carry nuclear warheads. The deal was said to be as high as 1.5 billion $ of which 100 $ had already been transferred to Otrag (quoted from Haaretz; 11 June 1981).

378   Haaretz, 29 March 1981.
379   J. Vinocur, IHT, 13 March 1981.
380   K.B., FAZ, 21 March 1981; J. Miller, IHT, 14 June 1981.
381   Ibid.
382   J. Miller, IHT, 14 Sept 1981.
384   In a British TV program quoted from J. Melman, Haaretz, 1 June 1981.
385   J. Miller, IHT, 14 Sept 1981.
386   J. Miller, IHT, 14 Sept 1981; also government spokesman Kurt Becker (K.B., FAZ, 21 March 1981); Haaretz, 29 March 1981.
387   B. Graham, IHT, 5 Aug 1981.
388   K.B., FAZ, 25 April 1981.
389   gl., FAZ, 7 Nov 1981. Balance-sheet loss for 1980/81: 515.9 million DM.
390   K.B., FAZ, 25 April 1981. He referred to the new § 15a of the income tax law, limiting the tax advantages of losses (Verlustzuweisungen).
391   See interview of FAZ with Franz Wukasch who replaced Otrag's founding father Lutz T. Kayser as chairman of the board in the latter half of 1981 (gl., FAZ, 7 Nov. 1981).
392   FAZ, 4 Nov 1981.
393   Ibid.
394   J. Melman, Haaretz, 27 Dec 1981.
395   SIPRI 1981.
396   J. Tal, Haaretz, 8 March 1981; Bry. (= K. Barry), FAZ, 9 March 1981; FR, 9 March 1981.
397   Der Spiegel, 6 July 1981, p.49; Haaretz, 8 July 1981.
398   Der Spiegel, 6 July 1981, pp.48-51.
399   SIPRI, 1981, p.238. "Some" were destined for the police force" (ibid.).
400   Der Spiegel, 11 Aug 1980, p.29. No details as to the kind of these "most modern weapons" (ibid.).
401   FAZ, 30 April 1981. The general was a counselor to the Sudanese General Staff. He should know what he was talking about. Bonn kept silence on that subject.
402   SIPRI, 1981, p.238.

403 J. Melman, Haaretz, 21 April 1981.

404 D. Degan, Haaretz, 4 Aug 1981.

405 SIPRI, 1981, p.240 had no authoritative confirmation (see the parantheses there). The Institute of Strategic Studies was unequivocally about the deal, see note 406.

406 The Military Balance 1981-1981, London 1981, p.116; letter by Christoph Bertram to the author, 7 June 1982. No details were available as to the costs.

407 Loc. cit., p.114. The Institute did not refer to the costs but according to "Turkish Daily News" (18 Nov 1980), it ammounted to 600 million Deutschmarks.

408 SIPRI, 1981.

409 The West German constitution ("Grundgesetz") combines a vote of non-confidence with the simultaneous stipulation that a candidate for the chancellorship be nominated by the opposition ("constructive vote of no-confidence"). Helmut Kohl, the parliamentary leader of the CDU/CSU and chairman of the CDU, was the candidate who won the vote on 1 October 1982.

410 "I cannot act like a virgin in this case," Chancellor Kohl told ZDF (German TV network) on 26 August 1983 in an interview with Hans-Joachim Reiche. In this domain, too, he said in January 1984, he could not begin from scratch; ckn.=Angela Nacken, FAZ, 27 January 1984.

411 R.M., NZZ, 7 October 1983; see also note 412.

412 ckn. (= A. Nacken), FAZ, 4 October 1983; interview with Peter Ellgaard, ZDF, "Bonner Perspektiven", 30 September 1983.

413 Note 411 and W.K. (= Köhler), FAZ, 5 October 1983.

414 **Der Spiegel**, 11 April 1983, pp.22 ff.

415 **Middle East Economic Digest**, Special Report, July 1983, p.32.

416 After the "Wende" the Bundestag was dissolved to pave the way for early elections which were won handsomely by the CDU/CSU and which brought the FDP back into the federal legislature.

417 **Loc. cit.**, p.37.

418 Der Spiegel, 11 April 1983, p.24.

419 Der Spiegel, 25 February 1985, p.22.

420 note 413, FAZ.

421 Kuwait Times, 28 June 1983, quoting the West German daily Frankfurter Rundschau.

422 Israel was to have been the first Middle Eastern state on Kohl's itinerary in the region but Prime Minister Begin's resignation, announced in late August 1983, led to a postponned of this trip from late August 1983 to mid-January 1984.

423 Middle East Economic Digest, 14 October 1983, p.53.

424 International Herald Tribune, 12 October 1982, p.2; J. Buchan,

Financial Times, 12 October 1983; C. E. Buchalla, SZ, 12 October 1983; W.K.(öhler), FAZ, 12 October 1983.

425 Buchan, FT, note 424.
426 W.K.(öhler), FAZ, note 424.
427 Cf. FAZ and SZ, 6 October 1983, Die Welt, 7 December 1983.
428 D. Degan, Haaretz, 18 and 30 December 1983. Government response to a parliamentary inquiry by a member of the Bundestag (faction of the Greens). Other "areas of tension" mentioned in the response were Iraq, Iran, Syria, and Lebanon. Egypt, Saudi Arabia or the Gulf States were not enumerated.
429 Arab News (Jidda), 14 January 1984.
430 Cf. his interview in August 1983, note 410.
431 Der Spiegel, 25 February 1985, No.9, p.21. Taken by surprise (literally: "... vom Stuhl gefallen ...")
432 Cf. Ko., NZZ, 11 February 1984; the text of his statement as well as the reactions of all parties represented in the Bundestag Das Parlament, 25 February 1984, pp.1 ff.
433 Saudi Gazette (Jidda), 23 February 1984.
434 Saudi Gazette, 11 February 1984; cf. also Arab News, 12 February 1984; Saudi Press Agency, 9 February 1984 published in BBC Summary of World Broadcasts (SWB), 11 February 1984. This statement was a direct response to Chancellor Kohl's comments to the Bundestag (ibid.).
435 D. Degan, Haaretz, 5 March 1984.
436 Haaretz correspondent in the U.S. (G. Sammet?), 5 March 1984.
437 Der Spiegel, 16 April 1984 quoted by D. Degan, Haaretz, 16 April 1984.
438 This was reported (and not denied by the government) in Der Spiegel, 25 February 1985, p.22.
439 Ibid.
440 Loc. cit., pp.21 ff.
441 D. Degan, Haaretz, quoting unnamed "German sources at NATO headquarters in Belgium, 12 December 1984.
442 M. Rehm, SZ, 14 January 1985.
443 Prince Faisal bin Turki, a nephew of King Fahd, indicated this return to the status quo ante in an address to the Social Democratic "Friedrich-Ebert-Foundation" in Bonn (SZ, 7 March 1985).
444 Haaretz, 10 March 1985.
445 S. Zedaka, Haaretz, 14 March 1985.
446 For the earlier proposal during the late SPD/FDP era cf. footnote 244 in Part II.
447 D. Degan, Haaretz, 26 July 1983.

448 Ibid. and D. Degan, Haaretz, 10 July 1983; SZ 14 July 1983, D. Degan, Haaretz, 12 August 1983.
449 SZ, 15 July 1983.
450 SZ, 14 July 1983.
451 D. Degan, Haaretz, 30 October 1983.
452 W.K.(öhler), FAZ, 5 October 1983. In August 1984, Kuwait ("area of tension"?) got 8 W. German gunboats (SZ, 4 August and SWB, 3 August 1984).
453 D. Degan, Haaretz, 27 February 1984. The government was infuriated by Strauss' failure to coordinate his activities with the Foreign Ministry (R. Cornwell, FT, 16 February 1984).
454 Middle East Economic Digest, 17 February 1984, p.11; J. Buchan, FT, 15 February 1984. The request had been put forward by Egypt's Defence Minister Abu Ghazala during his visit to Germany in November 1983.
455 Ibid. and FAZ, 15 March 1984.
456 SZ, 8 March 1985.
457 fy (= Feldmeyer), FAZ, 7 March 1985.
458 D. Degan, Haaretz, 19 February 1985.
459 Cf. Haaretz, 20 March 1984.
460 A. Ben-Vered, Haaretz, 2 February 1984; Israel Defence Forces Radio, 1 February 1981 quoted in DW, 2 February 1984; Arab News (Jidda), 29 January 1984.
461 See note and text 193 to 199 in Part II.
462 Middle East Economic Digest, 13 July 1984, p.50.
463 SZ, 11 October 1984, cf. Wolfram von Raven, Allgemeine, 31 August 1984.
464 Cf. for an in-depth analysis of this aspect Jochen Schmidt: Die Problematik des Rüstungsexports der Bundesrepublik Deutschland dargestellt an der Nachfrage Saudi-Arabiens nach deutschen Waffensystemen, unpublished M.A. thesis, Munich: Hochschule der Bundeswehr (to be published in 1985).
465 M. Wolffsohn, "The European Community and the Middle East 1983", Middle East Contemporary Survey, ed. by Colin Legum et al., New York-London (forthcoming in 1985); Arab News, 8 December 1984: German exports to Saudi Arabia fell by 17 % in 1984; SZ, 13 March 1985.
466 Wolffsohn, ibid.
467 cer., NZZ, 13 January 1984.
468 ckn., FAZ, 27 January 1984.
469 Wolfgang Hoffman, Die Zeit, 18 November 1983, p.33 and 24 February 1984, pp.17 f. In the latter article he described, among other activities, Krauss-Maffei's offers to Egypt.

470 W. Hoffmann, Die Zeit, 24 February 1984, loc. cit.; Middle East Economic Digest, 17 February 1984, p.11. The MEED report preceded the Zeit article.

471 Krauss-Maffei assured the public in August 1983 that it had not been to Saudi Arabia for a year (SZ, 26 August 1983). The problem which existed for Krauss-Maffei consisted in getting orders from 1987 onwards (fy. = Feldmeyer, FAZ, 8 October 1983; J. Schmidt, loc. cit.) In February 1985 prospects seemed bleaker than before, and the company announced that planning a new Leopard generation (Leopard 3) had been stopped (SZ, 13 February 1985) and that it saw its future in civilian production (GM, FAZ, 13 February 1985). According to confidential information this author has received, planning of the Leopard 3 has continued without interruption.

472 Allgemeine, 16 March 1984.

473 Deutsche Presse-Agentur (dpa) quoted by SWB, Middle East, 3 August 1984.

474 Ibid.

475 SZ, 4 August 1984; FAZ, 7 August 1984; Newsweek, 10 September 1984, p.27.

476 Newsweek and FAZ, loc. cit.

477 SZ and FAZ, 19 August 1983; L.B.(ewerunge), FAZ, 8 February 1984.

478 D. Degan, Haaretz, 7 September 1983.

479 Allgemeine, 13 January 1984 quoting dpa reports published a week earlier; SZ, 6 February 1984.

480 Newsweek, 27 August 1984, p.14; Der Spiegel, 6 August 1984, pp. 23 f.; Haaretz, 21 August 1984.

481 S. Shamir, Haaretz, 1 February 1985.

482 Newsweek and Spiegel, loc. cit.

483 Der Spiegel, 25 February 1985, pp.20 ff.

484 ZDF, ibid., and his position before his trip to Egypt in March 1985 Wörner intensified informal cooperation with Israel (D. Degan, Haaretz, 12 August 1983).

485 Cf. Frankfurter Rundschau, 29 November 1982. He was basically a "friend of Israel".

486 Interview with "Deutscher Depeschen Dienst (ddp), SZ, 25 April 1983.

487 W.K(öhler), FAZ, 12 October 1983, p.2. On the other hand, Möllemann's statements infuriated Israel (cf. SZ, 30 November 1982 and below: Möllemann).

488 Der Spiegel, 25 February 1985, p.23.

489 Der Spiegel, 20 February 1984, p.22.

490 For the political leverage of his post to the German-Arab Association cf. Klaus Broichhausen, FAZ, 11 August 1983.

491 A. Nacken, FAZ, 24 January 1984.
492 Der Spiegel, 18 June 1984, pp.23 ff.
493 Cf. SZ, 19 and 28 June 1984.
494 Der Spiegel, 6 August 1984, pp.28 ff.
495 C.G(enrich), FAZ, 16 August 1984.
496 SZ, 21 August 1984.
497 See CSU paper for the negotiations published by "Frankfurter Rundschau", 30 March 1983. The party wanted to include security as well as financial interests of the Federal Republic in the guidelines. Süddeutsche Zeitung (23 March 1983) wrote that Strauss also favored dropping the concept of "areas of tension", but this cannot be found in the written position of the party.
498 Published by Bayernkurier (= CSU weekly), 2 April 1983.
499 eb./hen./for., SZ, 24 March 1984.
500 Herbert Riehl-Heise, SZ, 23 March 1983, never very friendly toward Strauss spoke of the "End of the Strauss Myth". Nevertheless, his opponents continued to use/misuse/abuse this myth (depending on the point of view).
501 Cf. SZ, 2 December 1983; Arab News, 5 February 1984; in early 1985 he escalated his campaign SZ, 21 February 1985, 25 February 1985 (cf. A. Ponger, SZ, 27 February 1985; D. Degan/Dan Margalit, Haaretz, 26 February 1985; Hr.=Heimrich, FAZ, 2 March 1985.
502 Cf. note 497 with the February 1985 quotations.
503 For the emphasis of the importance he attached to this trip cf. **Bayernkurier** (CSU weekly) at the end of the visit (p.1 and 14). The coverage was unusually wide in this periodical.
504 Cf. for his visit to Damascus SZ, 21 and R.M., NZZ, 17 February 1984.
505 Sza. (= Szandar), SZ, 26 February 1985.
506 On the eve of Kohl's visit to Saudi Arabia there was a public appeal to the Chancellor signed by Bundestag members Riedl, Glos, Rose (ckn. = Nacken, FAZ, 6 October 1983).
507 FAZ, 8 April and dr. (= Dreher), SZ, 11 April 1983.
508 See above and sza (= Szandar), SZ, 6 October and ckn (= Nacken), FAZ, 29 October 1983.
509 Der Spiegel, 13 February 1984, p.19; SZ, 2 February 1984, SZ, 12 April 1984 and the section on the era of the SPD-FDP coalition.
510 Der Spiegel, loc. cit.
511 Ibid. and D. Degan, Haaretz, 10 August 1984. Genscher also criticized Britain's willingness to sell "Tornado" planes to Saudi Arabia (Haaretz, loc. cit.). On behalf of his parliamentary group the foreign policy spokesman of the FDP, Helmut Schäfer repeated the position of his party (SZ, 12 April 1983). In his farewell speech as chairman of his party Genscher once again criticized

those who wanted to change arms export guidelines and those who favored the delivery of the Leopard 2 tank. This, he said, was a fundamental question having less to do with production capacities but rather with "historical and moral responsibility" (U. Bergdoll, SZ, 25 February, 1985). He did not mention F. J. Strauss by name but everybody knew that his remarks were directed against the Bavarian Prime Minister who had once again spoken in favor of the delivery.

512 Cf. fy. (= Feldmeyer), FAZ, 7 October 1983; ckn. (= Nacken), FAZ, 17 October 1983; SZ, 13 October 1983; FAZ, and SZ, 28 December 1983; Ko., NZZ, 11 February 1984; Das Parlament, 25 February 1984 (with the discussion and statements at the Bundestag on 9 February 1984); SZ, 22 February 1985.

513 ZDF, TV, interview with Peter Elgaard, 30 September 1983.

514 Telegramm of the Israel Labor Party parliamentary leader, Moshe Shahal, to his SPD counterpart, Hans-Jochen Vogel, SZ, 28 January 1984.

515 Das Parlament, 25 February 1984, pp.3 f.

516 Hans Mayr, the chairman of IG Metall, Klr., FAZ, 27 February 1985.

517 Allgemeine, 16 and SZ, 20 March 1984.

518 Information given the author by persons who were in the audience at some of Nachmann's speeches.

519 Middle East Economic Digest, Special Report West Germany, March 1984, p.4.

520 SZ, 31 January 1984.

521 SZ, 8 March 1984.

522 D. Degan, Haaretz, 5 August 1983.

523 sza (= Szandar), SZ, 3 January 1984.

524 Quoted from D. Degan, Haaretz, 14 November 1983 (after Kohl's visit to Saudi Arabia).

525 Der Spiegel, 20 February 1984, p.23; mes., SZ, 14 February 1984.

526 Dieter Schröder, SZ, 7 March 1984 commenting Kohl's visit at the White House.

527 J.R. (= Jan Reifenberg, a very well-informed then Washington-based Journalist) and C.G. (= Claus Genrich, very well informed about the political scene in Bonn), FAZ, 7 March 1984.

528 Background briefing to ckn. (= Angela Nacken), FAZ, 15 February 1984. Mertes reacted especially to Vogel's allegations and observations.

529 Near East Report, 24 February 1984, p.30.

530 Cf. SZ, 6 March 1984.

531 C.G.(enrich), FAZ, 6 March 1984; Allgemeine, 9 and 16 March, 1984.

532 Allgemeine (the weekly of the German Jewish community, "Zentralrat der Juden in Deutschland"), 30 March 1984.

533 Ibid.

534 Ernst Cramer, Die Welt, 27 February 1984; BZ (a boulevard daily with the highest circulation in West Berlin), 28 February 1984.

535 B. Halsig, Allgemeine, 30 March 1984.

536 See note 108 in Part II with text.

537 D. Degan, Haaretz, 12 August 1983.

538 D. Degan, Haaretz, 5 August 1983.

539 Jerusalem Post, overseas edition, 4 February 1984, p.1.

540 A. Ponger, SZ, 27 and 30 January 1984; Der Spiegel, 30 January 1984, p.28; Bry. (Knut Barrey), FAZ, 30 January 1984.

541 Quoted indirectly from Jerusalem Post (note 535).

542 D. Degan, Haaretz, 20 September 1984.

543 Cf. for a short summary of the endless discussions: Newsweek, 11 February 1985, p.14.

544 SZ, 4 March 1985.

545 In a conversation with the author, Hamburg, 14 December 1984.

APPENDIX

1. Statistics for 1980 from the **American Jewish Year Book 1982** of the American Jewish Committee, M. Himmelfarb **et. al.**, ed., Philadelphia, Jewish Publication Society of America, 1982. p.215 (for Jews in the Federal Republic of Germany), 282-286. For 1939 in: Arieh Tartakower, Jewish Society (Hebrew), Tel Aviv and Jerusalem, Massada, 1965, p.50.

2. Tartakower (op. cit., p.53) counted 503,000 German Jews in 1933.

3. In the mid 1930s there were 500,000 Jews living in the states of the Middle East (excluding Palestine) and 509,000 in North Africa. (Tartakower, op. cit., p.54 f.)
   In 1980 there were 45,000 Jews in Asia (excluding Israel) and 21,000 in North Africa. (American Jewish Yearbook, loc. cit.)

4. These numbers were obtained from the Central Council in Germany. The American Jewish Year Book 1982 (ibid.) counts approx. 33,000.

5. H. Haibach, Frankfurter Allgemeine Zeitung (FAZ), 12 July 1980.

6. E. Stock and J. Wenkert, ed., The Jews of France in Troubled Times (Hebrew), Tefutsot Israel Vol.20 Nr.4, American Jewish Committee Center for Jewish Community Studies, 1982. p.22. On the situation of French Jews see:
   L. Rosenzweig, La Jeune France Juive, Paris, Editions Libres Hallier, 1980.
   A. Harris and Alain de Sédouy, Juifs et Français, Paris, Grasset, 1979.

7. On developments during the Weimar period in Germany see: M. Richarz, ed., Jüdisches Leben in Deutschland. Selbstzeugnisse zur Sozialgeschichte 1918-1945, Stuttgart, Deutsche Verlags-Anstalt, 1982, p.14 ff.

8. G. Wigoder (Jerusalem Post, 5 August 1977) summarizes an essay by D. Elazar which appeared in Tefutsot Israel.

9. E. Deutsch, "Radiographie d'une communauté" (Hebrew) in: Tefutsot Israel Nr.4, 1982. p.85.
   According to the Chief Rabbi of France, 70 % of French Jews marry non-Jews (Haaretz, February 19, 1982).

10. Arthur Hertzberg, "The Present Position of Jews in America", Christianity and Crisis, March 7, 1983. p.58.

11. I do not mean the type of "community" Jew as described by authors such as Schultz, Broder and Lang. See:
    Hans Jürgen Schultz, ed., Mein Judentum, Stuttgart and Berlin, Kreuz Verlag, 1973.
    H. M. Broder and M. R. Lang, ed., Fremd im eigenen Land. Juden in der Bundesrepublik, Frankfurt/Main, Fischer, 1979.

12. The British sought to avoid encouraging pro-German sentiments in the Middle East by refusing to tolerate Jewish immigration into Palestine. This was a pragmatic rather than a "moral" or "antisemitic" decision.

12 The British sought to avoid encouraging pro-German sentiments in the Middle East by refusing to tolerate Jewish immigration into Palestine. This was a pragmatic rather than a "moral" or "antisemitic" decision.

13 British attitudes were, of course, not free of antisemitism. See: B. Wasserstein, Britain and the Jews of Europe 1939-1945, London, Oxford Univ. Press, 1979.
Marrus and Paxton discuss the extent of voluntary participation in the Vichy regime on the part of the French population. M. R. Marrus and R. O. Paxton, Vichy et les Juifs, Paris, Calmann-Lévy, 1981.
In contrast, on the unpopularity of antisemitism in fascist Italy see: M. Michaelis, Mussolini and the Jews. German-Italian Relations and the Jewish Question in Italy 1922-1945, London, Oxford Univ. Press, 1978.
On the generally desperate situation of the Jews in those years and the worldwide lack of support see: A. D. Morse, While Six Million Died, London, 1968.
On the controversy over the possibility of destroying Auschwitz see: M. Gilbert, Auschwitz and die Alliierten, München, Beck, 1982.
For the American historian G. M. Mosse, France remains the "classic antisemitic country" (Newsweek, 20 October 1982).

14 The FAZ (March 7, 1983) quotes Werner Nachmann, Chairman of the directory of the German Jewish Council.

15 Lea Fleischmann, Dies ist nicht mein Land. Eine Jüdin verläßt die Bundesrepublik, Hamburg, Hoffmann und Campe, 1980. S.25.

16 Henryk M. Broder, "Ihr bleibt die Kinder Eurer Eltern", Die Zeit, February 27, 1981. p.9.

17 Der Spiegel, April 20, 1981. p.39, 44.

18 The term comes from Karl Mannheim. I have applied it to Israel in Politik in Israel (Leverkusen, Leske & Budrich, 1983), where the theoretical aspects are discussed in detail in the second part.

19 See: L. Fleischmann (op. cit., p.68 ff), where she describes her experiences as a student. She recalls a protest meeting on the campus of the Frankfurt University: "It was the first time I had ever shouted "we" with a German group: 'We don't want cops, we don't want emergency legislation, we want freedom.'"

20 Excerpted from W. Wiegand, FAZ, February 17, 1981. On the 1968 generation in France see: Harris and de Sédouy (op. cit., Note 6).

21 E. Deutsch, op. cit. (Note 9).

22 See my book: Politik in Israel, esp. chap. 14, 34 with numerous examples.

23 See, for ex., my essays "The European Community and the Middle East" in: Middle East Contemporary Survey Vol. V and VI (C. Legum et al., ed.), New York and London, 1983 and 1984.
See also: B. Panahi, Vorurteile, Rassismus, Antisemitismus, Nationalismus in der Bundesrepublik heute. Eine empirische Untersuchung, Frankfurt/Main, S. Fischer, 1980.

For comparative data on other European nations see:
A. Silberner, Sind wir Antisemiten? Ausmaß und Wirkung eines sozialen Vorurteils in der Bundesrepublik Deutschland, Köln, Verlag Wissenschaft und Politik, 1982.

24 Y. Gorni, Ahdut Haawoda 1919-1930. The Ideological Principles and the Political System (Hebrew), Tel Aviv, Tel Aviv Univ. and Hakibbutz Hameuchad, 1973. p.177.
See also my Politik in Israel. p.146 f., 399.

25 The left-leaning Jewish critic, D. Diner, who disputes this thesis, is brilliantly argued and worth reading, even his factual presentation is sometimes flawed. See: D. Diner, "Israel und das Trauma der Massenvernichtung" in: D. Wetzel et al., ed., Die Verlängerung von Geschichte. Deutsche, Juden und der Palästinakonflikt, Frankfurt/Main, Verlag Neue Kritik, 1983, p.30 ff.

26 Among the many titles see esp.: M. Davis, ed., World Jewry and the State of Israel, New York, Arno Press, 1977. (Esp. part III) and also: M. Davis, ed., The Yom Kippur War. Israel and the Jewish People, New York, Arno Press, 1974.
These premises are analyzed and criticized by Diner and Brumlik from their "German-Jewish-leftist" and thus atypical German Jewish perspective in Wetzel, ed., opt. cit. (Note 25).
Fro an empirical-analytical (and either not critically normative or uncritically normative) view see: S. N. Herman, Jewish Identity. A Social Psychological Perspective, Beverly Hills and London, Sage, 1977. The book contains polls of Israeli schoolchildren, American students and immigrants from the Soviet Union.

27 A.K., Le Monde, May 9, 1978. (Report on a major celebration of organized French Jewry on the occassion of the thirtieth anniversary of the founding of the State of Israel).

28 For one recent example see: Thomas Ross (correspondent in the Near East), FAZ, April 25, 1983.

29 Compare: Louis Harris and Associates, A Study of the Attitudes of the American People and the American Jewish Community toward the Arab-Israeli Conflict in the Middle East, New York, September 1980. Here, the numbers for the years 1975, 1976 and 1980. The Holocaust, as given by jews and non-Jews as a justification for Israeli behavior: Jews in 1975 - 95 %, in 1976 - 93 %; in 1980 - 93 %; non-Jews in 1975 - 79 %; in 1976 - 80 %; in 1980 - 80 % (p.67).
In the summer of 1980 76 % of French Jews expressed support for the "Jersualem Law" just passed by the Knesset legalizing (for the seoncd time since 1967) the annexation of East Jerusalem. Only 15 % expressed disapproval. IFOP poll for the weekly Le Point quoted in: E. Maisi, Haaretz, September 21, 1980.
A KONSO poll of Swiss Jews in the fall of 1980 showed "combating antisemitic tendencies" to be their highest priority, followed by "supporting Israel", "combating anti-Israeli tendencies", "maintaining good relations with non-Jews", "supporting Jewish education", "maintaining religious traditions" and "combating mixed marriages". In: Jüdische Rundschau, Basel, January 22, 1981. p.1, 14.

30 On the definition of "identity" see D. R. Miller, "The Study of Social Relationships" and Erik Erikson, "Childhood and Society", both in: Herman, op. cit.

31 See Note 29.

32 M. Brumlik, "Begin and Schmidt. Oder: Die Unfähigkeit zu trauern", in: D. Wetzel, op. cit., p.94. Brumlik speaks of a "God to be touched and admired" ("Gott zum Anfassen und Bewundern"). His intention is more polemical than mine, but we agree in the diagnosis.

33 According to P. Martin (Newsweek, April 7, 1980) there were initially 21 students in 1980. George Heuberger, Assistant to the Rector, reported 22 students majoring, 18 minoring and 120 others visiting courses in the field in the summer 1982. The large non-Jewish majority is, according to Heuberger, already causing concern, as it is the intention of the institution to have non-Jewish students learn about Judaism through observation and participation in Jewish self-expression, rather than through an academic, theological or ideological filter. (Südwestpresse, Ulm, July 39, 1982).

34 G. Wigoder, Jerusalem Post, August 5, 1977.

35 G. Kröncke, Süddeutsche Zeitung, June 26/27, 1982.

36 Deutsch, op. cit., p.83 (Note 9).

37 The Times, December 2, 1976.

38 Haaretz, February 13, 1980. Le Monde, February 20, 1980.

39 Süddeutsche Zeitung, July 9, 1982. According to information supplied by the Jewish community in Berlin, a mere 9 of its members were among the 43 signatories of an "anti-Israeli" declaration on Lebanon. The Berlin Community itself had sponsored a "major demonstration of solidarity" for Israel. The arguments presented there closely followed the official line of the Israeli government. (See: U. Zelle, Allgemeine Jüdische Wochenzeitung, July 2, 1982. The same applies to the commentaries in this weekly newspaper throughout the war and its aftermath).
The Jewish student organization BJSD declared it stood "behind the efforts of the Jewish soldiers ... to achieve peace and security in the north of Israel and in Lebanon." (Resolution of the BJSD appearing in the Allgemeine Jüdische Wochenzeitung July 2, 1982).
In France, the otherwise strongly pro-Israel "Renouveau Juif" was highly critical. See the interview with its chairman, Henri Hajdenberg in Le Monde (September 24, 1982). Many members of the 1968 generation belong to the Renouveau Juif, and especially those Jews who can not be counted among the typical community Jews protested, among them many writers and professors. (P. Balta, Le Monde, June 17, 1982, and before that in Le Monde, March 29, 1980).
In Great Britain, the Council of Jewish Communities demanded that those responsible for the Beirut massacre be brought to Justice. (Haaretz, September 28, 1982, and also: J. Melman, Haaretz, September 20, 1982). The event brought into the open a split among the Zionist organizations (J. Melman, Haaretz, February 28, 1983)

that had already been developing (J. Melman, Haaretz, January 12, 1982).
In Switzerland, the situation was much the same. Of the 34 signatories of a declaration critical of Israel in the Neue Zürcher Zeitung 33 were not members of any Jewish community. (A. Kohn, Haaretz, July 5, 1982). Following the massacre, the Swiss association of Jewish communities (Schweizerische Israelitische Gemeindebund) demanded a "complete and relentless investigation" in order to bring those responsible to account. (FAZ, September 25, 1982).
The same applies to Finnland's Jews (Jerusalem Post, October 1, 1982).
See G. Kröncke (Süddeutsche Zeitung, June 26/27, 1982) on the embarrassed silence of the Jews in the Netherlands.
On their loud protest see:
H. Boaz, Haaretz, September 28, 1982.
The Organization of Jewish communities in Italy, usually not critical of Israel, at least in public, also demanded the punishment of these responsible for the massacre. (Haaretz, September 21, 1982) U. Diehl reports in the FAZ (July 24, 1982) on the "disappointment" over Israel even among the Jews of Rome, who are said to be especially hawkish and willing to approve Israel's every action. See C. Widmann, Süddeutsche Zeitung, October 16/17, 1982 on the massacre and the attack on the Synagoge in Rome. All of these tensions were reflected in the polarization between Israeli and Diaspora Jews at the World Congress of Zionist Organisations (Haaretz, December 9 and 16, 1982; Süddeutsche Zeitung, December 9, 1982).

40   This is made especially clear by the already cited Harris poll. Compare the results of a poll for Haaretz among U.S. Jews (E. Salpeter, Haaretz, April 10, 1983). It documents the political genius of the assassinated President Sadat of Egypt, who employed the polarization of the Diaspora Jews to generate Jewish pressure on Israel as a means to achieve his own political ends. (See: Le Monde, April 4 and 25, 1978) Sadat developed close contacts with American, French and British Jews for precisely this reason. On the day of Sadat's speech to the Knesset, on November 20, 1977, I stated in a commentary on German television (ZDF) that the Egyptian President might possibly want to (and have to) drive a wedge between Israel and the Diaspora in order to achieve his goals in the face of the Begin government. I added that he would have to employ the same political strategy with regard to Israel's domestic politics. He accomplished both, proof of both his political mastery and courage.

41   The return from Exil to Zion began in the year 537 B.C. and increased under Ezra and Nehemiah (457-428 B.C.). The Second Temple was rebuilt under Zrubabel in 516 B.C.

42   If one also includes the exile of the "children of Israel" in Egypt up to the conquest of Canaan, the history of the Diaspora then becomes much longer.

43   Jerusalem Post, June, 1978.

44 Compare the dialogue between Jürg Altweg und George Steiner (FAZ, September 18, 1982).

45 For example from the years 1980-1982 see my essays in Middle East Contemporary Survey (op. cit., note 23).
For Abu Nidal, chief of the "Al Fatah Revolutionary Council" (no longer part of the PLO), the Diaspora Jews are "de facto Israelis" and "Zionists". He declares that French or Italian interests have never been nor will ever be attacked inside or outside these countries, but that "Zionist terror" in these countries will receive a "firm reply" without affecting the "native citizens" (FAZ, April 26, 1983).
Because of the controversial nature of the topic, it must be once again stated that I am attempting to describe the perspective of both parties in the Middle East conflict without passing judgement.

46 Take for example the statement of former Defence Minister Sharon to the effect that Israel cannot tolerate attacks by the PLO on Jews in Europe or on Israelis either inside or outside Israel, and that Israel views itself as the protector of the Diaspora Jews. (BBC Monitor Service for the Middle East, June 21, 1982).
On the moral aspect see: S. Rosenfeld, "Newspaper Editors' Dilemma", Jerusalem Quarterly Nr.25 (Fall, 1982), p.101. Prime Minister Begin assumes Israel's "right" to intervene in order to protect Jews "whereever they may be." (Le Monde, August 14, 1982).
Heinz Galinski, head of the Jewish community in Berlin, accepts this protective function: "Those who know the sufferings of the Jewish People know how terribly important the protection offered by the Jewish state is for every Jew in the world at the present." (Allgemeine Jüdische Wochenzeitung, July 2, 1982).

47 Following the attack in the rue Copernic: Haaretz, January 26, 1981. Following the attack in the rue des Rosiers: Haaretz, September 6, 1982.
It is significant that Minister Aharon Uzan was sent to France. Uzan, born in 1924 in Tunis and immigrated to Israel in 1949, embodies the Zionistic Oriental Jewry of North Africa, and thus one of the main target groups in the Jewish community in France. An Israeli politician marked by the Holocaust would certainly have been a far less effective salesman for this audience.

48 Le Monde, August 17, 1982.

49 Le Monde, August 12, 1982.
In an open letter to Begin in Le Monde (August 16, 1982) Marek Holter wrote: "Vos fonctions ne vous autorisent pas à parler au nom de millions de juifs qui ne vous ont pas élu." It is in Israel's long term interest to motivate all Diaspora Jews to immigrate to Israel, and thus eliminate the Diaspora. Since this is probably a utopian goal, however, Israel must, regardless of whatever Zionist party is in power, maintain good relations with the Diaspora and its leadership.

50 Broder and Lang, op. cit. (Note 11).

51 E. Deutsch, op. cit. (Note 9). p.80, 84.
The former WZO representative in France, Avi Primor, gave a much lower estimate of the number of organized Jews in an internal re-

port: 5 % (G. Allon, Haaretz, July 15, 1979).

52 Haaretz, February 18, 1983.

53 Le Monde, October 25, 1980.

54 See: FAZ, June 18, 1980 on the reaction of the Central council of German Jews to the Declaration of Venice. See also: n (Nachmann?), Allgemeine Jüdische Wochenzeitung, July 2, 1982.

55 The national-religious youth movement "Bne Akiva" is the most popular of such organizations in Israel (see: Politik in Israel, p.546 ff.) and is also successful in the Diaspora, especially in Berlin.

56 M. Schwarze, FAZ, May 14, 1982.
One observes that such waves of xenophobia occurr independent of cause and object in long term cycles of 50 to 60 years, at least in Germany. The object becomes some presumed enemy; Jews, for example. The most recent dates: 1878 (the Berlin antisemitism controversy was the tip of the iceberg), the 1930s, now the 1980s. The intensity of the waves varies, but their existence is undeniable. For a discussion of the short, middle and long term cycles and further secondary literature see: M. Wolffsohn, Die Debatte über den Kalten Krieg. Politische Konjunkturen – Historisch-politische Analysen (Leverkusen, Leske & Budrich, 1982) and "200 Jahre Außenpolitik der Vereinigten Staaten von Amerika. Entwicklungslinien und Erklärungsversuche" (Aus Politik und Zeitgeschichte, weekly supplement to Das Parlament, February 7, 1981, p.15.24).

57 Regarding the dream and its disappointment see: G. Kröncke, Süddeutsche Zeitung, June 26/27, 1982; A. Hertzberg, op. cit. (Note 10); U. Diehl, FAZ, July 24, 1982.

SELECTED BIBLIOGRAPHY

PART I

DANN, Uriel, ed.: **The Great Power and the Middle East**, 1919-1939, New York-London: Holmes & Meier 1985

DELUCA, Anthony R.: "'Der Grossmufti' on Berlin: The Politics of Collaboration", **International Journal of Middle Eastern Studies**, Vo.10 (1979), pp.125-138

HIRSZOWICZ, Lukascz: **The Third Reich and the Arab East**, London-Toronto 1966

LEATHERDALE, C. A.: **British Policy towards Saudi Arabia 1925-1939**, unpublished Ph. D. thesis Aberdeen University 1981

NEUBERT, Friedrich P. H.: **Die deutsche Politik im Palästina-Konflikt 1937/38**, unpublished Ph. D. thesis Bonn University 1977

NICOSIA, Francis F.: "Arab Nationalism and National Socialist Germany, 1933-1939: Ideological and Strategic Incompatability", **International Journal** of Middle Eastern Studies, Vol.12 (1980), pp. 364 ff.; see also his unpublished Ph. D. thesis on the same subject McGill University, Montreal Canada 1982 and the revised version "The Third Reich and the Palestinian Question", Texas University Press 1985

SCHRÖDER, Josef: "Die Beziehungen der Achsenmächte zur Arabischen Welt", Manfred Funke, ed.: **Hitler, Deutschland und die Mächte**, Düsseldorf: Droste 1976, pp.372 ff.

SILVERFARB, Daniel: "Britain and Saudi Arabia on the Eve of the Second World War," **Middle Eastern Studies**, Vo.19 (1983), No.4, pp.403 ff.

PART II

DEUTSCHKRON, Inge: **Israel und die Deutschen**, 2nd and enlarged edition, Köln: Verlag Wissenschaft und Politik 1983

NEUSTADT, Amnon: **Die deutsch-israelischen Beziehungen im Schatten der EG-Nahostpolitik**, Frankfurt am Main: Haag+Herchem 1983

WOLFFSOHN, Michael: "The European Community and the Middle East", **Middle East Contemporary Survey**, ed. by Colin Legum et al., New York-London, Vol.V, 1982, pp.80 ff. and Vol.VI, 1984, pp. 55 ff. and Vol.VII forthcoming in 1985

Deutsch-Israelische Beziehungen im Spiegel der Umfragen, 1952-1983, München: Landeszentrale für politische Bildung forthcoming 1985

Wolffsohn, Michael / Niederfeld, Reinhard

POLITIK ALS INVESTITIONSMOTOR?

Deutsche «Multis» in Lateinamerika

Frankfurt/M., Bern, New York, 1985. 141 S.
ISBN 3-8204-7487-0   br. sFr. 32.—

Anhand der gesamten sowie branchenspezifischen Investitionsentwicklung bundesdeutscher «Multis» in Argentinien, Brasilien und Chile wird für den Zeitraum 1961 bis 1981 geprüft, ob Zusammenhänge zwischen den politischen Veränderungen in den Gastländern einerseits und den Investitionen in diesen Staaten andererseits bestehen. Eine neue Methode zur Feststellung dieser Zusammenhänge wird vorgeschlagen, bisher unveröffentlichte Daten vorgelegt. Ziel: Ökonomische Absicherung politikwissenschaftlich-zeitgeschichtlicher Aussagen und politikwissenschaftlich-zeitgeschichtliche Ergänzung ökonomischer Analysen.

Aus dem Inhalt: Politik und Investitionsentwicklung in Argentinien, Brasilien, Chile 1961 bis 1981.

Verlag Peter Lang Bern · Frankfurt a.M. · New York
Auslieferung: Verlag Peter Lang AG, Jupiterstr. 15, CH-3000 Bern 15
Telefon (0041/31) 32 11 22. Telex verl ch 32 420